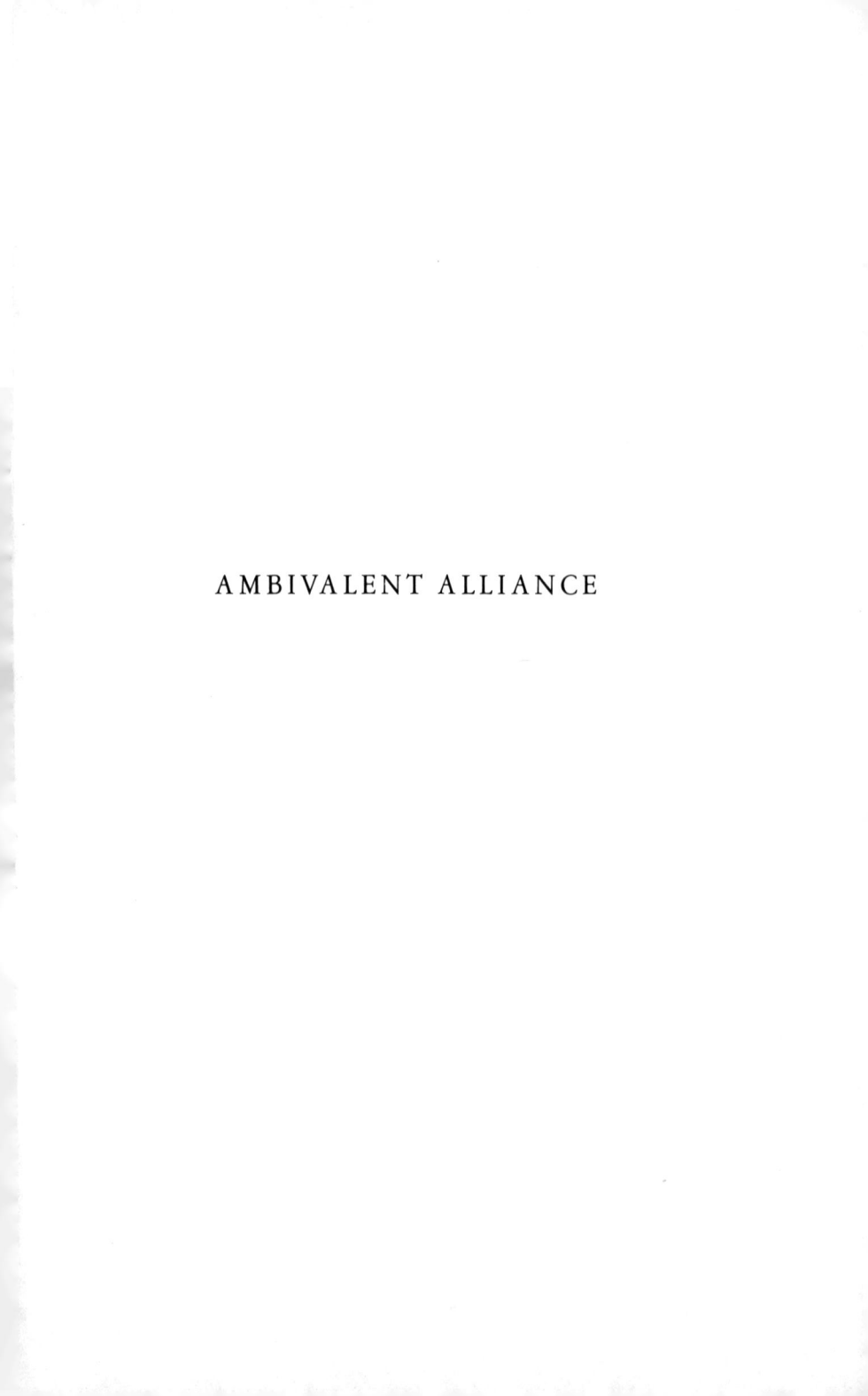

AMBIVALENT ALLIANCE

✝

Ambivalent Alliance

THE CATHOLIC CHURCH
AND
THE ACTION FRANÇAISE
1899–1939

✝

Oscar L. Arnal

UNIVERSITY OF PITTSBURGH PRESS

Published by the University of Pittsburgh Press, Pittsburgh, Pa. 15260
Copyright © 1985, University of Pittsburgh Press
All rights reserved
Feffer and Simons, Inc., London
Manufactured in the United States of America

Library of Congress Cataloging in Publications Data

Arnal, Oscar L., 1941–
    Ambivalent alliance.

    Bibliography: p. 221.
    Includes index.
    1. Catholic Church — France — History — 20th century.
2. Action française — History — 20th century.   3. Church and state — France — History — 20th century.
I. Title.
BX1530.A64   1985   282'.44   84-21961
ISBN 0-8229-3812-X

*To George and Naomi Arnal,
my beloved father and mother,
with thanks*

Contents

	Acknowledgments	ix
1.	A Church in Conflict	3
2.	The Birth and Pro-Catholic Values of the Action Française	11
3.	A Catholic Church Under Fire (1899–1906)	31
4.	Catholic Integrists Purge the Church (1906–1914)	49
5.	The Birth of a Friendship (1906–1914)	63
6.	The Apogee of a Friendship (1914–1925)	81
7.	The Winds of Change (1914–1925)	104
8.	The Church Condemns the Action Française (1925–1929)	123
9.	Shattered *Ralliement* and the Reprieve of the Action Française (1929–1939)	146
10.	The Final Reckoning	176
	Notes	187
	Bibliography	221
	Index	249

Acknowledgments

No thoroughgoing study of the relationship between the Catholic church and the Action Française has been published outside of partisan literature. To be sure, the basic works on the royalists by Eugen Weber and Edward Tannenbaum give serious attention to this matter, but only as one portion of their larger purposes. Adrien Dansette's monumental *Histoire religieuse de la France contemporaine* views the ties between Maurrasianism and Catholicism in the broader framework of 150 years of church-state conflict. Harry W. Paul narrows this theme by concentrating on the critical 1920s, and René Rémond examines interwar French Catholic pluralism in light of a Vatican *ralliement* which commenced by a condemnation of the Action Française. I am grateful for their pioneering labors and have built my work upon the scholarly foundation they have laid so well.

Nevertheless, this debt involves a corresponding critique as well. This book insists, against the more optimistic assertions of Dansette, Paul, and Rémond, that the brief *ralliements* of Catholic progressives during the period under consideration were fragile indeed. Further, it is contended that these so-called Catholic liberals were fewer and less significant in the events and decisions of French Catholicism than the above authors have asserted. Although I share their conviction that internal conflict between progressives and ultras has characterized French Catholic history since the French Revolution, I part company with them to the extent that they suggest that the French church chose democratic and social democratic values and programs in a significant fashion during the Third Republic. French Catholicism's shifting relations with the Action Française from 1899 to 1939 demonstrate that the most powerful sectors of the church pursued consistently a strategy of conservative political and social defense.

This book is neither a study of the ferment in Catholic intellectual circles from Dreyfus to Pétain, nor is it primarily biographical. To be sure, both these elements are present but only insofar as they serve the chief purpose of the book, namely, to analyze the public conflicts within the Catholic church that revolved around the relationship of its myriad organizational facets with the Action Française. Events in intellectual history, such as the Modernist controversy, are relevant to this larger issue, as are the lives and motivations of leading actors in the Catholic Church–Action Française drama. Nonetheless, the organizational and programmatic context of this drama and the public arena in which it unfolded remains the conscious and dominant concern of the book. Consequently, the source material used is overwhelmingly public in character, whether periodical publications or police materials, both of which are concerned with mass impact and manifestations. Even the interviews do not serve primarily a biographical purpose; they are rather supplementary material which serves to reinforce the written documentation. Ideological conflict and sociopolitical struggle within an evolving Catholic church remain the chief concerns of the book, especially as these come to bear on the right-wing league called the Action Française.

I wish to acknowledge my gratitude to all the historians who played an important part in encouraging me to research and produce this book. Brief contacts with Eugen Weber, René Rémond, Emile Poulat, Stewart Doty, Stuart Campbell, Joseph Moody, Robert Colodny, Richard Hunt, Francis Murphy, and Robert Young provided invaluable suggestions which contributed to the continuation of this project. The specialized assistance of Robert

Soucy of Oberlin College, Harry Paul of the University of Florida, and John Hellman of McGill University was especially profitable. William D. Irvine of York University aided me in matters of definitional refinement, and my good friend Joel Blatt of the University of Connecticut rendered precious advice which was the product of much fruitful discussion and common labors. To Seymour Drescher of the University of Pittsburgh, my dissertation adviser, I owe more than words can say. His precise scholarship and warm humanity have animated my academic work since I began graduate study under his tutelage fourteen years ago. It is my profound hope that this book will render to him some of the homage he deserves.

Many thanks are given to all those Frenchmen who permitted me to interview them and record their personal testimonies as participants in the events described in this work. To those Action Française militants and other living actors of the historical dramas in question I offer my gratitude and the promise that I have labored strenuously to insure a faithful use of the precious memories they have entrusted to me.

I acknowledge my debt for the following grants which enabled me to conduct the research for this book. The bulk of the investigation was made possible by two Ford Foundation grants which permitted me to spend a year in France (1972–1973) and a further few months to organize my primary materials. An Andrew W. Mellon predoctoral fellowship (1973–1974) allowed me to collect the remainder of the data necessary to complete my dissertation. A Wilfrid Laurier University Summer Research stipend (1977) assisted me in bringing my material up to date. Finally, two summer grants by the Social Sciences and Humanities Research Council of Canada (1979–1980), designated for a project on the French "worker-priest" movement, allowed me to return to France and spend some time in examining sources I had missed earlier.

I am grateful to Bob and Cyndy Gmeindl, Terri Peemoeller, and the late Mavis Lewin for their typing skills; also to Mavis Lewin and Jane Flanders for editorial scrutiny and expertise, and to Laura Gingerich, who compiled the index. Most of all, I am indebted to my beloved wife, Bunny, for her skillful editorial work, for all her sacrifices in sustaining my academic vocation, for her moral support and most of all, for her love. Above all, this book is my tribute to her.

AMBIVALENT ALLIANCE

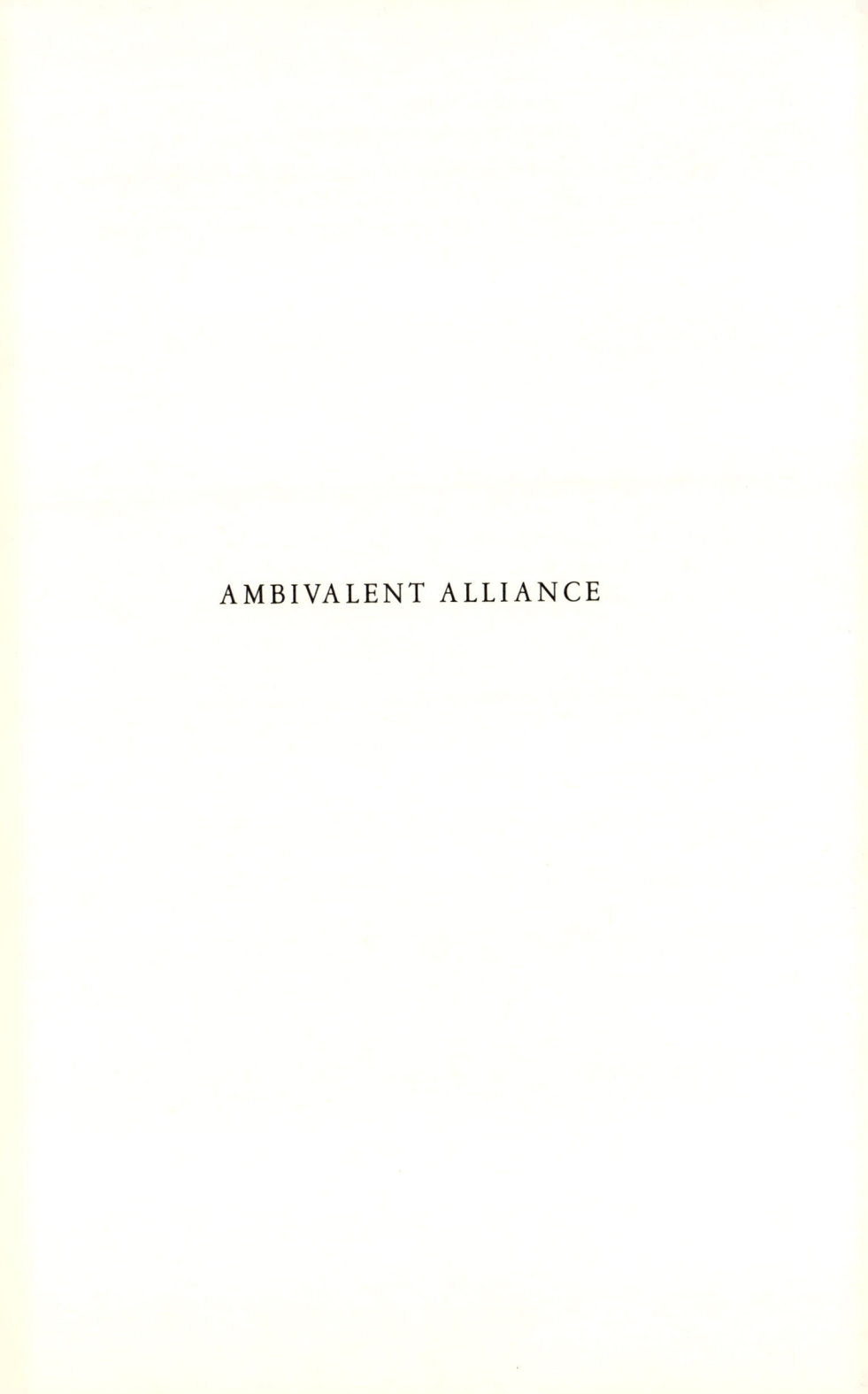

1

A Church in Conflict

For almost two centuries, the French Catholic church has been torn by conflicts brought about by the shock waves of the French Revolution and the social and political changes that followed it. Not only has it been forced to deal with hostile governments and anticlerical movements bent on its destruction; it has also been compelled to address itself to conflicting values and movements within its own ranks. Faced by the onslaughts of foes without, the French church became increasingly polarized from within. It has been a house divided. On the one hand were those who saw in the French Revolution and its aftermath the powerful forces of the demonic that could be resisted only with the weapons of a Catholicism loyal to the privileges, traditions, and values of its pre–French Revolutionary past. On the other hand were those Catholics who felt that the church's only hope was to abandon societal privileges, Christianize the Revolution's values and identify with positive forces for change within modern society. This struggle within the French church reached its height in the fierce clashes surrounding the Dreyfus affair and the Separation Law of 1905, and although it abated gradually, it took two world wars and Vatican II to soften it considerably. It is in this context of a beleaguered fortress environment that must be found the explanation of the ambivalent relationship between the French Catholic church and the Action Française.

A whole series of embarrassing or at least curious questions can be raised concerning the ties between these two groups. Why would a church becoming increasingly internationalist and ultramontane find a narrow superpatriotic group like the Action Française so appealing? Why would a church dedicated to traditional Christian doctrine find the Action Française's philosophy, which was created and shaped by an agnostic, so compelling? How could such a conservative institution as the French church tolerate the verbal and physical violence of a group which did not hesitate to advocate murder of prominent citizens and physical abuse against Jews and other groups deemed undesirable? These and similar questions portray the difficulties, indeed the incongruities, of any positive ties between these two organizations.

Nevertheless, such ties did exist, and very important sectors of the French church were sympathetic and even intensely loyal to the Action Française and its agnostic philosopher Charles Maurras, while others were overtly hostile to both. It will be the task of this book to describe and explain these intertwining and changing relationships from the birth of the Action Française in the wake of the Dreyfus affair through its growth among and influence over influential Catholics to its condemnation by Pius XI (1926–1927) and subsequent restoration by Pius XII (1939).

Although Action Française–Catholic ties are a direct outgrowth of the anticlerical struggles of the first years of this century, the roots of these conflicts draw from the soil of 1789. Of course, it cannot be denied that serious church struggles predated the revolutionary epoch; nonetheless the French Revolution became the great watershed of modern French Catholic history. Prior to it the church was a privileged corporation in French society. The eruption of 1789 changed all that. In a brief period of five years, the Gallican church was dashed from the heights of privilege to the position of a suspect, alien force within the new order. Legislation stripped the church of its wealth and power, and even the Napoleonic Concordat of 1801 offered domestic Catholicism only illusory promises of the church's privileged past. So abrupt had been the Revolution's assault upon the church that the result was the birth of a counterrevolutionary nostalgia within ecclesiastical circles which, though unable to stem the tide of modernity, was able to fight a desperate rearguard action. Caught between this crossfire was the tiny minority of social reformers and prodemocratic moderates within the church. Although these Catholic liberals were not spawned by the Revolution itself, they used its leverage to give greater voice to their increasingly democratic convictions. Imbued with the spirit of '89, they challenged the entrenched positions of their more conservative confreres. In such a fashion the French Revolution had come to define both church-state and interchurch struggles for almost two hundred years.

The uncertainty of the Catholic church in postrevolutionary France reflected the growing fears of a once secure institution rapidly finding itself vulnerable and without a secure place within a society of which it had been so recently an integral part. No wonder then that the next century and a half found French Catholicism caught in a tortured ambivalence. At one moment, it could yearn for that past society which gave it privilege and position. Ecclesiastical support and eulogy for the Bourbon restoration and Louis Napoleon's authoritarian reign were good cases in point. In other instances, church figures urged accommodation to new regimes and adaptation to democratic values and reforms. Appeals by bishops Félix Dupanloup and M.D.A. Sibour for moderate change and the Christian Democratic visions of Father Lammenais and his followers illustrated this minority position.[1]

Internal Catholic conflict continued and accelerated within the context of the Third Republic. Benefiting from the reentry of large sectors of the bourgeoisie into the church and experiencing a resurgence of some of its previous influence, the French church entered the Third Republic confident that it could enhance its already powerful educational and political position.

However, slippage had occurred. Since the ancien régime, when religious practice was obligatory, a perceptible decline in official church attendance was noted wherever episcopal studies were authorized. For example, Félix Dupanloup's Orléans diocese reported only approximately 25,000 Easter duties out of a population of 360,000. Again it was the Great Revolution that had set in motion those acts of ecclesiastical disestablishment which would reveal slowly but surely that the nation's Catholicism was becoming increasingly marginalized. The backward and more pastoral areas of France, such as Brittany, the Massif Central, and the eastern uplands, remained practising, but the urban sprawls caused by the industrial revolution were virtually lost to the church.[2] Nonetheless, the Catholicism that faced the Third Republic failed to see these signs and instead adopted a program according to recollections of its pre-1789 past. Under the slogan "Save Rome and France in the name of the Sacred Heart," Catholicism turned to the royalist National Assembly in the hope that it would restore the monarchy and pursue an ultramontane policy abroad. The church in France had adopted openly the reactionary *Syllabus* mentality of Pius IX.

The republican victory led by Léon Gambetta in the mid-1870s insured both the failure of the Catholic program and a governmental platform which would continue to weaken Catholic power at the political level in France. Jules Ferry, the minister of education, persuaded the French parliament to pass anticlerical legislation designed to establish a national school system based upon the French Revolutionary and republican principles upholding "free, secular and compulsory" education. Catholic outrage was predictable, but the tactics of reactionary Catholic monarchism accomplished little for the church during the next ten years.[3]

For this reason, Pope Leo XIII (1878–1903) called upon the French church to adopt a constitutional strategy in place of a monarchist one. This Ralliement, as it was called, was formulated in his public letter *Au milieu des sollicitudes* (May 3, 1892) which he addressed to the French cardinals. The pontiff was neither appealing to royalists to drop their political preferences, nor was he suggesting that French Catholics adopt republican and democratic values. He did not criticize the religious program of the reactionaries but only their means to achieve it. In place of counterrevolutionary rhetoric, he insisted that the French church employ the weapons of republican legality against the anticlerical republicans. Most of French Catholicism's powerful leadership refused to be flexible. The hierarchy was decidedly uncooperative, and the Catholic popular press, notably *La Croix* and *La Libre Parole*, turned its back upon the papal pleas. Even those laymen who sought to implement the pontiff's policy in the public arena failed miserably.[4]

In spite of its twin failure to stem the anticlerical tide and moderate the Catholic ultras, the Ralliement was successful in awakening the church's progressive values and programs that had gone underground for almost forty years. This resurgence of Catholic creativity took two basic forms. The first of these, social Catholicism, was led by two reactionary aristocratic and monarchical army officers, René La Tour du Pin Chambly and the imperious superpatriot Albert de Mun. For them, virulent religious defense would never return the church nor French society to the halcyon days prior to 1789. Only a charitable love of the abused toiling masses by God-ordained aristocrats could accomplish that divine task.[5] De Mun's *Oeuvre des cercles d'ouvriers* gave itself "the mission to 'propagate the devotion of the directing class to the popular class'" in the name of Jesus Christ.[6] In time this counterrevolutionary noblesse oblige would evolve into programs using grass-roots methods and more democratic ideas. Organizations such as the Association Catholique de la Jeunesse Française (ACJF), the Jesuit-based Action Populaire, and the laity-led Semaines Sociales are some examples of this.[7] The ACJF was founded by de Mun himself, among others, in 1886. Its goal was "to cooperate in the reestablishment of the Christian social order, to return in submission to the church and to fight by any means the enemies of Catholicism." Within a year forty of these youth groups existed, and by 1908 there were more than two thousand. By this time it had become a militant support of the pro-Catholic party Action Libérale Populaire, a party led, in part, by de Mun himself.[8] Action Populaire, which would continue Tour du Pin's and de Mun's *Association Catholique* review after 1908, was the creation of a socially sensitive Jesuit father from Lille named Henri-Joseph Leroy who soon won the collaboration of a younger Jesuit, Gustave Desbuquois. Eschewing political action, they suggested that the chief issue was the social question, which included such problems as the proletarian's "work instability," "the decay of his family," "the desertion of the countryside," "the weakening of his beliefs," and so forth. The heart of Action Populaire became rapidly the publication of periodical and specialized literature on social Catholic concerns especially as they impinged on the working class. Indeed, Action Populaire was "a team of religious, aided by some laity, animating a center of study and social information" whose ambition was to aid Catholics "by furnishing materials for their reflection and action." From its center in Reims, it produced documentation which in one year alone amounted to sales of 13,000 volumes, 340,000 reviews, over 100,000 brochures, and over 600,000 tracts and information sheets. From the initial book written by Father Leroy in 1903, Action Populaire became a formidable source of social Catholic propaganda shorn of the blatant counterrevolutionary origins promulgated by Tour du Pin and de Mun.[9] Even less inclined to social Catholicism's reactionary roots were the Semaines Sociales. These study weeks on the social question originated in 1904 at Lyon under the inspiration of dedicated laymen who formed a team which had been publishing a social Catholic review since the 1890s called *Chronique des Comités du Sud-Est*. They were led by a warm Christian humanist named Henri Lorin, but the real inspiration for both the review and the Semaines Sociales was Marius Gonin, a tiny, thin mystic and lay celibate whose origins were among Lyon's silk workers. Initially he worked with the regional *La Croix*, but his own republican sympathies led to the creation of reviews and activities that became linked to the rising consciously democratic manifestations of Catholicism.[10]

However, it was the rebirth in the 1890s of Christian Democracy per se that unchained social Catholicism irrevocably from its reactionary moorings. This second form of Catholic liberalism, which arose in the wake of the Ralliement, moved beyond the intentions of Leo XIII. Although they too emerged from older social Catholicism, Catholic democrats were committed openly both to their Christian faith and to the French Revolution. Father Paul Naudet's affirmation, "God has blessed the movement of 1789" and "the reign of democracy," could have been the public profession of any of these Christian Democrats found throughout France.[11] Some Catholic republicans were prominent laymen like the factory owner Léon Harmel and the Breton naval officer Emmanuel Desgrées du Loû. Others were priests, appropriately called *abbés démocrates,* who either served in Parliament like Hippolyte Gayraud and Jules Lemire or became leading figures in the Christian Democratic press like Paul Naudet, Pierre Dabry, and Félix Trochu. Opposition to their position and internal divisions blocked their organizational attempts. Consequently, the Christian Democratic presence was reduced to a string of lone voices speaking through newspapers or from the Chamber of Deputies.[12]

The sole exception to this state of affairs was the Sillon of Marc Sangnier. This Christian Democratic movement combined Catholic mysticism with republican values and proclaimed publicly its crusade dedicated to "the reconciliation of Christ and the people, of Catholicism and the suffering of the revolutionary masses."[13] In many respects the Sillon was an extension of Sangnier himself. This short stocky man embodied the very spirit of his organization. He was warm and inspiring, a visionary who brought to his mystical faith all the faults and virtues of a popular tribune. By the end of the 1890s, Sangnier had achieved some measurable results. Local Sillonist societies were formed and organized into five regional federations. In addition, study groups, cooperatives, hostels, popular institutes, and publishing facilities were created. With the dawn of a new century, a monthly review *Le Sillon* and a weekly newspaper *L'Eveil Démocratique* began to promulgate the social democratic programs of this budding mass movement.[14] It was no accident that Marc Sangnier, the Sillon, and Christian Democracy would be singled out for demolition by both Catholic ultras and the reactionary royalists of the Action Française. Indeed, the waxing and waning of the respective fortunes of Maurrasians and Christian Democrats would be interrelated inexorably.

Although the Ralliement had failed in its original purpose to unite French Catholics behind a republican or constitutional strategy of religious defense, it released forces that would begin the long task of demonstrating to French society, Christian or otherwise, that one could be devoted to both the principles of 1789, as embodied in the Declaration of the Rights of Man, and the doctrines of the Catholic faith. That few believed this at the turn of the century is an indicator of the deep and abiding fissures that remained between the heirs of the French Revolution and the Catholic church. The Ralliement was doomed from the very beginning, and the trauma of the Dreyfus affair only exposed the failure of Vatican moderation to harsh public display. The events surrounding the questionable condemnation of a Jewish army officer to life imprisonment and his subsequent pardon accentuated internal Catholic divisions. This gave birth to a successful anticlerical offensive that forced the church into a hopeless rearguard action and intensified the proliferation of sectarian nationalist leagues, chief of which was the Action Française. This atmosphere of polarization among Catholics and between Catholics and anticlerical republicans was the immediate context of the origins of the Action Française and its ties with the Catholic church.

+ 2 +

The Birth and Pro-Catholic Values of the Action Française

In 1945, almost fifty years after the Dreyfus affair had rocked the French nation, the aged Charles Maurras was convicted of treasonous collaboration with the German enemy. His poignant outburst, "This is Dreyfus's revenge," is testimony to how deeply intertwined were the events surrounding the case of Alfred Dreyfus and the birth and development of the Action Française. By the time the court martial of a Jewish captain had erupted into a cause célèbre, the public sectors of the nation had chosen sides, each advancing its cause as a crusade. On the side of Dreyfus were ranged most of the outspoken secular friends of the French Revolution. Such figures as Georges Clemenceau, Jean Jaurès, and most of the Radical leadership suspected that behind the charge of Dreyfus's guilt lay a sinister plot of the army, the patriotic leagues, and the Catholic church to overthrow the republic. Those who stood against the Jewish captain were convinced that behind the democratic slogans used so glibly by the Dreyfusards could be found alien forces bent on either dividing or destroying the nation. France had to be protected from internal and external enemies. For the anti-Dreyfusards, the polarization of the nation over one man was a mortal sin; the conviction of a possibly innocent man was a venial one. The grandeur of France was infinitely more important than the fate of one man, and a Jew at that. Time, however, was on the side of the Dreyfusards. Within a few years of the onset of the affair, a presidential pardon freed the captain, and a legislative election brought a coalition of anticlerical Radicals and Socialists to power. This electoral victory dealt a serious blow to superpatriots, militarists, xenophobes, anti-Semites, and traditional Catholics. Their loss, however, served only to increase the tempo and virulence of their attacks.[1]

It is in this context of anti-Dreyfusard defeat and the continued conflicts which followed it that the Action Française was born and would become the leading voice of strident nationalism in France. As an inflammatory patriotic league on the far right of French political life, the royalist movement was not unique. Extreme nationalism and right-wing leagues, such as the Ligue des Patriotes, the Ligue Antisémite and the Ligue de la Patrie Française, were earlier rivals of Maurras's and Daudet's monarchists. Indeed, most of them had predated the Action Française and had appeared more likely to succeed than the new royalists.

By the 1880s, when it had become apparent that republicanism could not be dislodged, the political right turned to mass politics in order to enter the halls of power once again. In some instances former traditionalists were prepared to adopt the style of street politics, demonstrated by the welcome they gave to the campaigns of Georges Boulanger and Paul Deroulède. At other times, these neophyte militants attempted to attract popular support by forming leagues and by publishing newspapers. The activities of the anti-Semite Edouard Drumont and the reactionary Assumptionists who created *La Croix* are two cases in point. Faced with the inability to retain past privileges, the conservative and ultraconservative right had turned to the people even before the Dreyfus affair in an attempt to use democratic means for elitist and counterrevolutionary ends. Former ideologies were intensified in tone by the injection of militarism, xenophobia, ethnic hatred, authoritarianism, and the rejection of parliamentarianism. Strategies were adopted to appeal to a mass public. Violent histrionics and sensationalist journalism replaced the aloofness and snobbery of the traditional right. Counts and literary elitists sought to be tribunes of those marginal sectors of the populace who felt uprooted from the minimal economic security and questionable social status to which they had clung desperately.

After the collapse of Boulangism and with the rise of Leo XIII's Ralliement, there was a marked decline in power of these groups. An important number of their Catholic supporters heard the papal call and entered constitutional politics seriously. Two such examples were the devout Albert de Mun, who took up the Ralliement as a sacred cause, and Jacques Piou, a provincial lawyer who provided a more pragmatic contrast to his crusading comrade. By the end of the 1890s, both men had moved from royalism to Boulangism and from there to the Ralliement. No new political temptation would ever again shake them from their commitment to conservative and Catholic goals via the strategy of constitutionalism. Nevertheless, this was not true for many other traditionalists or reactionaries, and by the time of the Dreyfus affair, there was a resurgence of the mass right-wing activity that had characterized the Boulangist era. This foray into mass politics would serve as a model which would be used so effectively by both the twentieth-century fascists and the Action Française.[2]

As the new century dawned, most of the older patriotic leagues were in a state of decline. Such was not the case for the Action Française. Indeed, by 1900 it was barely one and one-half years old. Founded by Henri Vaugeois, Maurice Pujo, and a handful of other superpatriotic intellectuals, the new league adopted as its task the radical purification of the republic from corrupt politicians and financiers. The organization's initial years were inauspicious. Its members wrote articles for several journals of the ultraright, and soon the league began to publish a biweekly review which came to be called *Revue de l'Action Française*. Although this fortnightly never reached a mass audience, during its fifteen-year life (1899–1914) it did provide a forum in which the unified world view of the Action Française would be forged. (Beginning in 1908, a daily *L'Action Française* was published.) Further, the league was narrowly intellectual; its leaders were too eclectic; and its competitors were older, larger, wealthier and better organized. In spite of these handicaps, the Action Française survived and within a decade was a serious voice of the extreme right in France.[3] There were several internal reasons for this.

Chief among these was the philosophical dominance of Charles Maurras. This lonely lover of classical antiquity, shaped both by the early death of his father and a deafness which began at age fourteen, brought to the rising Action Française an intellectual credibility which few other ultrarightist groups could claim. To the fledgling league, this Provençal poet contributed an amalgamation of Comtian positivism, the classical tradition, and his own distinct brand of monarchism. In fact, Maurras was the sole royalist among the founders of the new organization, and he took it upon himself to convert the league to the cause of the king. He succeeded in this task by the early 1900s when his *L'Enquête sur la monarchie* was published. His royalism was neither a carbon copy of traditional monarchism nor was it a continuation of the philosophy espoused by the dwindling circle of devotees surrounding the Orleanist pretender. For Maurras, royalty was not an end in itself. Rather, it was a symbol of a greater good, namely France itself. The monarchy meant stability, unity, and "a permanent expression" of national love, virtues so lacking in the midst of Dreyfus-polarized France. Thus the throne would be in servitude to that militant patriotism called "integral nationalism" which demanded an intense devotion to the "cult of the fatherland" before which even the king was expected to bow.[4]

When he spoke of "politics above all else" (*politique d'abord*), Maurras meant that the monarchy, religion — indeed all the traditional values he cherished — were subservient to the nation. For him, France was no vague notion. He contrasted what he called the "legal nation" (*pays légal*) and the "real nation" (*pays réel*). The former was the Third Republic, child of the French Revolution, and all its Dreyfusard friends. The latter was the true and authentic France worthy of all loyalty and devotion, a France that predated 1789. This nation was the beneficiary of Graeco-Roman civilization and had defended this heritage via throne and altar for a thousand years of medieval history. The French Revolution had upset this delicate balance of authority, tradition, and order by unleashing the demons of destruction and chaos. Consequently,

Maurras's call to action was "reaction, first of all" (*réaction d'abord*), for he sensed that the *pays réel* could be salvaged only by a return to a political order which existed prior to the French Revolution. It was within this general framework that the Action Française and its leading philosopher found a significant place for the Catholic church.

By his blend of empirical positivism with traditional French royalism, Maurras offered the budding Action Française a consistent, unified ideology that would guide it through the years ahead. Within a few years his positions had become the official ideology of the young league, and he had become the organization's philosophical authority. He would maintain this role for the next forty years through the writing of books and his editorial column "Politique" which appeared regularly in the daily *L'Action Française*. Charles Maurras was undoubtedly the philosophical overlord of the Action Française, and his intellectual prestige catapulted the reputation of this superpatriotic organization above that of its competitors. The Action Française became not simply another rightist group; in addition, it constructed an entire value system for the new nationalism of the far right. All the fragments of this new virulence were brought into a unified whole by the Action Française, and this was, in no small measure, the work of Charles Maurras.[5]

In addition, the fledgling league had developed its highly effective organizational apparatus by 1908 and had used it in such a way as to insure the maximum of public notoriety. By 1905 the Action Française had penetrated the rightist student movements of the Parisian Left Bank and was being noted on the police lists as an organization to be watched carefully. An Institut d'Action Française was created in 1906 to raise money for the review and to propagate integral nationalism among the members of the right-wing intelligentsia. Designed according to the pedagogical precepts of Auguste Comte, the institute's programs attracted prominent speakers and participants which thus enhanced the prestige of the entire organization. Finally, in the autumn of 1908, the Camelots du Roi came into being. Led by Maxime Réal del Sarte and Maurice Pujo, this melange of upper-class and petty-bourgeois youth became the most visible expression of the Action Française. With their lead-tipped canes, they were the royalists' street fighters who defended the name of Joan of Arc, served as parade sergeants in right-wing demonstrations, faced arrests, disrupted the courts, heckled public speakers, and beat up the foes of integral nationalism.[6]

However, their chief function was to sell the newspaper *L'Action Française,* and it was the creation of this daily on March 21, 1908, and its methodological dissemination in the years to follow that made the Action Française one of the French right's leading voices for over two decades. The force behind the paper and the reason for its mass success was the charismatic Léon Daudet. If Charles Maurras was the philosopher of the league, Léon Daudet was its popularizer. He soon replaced Edouard Drumont as France's most well-known hater. Daudet was the son of one of France's greatest literary figures and an intimate associate of the noted republican family of Victor Hugo. By the time of the Boulangist crisis, this young provincial had become a nationalist agitator and a member of Drumont's Ligue Antisémite. His hatred of the Jews was inflamed by the Dreyfus affair, and the influence of his second wife had converted him to Catholicism and monarchism by 1903. Mme. Daudet was a royalist firebrand in her own right, and she led her husband a year later into the ranks of the Action Française. It was largely through Daudet's initiative that the newspaper was born. He raised the initial monies necessary for the paper's appearance, largely through capital furnished by his wife and a few other important contributors, and once the initial hurdles had been overcome, *L'Action Française,* despite perennial financial difficulties, became one of the most well-known Parisian dailies for the duration of the Third Republic. Though its circulation probably never exceeded 150,000, its impact upon the political right and the government elite was notable, primarily because of its capacity to create and exploit scandals and its unique integration of philosophical refinement and yellow journalism. This balance of sophistication and demagogy were exemplified by the complementary personalities of Charles Maurras and Léon Daudet.[7]

For these reasons, the childhood of the Action Française was not a wasted decade. The organizational apparatus had been set in motion; Charles Maurras had contributed his philosophy of royalist nationalism, and Léon Daudet had launched the inflammatory daily which would become a dominant voice of the French extreme right for more than twenty years. Not only had the Action Française survived; it was also on the threshold of becoming a serious leader of right-wing nationalism in France.[8]

Initially the Action Française's ties with French Catholicism were practically nonexistent, although many of the earlier members were practicing Catholics. Chief among these were Louis Dimier, a Catholic art historian; Léon de Montesquiou, another Catholic intellectual; and Bernard de Vésins, a devout military man. They assisted Charles Maurras in developing the pro-Catholic politics of the royalist league. In fact, it was this integration of Catholic values into the overall philosophy of the Action Française that laid the groundwork for the later ties between influential French Catholics and the integral nationalists.

Every new member of the league not only pledged his loyalty to the monarchical restoration but also his commitment to the destruction of the Republic because it favored "religious influences directly hostile to traditional Catholicism."[9] In such a way, entry into the ranks of the Action Française was linked to a defense of the Catholic heritage as it was embodied in prerepublican France. At issue was neither one's internal convictions, nor one's devotional piety nor even one's firm belief in the verity of Catholic dogma. After all, Maurras was himself an agnostic. Rather, the oath demanded an intense conviction that traditional Catholicism was inexorably tied to France. Integral nationalism meant devotion to every institution that was part of the essential fabric of medieval France. Naturally, this included the Catholic church. "France is 'by heart Catholic,'" affirmed Maurras, "and also by tradition, habit, morals and spirit."[10] Both believers and unbelievers "are born Catholic," he argued, because "France was the product of its bishops and monks." Moral and spiritual habits were part of the social and historical fabric of a nation, and this was especially true of Catholic France. Ecclesiastical labor, symbolized by monasteries and altars, was part and parcel of the organization and conservation of authentic France and remained so to the present day. Without the medieval church and its heirs, civic and social values would be lost, and the modern heresies of liberalism, egalitarianism, and internationalism would be free to wreak havoc and anarchy on fragile France. Such a resolute dike against the revolutionary forces of darkness was at the "very marrow of Catholic teaching."[11] No wonder then that Maurras called for a French religious policy which would be officially Catholic, that is, a program which promised "a privileged position for Catholicism in society as well as in the state."[12] Maurras had set the tone. By the outbreak of the Great European War, the Action Française had adopted his religious politics. Catholicism had become interwoven with integral nationalism: "French national interest is indissolubly linked to Catholicism. Thus, insofar as the Action Française takes cognizance of itself, it finds itself necessarily Catholic."[13] This amalgamation of a religious tradition into reactionary nationalism was the very heart of the Catholic-royalist marriage as the ideologues of the Action Française perceived it.

For Maurras and his disciples, the Catholic church was the epitome of order, that civil and societal virtue to be admired by believer and unbeliever alike. "Catholicism is above all an order," asserted the royalist philosopher. "It is in this most general notion of order that its religious essence harmonizes with its outside admirers."[14] More specifically, Catholic order provided a dike to hold back the threatening flood of civilization's enemies:

> The Roman order. The Roman Church is the only force of organization, of clustering and of hierarchy which stands against the Jewish army. . . . Etymologically, religion signifies reunion, bonding, cohesion. By all its exterior brilliance and by its intimate gentle splendor, Rome exemplifies this glorious etymology. It frames and coordinates. . . . It resists two invasions, the one materialistic, the other ideological. It repulses victoriously the assaults of anarchic individualism.[15]

Order also meant hierarchy and discipline. The Action Française admired greatly the authoritarian structure of the traditional Catholic church. It called this organizational pattern "a perfect of authority and tradition. To call the spirit of the Revolution classical is to adulterate the natural sense of that word.

The Revolution has entirely different origins: the Bible of the Reformation, the statutes of Geneva's republic, the Calvinistic theologians.[31]

Republicanism and the revolutionary values emanating from it were the final adversary that the Action Française claimed to share with traditional Catholicism in France. The potential member of the league was confronted with this challenge: "You decide . . . Monarchy or Republic," or to put it another way, the French were expected to choose between "divine right or the rights of man."[32] The very pledge made by every new member included the desire to restore the monarchy upon the corpse of republicanism precisely because this latter form of government was held to be detrimental to Catholicism. For Charles Maurras, republicanism is the natural child of revolution and sociopolitical disorder. Its principles violate the natural order of things: "Political liberty, basic to the republican system," has destroyed civic respect; being a citizen has lost its meaning. Equality has shattered the natural pyramid of authority by allowing power to reside with the lowest common denominator. Talented and productive forces have been supplanted by "the inferior elements of the nation." Finally, the republican virtue of fraternity has been replaced by its opposite—civil war.[33] The history of republicanism in France was proof plenty for Maurras that behind all the lofty ideals espoused by democrats lurked the inevitability of revolution and anti-Catholicism. He pointed out that even the participation of Catholics in the French Revolution could not prevent the spirit of 1789 from degenerating into the regicide and Jacobin tyranny of 1793 and 1794. Subsequent events demonstrated further that republicans of good will were powerless to prevent the revolutionary bloodshed and anarchy that inevitably followed. This was as true of the Second Republic of 1848 and the socialist Paris Commune of 1871 as it was of the Grand Revolution itself. The long anticlerical campaign of the present Third Republic was, for Maurras, a current reminder of the veracity of his contentions. This historical recital was followed by a grim and simple conclusion: "It cannot be said that the French Republic is not the offspring of the revolutionary and insurrectional spirit."[34] Because republican insurrectionism needed a spiritual foundation, this "religion of revolution" was compelled to combat "every other religion" and transform itself into a counterchurch. This alternative religion needed to be shattered in the name of integral nationalism and the Catholic church. Such was the contention of the Action Française.[35]

With such wide-ranging positions reflecting solidarity with the French church, Charles Maurras and his followers hoped to reap a glorious harvest of Catholic members and sympathizers for the Action Française. On the one hand, the royalist league espoused values of order, authority, hierarchy, and civilization which it found inherent to traditional Catholicism. On the other hand, it declared war against individuals, groups, and principles which were hostile to the French church. Its devotion to the anti-Dreyfusard cause and its damning of the Republic's anticlerical campaigns made it a prime contender for the winning of Catholic sympathies.

However, the matter was more complex than these apparent parallels seemed to warrant. Elements of the philosophy of Charles Maurras were in direct conflict with traditional Catholic dogma and piety. Most blatant of these was the professed agnosticism of the royalist leader, a skepticism gleaned in large part from his interpretation of the positivism of Auguste Comte. Maurras recognized the possibility that Catholics might hesitate to form alliances with unbelievers. For this reason, he constructed a rationale to offset Catholic uncertainties about his position by expanding upon the following axiom: "Divided on heavenly things, positivism and Catholicism are often in accord on temporal matters."[36] He urged Catholics to rally to the appeal of the positivists, because "deism, Protestantism and, for a stronger reason, Judaism" have united for the purpose of destroying the French church. In order to resist this Protestant, secular, and Jewish menace, a coalition must be marshaled that would include all forces dedicated to defending the Catholic church. For Maurras, one society eminently and delicately hierarchized."[16] Such a natural chain of authority, cemented by religious discipline, served as a vital model for the basic unit of French society, the patriarchal family. Owing Catholic training, this social embodiment was able to resist attempts by the revolutionary state to claim a monopoly over the education of children. What made this family so strong was the Catholic insistence that its essence was "an indissoluble union between father and mother" built upon a "respect for all the obligations, functions and conservative hierarchies" that embodied it.[17]

Finally, Catholicism stood as a bulwark of civilization against barbarism. "Good Church of Rome," eulogized Maurras, "Church of civilization, of politics, of letters, of science, of morals, Church of order, you have been a natural providence for humanity."[18] In particular, the medieval Catholic church was seen as a channel through which classical values and traditions could be transmitted, without adulteration, to modern times. Catholic philosophers and theologians received from Rome and Athens "the wisdom of the human race." By amalgamating the Christian spirit with "Greek science and Roman empiricism," they forged those weapons which could resist resolutely "every revolutionary idea."[19] Put another way, the Catholic church adopted the classical tradition, uprooted and removed all Semitic notions from the primitive Christian gospel and created a transformed value system which Léon de Montesquiou called "Christian civilization."[20] The Latin-Catholic nations, especially France and Italy, were both the repositories of civilization's benefits and the defenders of its priceless heritage. Bernard de Vésins described these nations as "Catholic by a great majority." Their civilization, indeed their very soul, was "impregnated with the Catholic and Roman culture." For this reason, they were "indebted to the Church . . . for what they are."[21]

Consequently, the Action Française felt that its principles and rhetoric were embodied in the prerevolutionary Catholic tradition. This conviction enabled Charles Maurras to make the following judgment: "All our favorite ideas—*order, tradition, discipline, hierarchy, authority, continuity, unity, work, family, corporat-*

ism, decentralization, autonomy, worker organization — have been conserved and protected by Catholicism."[22] For Maurras and his royalist followers, the Roman and Gallican Catholic churches were a very real manifestation of what "authentic France" was all about in the midst of the alien nation which officially governed the French. Both the church and the Action Française shared common visions of a good society, or so it seemed, and both found a common symbol of what constituted the national purpose, the patron of the fatherland, Joan of Arc. For the Action Française, she brought together those two basic foci of the nation, the monarchy and the Catholic church. In this way, she incarnated the reality of France and thus could be called "the angel of the French fatherland."[23] She was a figure of beauty, devotion, and piety, but, as guardian of the nation, she did not hesitate to enter the fray to do battle with the enemies of the *pays réel*.[24]

It is in the identification of these foes that the Action Française found its second major area of alignment with French Catholicism. Charles Maurras and the royalists were convinced that their opponents were also those of the Catholic church. Maurras saw this proven in the fact that "very few Catholics supported Dreyfus" and in the perception that the pro-Dreyfus republic of "Jews, Protestants, Masons and foreigners [*métèques*]" was dedicated resolutely to the destruction of Catholicism in France. He called the church "their unique rival."[25] The Action Française railed against these common adversaries and sought to demonstrate why they were alien to the essence and purpose of French Catholicism.

First of all, the Freemasons were described as enemies of both France and the church. In fact, the Catholics were called their "most resolute adversaries." And no wonder, for the Masons had mobilized republican institutions for twenty-five years in order to isolate the Catholic church from "the national family." It was in the arena of educational politics that the two forces had clashed most directly. On the one side were the Masons who were seeking to dismantle the Catholic schools with their emphasis on spiritual and character formation. Masonic education meant a pedagogy "smitten with 'liberal' Protestantism," scholastic values that originated in the Geneva of John Calvin and Jean-Jacques Rousseau. On the other side were ranked the Catholics, whose educational principles were built upon discipline and the pedagogical role of the family. A victory for the Masons would mean the certain destruction of "the French schools." The Action Française described this struggle as "a war of religion, . . . the direct heir of the *wars of religion* which have divided our nation since the Reformation."[26] This sense of a religious crusade inspired the Catholic royalists of the Action Française to label the Masonic movement as a "counterchurch," a religious establishment impregnated with the values not only of Protestantism but also of hated Jewry. Judaism had usurped and misued the biblical promises, and by so doing, it became an enemy brother of Catholicism. The subversive plot of the Masonic church to overthrow the genuinely French Catholic church made necessary an alliance of religion and patriotism: "This time, as always, our duty as Catholics accords perfectly with our duty as Frenchmen, for the same Jewish and masonic sectarians desire both the body and soul of France."[27]

Second, the Jews were singled out as common foes of both the Action Française and the French church. From the beginning, the royalist league was resolutely anti-Semitic, but in this respect, it was hardly unique. Hatred of the Jews was intrinsic to the new and rabid nationalism which had originated with Boulangism, and it was deeply rooted in French Catholic tradition itself. However, the anti-Semitism of the Action Française was particularly virulent. It was often as ugly as that expressed by Edouard Drumont, and it could be as violent as the pogrom mentality found in Algiers at this time. One leaguer called the Jew "an intermediate creature between animals and man," and another royalist aristocrat insisted that "our duty as French Catholics is to struggle . . . against the Jewish-Masonic octopus."[28] It is very difficult to determine whether Action Française anti-Semitism was primarily theological, economic, or racial. In some instances, the rationale used against the Jews was religious; in other cases, emphasis was placed upon the Jew's "subhuman" character and the presence of "alien" blood in the French body politic. Finally, Jewry was charged with financial greed and responsibility for the economic woes of the nation, witnessed to by the continuing euphemism found upon the lips of royalists who spoke of Jewish wealth as "anonymous and vagabond fortunes." However, for the most part, Jews were deemed to be subversive because they imported alien and competitive values into France. Charles Maurras articulated this philosophy in his political writings. For him the "anarchic" Hebrew prophets had undermined the stability of society by their individualistic protests. They had infected their countrymen and had created the Jew as "a revolutionary agent." In this respect, Jews were regarded as no different from Protestants who were called their ideological brothers along with the Masons and other revolutionaries.[29] As often as not, the Jew was charged with linking together those enemies which the Action Française and the Catholic church supposedly shared in common.

To list Protestantism as the third enemy of royalist patriots and Catholics was hardly surprising. The Gallican church had a long history of enmity against the sixteenth-century Reformation, and traditional Catholic theology was rife with the polemics of the Counter-Reformation and the Council of Trent. Once again, however, the Action Française was able to link together its other enemies with the traditional Catholic enmity against Protestants. The way in which Masonic educational policy and revolutionary Jewry were linked to the Reformation has been noted already. In addition, Protestantism was branded as a heresy with uniquely German colors. After all, was not "the Protestant disease" created in Germany by Martin Luther who disseminated ideas of liberty and equality which were carried by Voltaire and Rousseau into France immediately prior to the French Revolution. Protestantism was a value system alien to France, the spirit of revolution imported into France from Germany.[30] For Maurras the alternative to this danger was the Catholic and classical world view:

> In the modern era Catholic philosophy models itself upon Aristotle; Catholic politics appropriates Roman politics. Such is the character of the classical tradition. The classical spirit is properly the essence of the doctrines of high humanity. This is the spirit

of authority and tradition. To call the spirit of the Revolution classical is to adulterate the natural sense of that word.

The Revolution has entirely different origins: the Bible of the Reformation, the statutes of Geneva's republic, the Calvinistic theologians.[31]

Republicanism and the revolutionary values emanating from it were the final adversary that the Action Française claimed to share with traditional Catholicism in France. The potential member of the league was confronted with this challenge: "You decide . . . Monarchy or Republic," or to put it another way, the French were expected to choose between "divine right or the rights of man."[32] The very pledge made by every new member included the desire to restore the monarchy upon the corpse of republicanism precisely because this latter form of government was held to be detrimental to Catholicism. For Charles Maurras, republicanism is the natural child of revolution and sociopolitical disorder. Its principles violate the natural order of things: "Political liberty, basic to the republican system," has destroyed civic respect; being a citizen has lost its meaning. Equality has shattered the natural pyramid of authority by allowing power to reside with the lowest common denominator. Talented and productive forces have been supplanted by "the inferior elements of the nation." Finally, the republican virtue of fraternity has been replaced by its opposite — civil war.[33] The history of republicanism in France was proof plenty for Maurras that behind all the lofty ideals espoused by democrats lurked the inevitability of revolution and anti-Catholicism. He pointed out that even the participation of Catholics in the French Revolution could not prevent the spirit of 1789 from degenerating into the regicide and Jacobin tyranny of 1793 and 1794. Subsequent events demonstrated further that republicans of good will were powerless to prevent the revolutionary bloodshed and anarchy that inevitably followed. This was as true of the Second Republic of 1848 and the socialist Paris Commune of 1871 as it was of the Grand Revolution itself. The long anticlerical campaign of the present Third Republic was, for Maurras, a current reminder of the veracity of his contentions. This historical recital was followed by a grim and simple conclusion: "It cannot be said that the French Republic is not the offspring of the revolutionary and insurrectional spirit."[34] Because republican insurrectionism needed a spiritual foundation, this "religion of revolution" was compelled to combat "every other religion" and transform itself into a counterchurch. This alternative religion needed to be shattered in the name of integral nationalism and the Catholic church. Such was the contention of the Action Française.[35]

With such wide-ranging positions reflecting solidarity with the French church, Charles Maurras and his followers hoped to reap a glorious harvest of Catholic members and sympathizers for the Action Française. On the one hand, the royalist league espoused values of order, authority, hierarchy, and civilization which it found inherent to traditional Catholicism. On the other hand, it declared war against individuals, groups, and principles which were hostile to the French church. Its devotion to the anti-Dreyfusard cause and its damning of the Republic's anticlerical campaigns made it a prime contender for the winning of Catholic sympathies.

However, the matter was more complex than these apparent parallels seemed to warrant. Elements of the philosophy of Charles Maurras were in direct conflict with traditional Catholic dogma and piety. Most blatant of these was the professed agnosticism of the royalist leader, a skepticism gleaned in large part from his interpretation of the positivism of Auguste Comte. Maurras recognized the possibility that Catholics might hesitate to form alliances with unbelievers. For this reason, he constructed a rationale to offset Catholic uncertainties about his position by expanding upon the following axiom: "Divided on heavenly things, positivism and Catholicism are often in accord on temporal matters."[36] He urged Catholics to rally to the appeal of the positivists, because "deism, Protestantism and, for a stronger reason, Judaism" have united for the purpose of destroying the French church. In order to resist this Protestant, secular, and Jewish menace, a coalition must be marshaled that would include all forces dedicated to defending the Catholic church. For Maurras, one of these natural allies of the beleaguered church was the philosophy of Auguste Comte, a philosophy vindicating "Catholic civilization against the forces of anarchy and barbarism." Had not Comte himself cherished Catholicism "as a necessary ally of science" against these very minions of hate?[37] In detail, the world views and foes shared in common by both traditional Catholics and agnostic positivists were sufficient cause for Maurras to justify an alliance short of unified theistic convictions: "The Church and positivism tend to fortify the family. The church and positivism promote the idea that public authority comes from God or at least springs from the most basic natural laws. The Church and positivism are friends of tradition, order, the fatherland and civilization. In a word, the Church and positivism have enemies in common."[38]

That patriotic positivists do not believe in the God of the Catholic church should not be an insurmountable problem, argued Maurras, for the very good reason that there lived within the heart of "every true Frenchman" what he called an "instinctive Catholicism."[39]

Relationships with the French church were complicated further by the harsh polemics which appeared regularly in the league's review against particular Catholics. Inflammatory language was not unique to the Action Française; vitriolic broadsides against one's enemies were also characteristic of the mass-oriented Catholic press, graphically displayed by the Assumptionist *La Croix*. Nevertheless, the appearance of such attacks against Christian persons and groups in a journal whose leading philosopher was an agnostic might be expected, at least, to raise traditional eyebrows.

Unsurprisingly, the Action Française directed most of these polemics against those Catholics who were avowed republicans, namely the Christian Democrats. Very early in their career, the new royalists were accusing these Catholic republicans of rallying to the cause of Dreyfus. Although they were a "tiny sect," the "liberal Catholics" were viewed as a dangerous subversive element within the body of the traditional church.[40] Henri Vaugeois warned Catholic families that Christian democratic ideas were infiltrating the young and were seriously undermining the traditional values of most Catholic parents. Should this trend continue, one would soon find that a "Christian" army would be supplanted by a "Jewish" and democratic one. Instead, pleaded Vaugeois, let the Christian Democratic ideas be posted where they belong, "on the outside of urinals."[41]

Particular Catholic democrats and their organizations were singled out for special attack. Hippolyte Gayraud, a Christian Democratic priest in the French Chamber of Deputies, was one of these. His book *La République et la paix religieuse* was criticized roundly by Jacques Bainville, a noted reactionary historian and early sympathizer with the royalist league. He regretted that Catholics like Gayraud and his supporters chose to place themselves "under the protection of the 'Declaration of the Rights of Man'" rather than under the traditional authoritarian hierarchy of the Catholic church. Further, the social catholicism advocated by this questionable book originated in Britain and Geneva, havens of Protestantism, rather than at Rome, which should have been its source.[42]

However, no person or group in this category received such massive assaults from the Action Française as Marc Sangnier and the Sillon. This is understandable, since both this vigorous group of Christian Democrats and the Action Française competed for the same mass clientele, especially the Catholic youth.[43] As early as 1902, the Action Française was warning Catholics to beware of the seductive words of Sangnier. His "vaguely humanitarian and pseudo-democratic declarations" were subtle means used to undermine the French army.[44]

During this same period letters were exchanged between Charles Maurras and Marc Sangnier. In this correspondence, the royalist leader attempted to demonstrate to the Christian Democratic tribune that both the course of human nature and the French national interest demanded a monarchy. When these arguments failed to convince Sangnier, Maurras published his most important work on Christian Democracy in the royalist fortnightly review. This series of articles, which appeared in *L'Action Française* during 1904 and 1905, were an edited collection of the above letters entitled "Le Dilemme de Marc Sangnier."[45]

According to Maurras, the issue posed by Sangnier between "the positivist monarchy of the Action Française [versus] the social Christianity of Sillon" avoided the basic question. The Sillon had no monopoly on social Catholicism, Maurras charged. In fact, both medieval, traditional Catholicism and positivism upheld a societal philosophy structured according to the natural laws of order, family, tradition, hierarchy, and the like. Consequently, a Catholic-positivist alliance could find its historic facsimile in the Middle Ages when Catholicism was drawn by a logical affinity to the philosophy of Aristotle. For Maurras, there was a problem, but it was not "the dilemma" suggested by Marc Sangnier: "A sole dilemma exists, but it is between those who wish to build society on the virtue of citizens and those who place the frailty of men within a social organization. Social Christians, historically and rationally, are ranked in this latter group with the Action Française. Sillon is unhappily on the other side in bad company."[46]

Maurras did not deny that Sangnier possessed admirable qualities. He was magnanimous, generous, a spirited orator, and a man of action, but these characteristics were offset by his similarity to the socialist demagogue Jean Jaurès and his faith in democracy. By judging every voter to be a saint, Maurras argued, Sangnier acts against the social, moral, and political order and, by so doing, strikes a blow against France. Such naïveté, charged Maurras, did not take into account that behind the glorious theory of democracy lay a tyranny under the domination of vested interests. Sangnier was intoxicated by false dreams and chimeras, while the Action Française and its leadership were dedicated to such principles as "love of the fatherland, love of religion, love of tradition, love of material and moral order, hatred and fear of anarchy and of the foreigner, whether internal or external." Only a king could provide such order against the forces of chaos. For this reason, it was imperative that all "patriots, Catholics, traditionalists and men of order" unite in order to restore the monarchy.[47]

So began a conflict between two men and two ideas, a battle waged within the Catholic camp for the duration of the Third Republic and beyond. On the one side were those who looked backward to a society of order and ecclesiastical privilege that predated the French Revolution. Their views found a voice in the reactionary nationalism of Charles Maurras and the Action Française. On the other side were those believers who felt that Catholicism could integrate the more positive elements found in modern values of democracy and social justice. These were the Christian Democrats, and their most articulate tribune was Marc Sangnier.

Not all Catholics fell exclusively into either of these two camps. Many, perhaps most, Catholics were traditional—even conservative—in their political positions. However, this did not mean that they were open monarchists. Certainly they were not attracted to the positivism of Auguste Comte. More or less reluctantly, they had joined the Ralliement program of Pope Leo XIII in the hope that they might use the constitutional and republican machinery of France to restore the flagging fortunes of the Church. In spite of the massive assaults of the anticlerical government elected in the wake of the Dreyfus affair, the majority of Catholic political elites clung stubbornly to some form of Ralliement strategy and ideology. Only the shock of the Separation legislation voted at the end of 1905 would jolt the church into a decided policy shift.

In the interim, the Action Française treated some of these very important sectors of the French church with less than diplomatic finesse. *La Croix,* the most influential Catholic newspaper of that era, was judged to be a false friend of the conservative Catholic cause because it vacillated in its attitude toward monarchism and republicanism.[48] Further, the Action Française criticized those elements within the French episcopate which supported the Ralliement. In one instance, a *rallié* bishop was charged both with destroying "the ancient cadres of religious and social defense" and with reinforcing "the antisocial and antireligious army" that governed France.[49] Finally, the integral nationalists criticized publicly the Vatican policy of compromise with the Third Republic which Leo XIII had inaugurated. Although the league's review declared emphatically that Christian Democrats had attempted dishonestly to manipulate papal statements in defense of their personal programs, the royalist position was opposed unequivocally to the Ralliement. From the Action Française point of view, the conservative Leo had made a serious tactical blunder. By ordering French Catholics to abandon their royalist militancy and to abstain from combating the republican constitution, he had opened the door to civil war among Catholics. The ensuing internal divisions in the church augmented the church's vulnerability in the face of the anticlerical republican onslaught.[50]

Thus, from the very beginning, the loyalty of the Action Française to the Catholic church was tempered by Maurras's particular brand of patriotism. The Catholicism it revered was so sharply and narrowly defined that it excluded all Christian Democrats and many nonroyalist conservatives with the best of ecclesiastical credentials. Even bishops and popes were not necessarily exempt from the polemical barbs of the royalist review. Add to this behavior the agnostic positivism of Charles Maurras, and one has those ingredients that called into question, for some, the feasibility of an Action Française–Catholic church alliance.

Nevertheless, some Catholics did join, and many of them were dedicated and loyal practitioners of their faith. Their reasons for enlisting in the new royalist organization were conscious and, in many cases, ably articulated. One priest put it this way: "As a French citizen and as a Catholic priest, I have the duty to adhere to the *League of the Action Française*. . . . I do not intend to lose my way in the liberal . . . visions of Monsieur Sangnier."[51] Very clearly, his attraction to the disciples of Charles Maurras was built upon a world view that he and these royalist reactionaries shared in common, a system that he felt was alien to the species of Catholicism articulated by the Sillon. That Maurras was an agnostic or that brutal polemics were characteristic of the new group were, at most, only secondary concerns when compared with the ideological and psychological affinities he deemed to be essential. From the beginning, the Action Française attracted some Catholics who were prepared to unite militant patriotism with a monarchical restoration in order that the church and society they cherished could supplant the frightening values and structures they believed had emanated from the French Revolution. That an agnostic was philosophical leader of this group was either overlooked by these believers or deemed to be one of the mysteries of God.

For the most part, however, the Action Française was ignored in these early years by both French believers and unbelievers. Nevertheless, this brief inaugural period witnessed the ideological and structural organization that would lead to its significant impact on France in general and on the Catholic church in particular. The groundwork had been laid by the royalist league which would attract some Catholics and repel others. Its pro-Catholic medievalism and social values, combined with its relentless opposition to elements commonly viewed as hostile to the traditional church, made it especially appealing to those Catholics who sought refuge in a glorious prerevolutionary past. These same principles, combined with violent polemics and elements of positivistic agnosticism, rendered it alien to Christian Democrats and suspect to many traditional believers. Such a contradiction not only was manifest within the league itself but also was part and parcel of the conflicting divisions within French Catholicism. These mutual paradoxes would define, color, and decipher the stormy relationship that existed between the Action Française and the Catholic church from Dreyfus to Pétain.

The Dreyfus affair and the triumph of anticlerical republicanism in the elections of 1899 had been instrumental in the birth of royalist integral nationalism. For the next five and one-half years the victorious Dreyfusard government waged a relentless campaign against the French church which the anticlericals had judged to be compromised hopelessly in the wake of the Dreyfus conflict. These anti-Catholic attacks forced the church into a defensive posture which threatened the unity so firmly sought by Leo XIII. Not only had the affair and the new governing coalition it spawned given birth to the Action Française, but also these and subsequent events alienated French Catholicism from the republic and made it more susceptible to antidemocratic elements within both the church and the nation.

a blend of republicanism, social Catholicism, and anti-Semitism. Throughout the Dreyfus affair his commitment to the democratic values of 1789 did not prevent him from advocating a two-France position similar in some ways to that of both *La Croix* and the Action Française. Dreyfus was called "the traitor," and the newspaper advocated a program which would expropriate Jewish wealth legally.[5] Most of the other Christian Democrats paralleled the practice of *L'Ouest-Eclair*. Father Paul Naudet, a Breton comrade of Desgrées du Loû, affirmed the need to free French soil from alien Jewry in both its ethnic and economic aspects, and François Mouthon, the Christian Democratic leader of Lyon, called his weekly *France Libre* "Catholic youth's anti-Jewish and anti-Masonic newspaper."[6]

Nevertheless, it was among the Christian Democrats that the Dreyfusard cause found its first Catholic adherents. Father Jules Lemire, a parliamentary deputy from the Nord and a long-time devotee of republicanism, abandoned economic anti-Semitism as a political platform, and Marc Sangnier refused to allow the Sillon to be drawn into a campaign of ethnic and religious hate. In time, Father Naudet himself became disenchanted with anti-Semitism, published letters favorable to Dreyfus in his *Justice Sociale* and joined the Committee for the Defense of Right, the only significant Catholic group to espouse the Dreyfusard cause.[7] However, these few Christian Democrats were exceptions to the rule. In most instances, Catholic republicans had adopted the republic without abandoning that anti-Semitic populism which was integral to their socioeconomic programs.

Meanwhile, other leading Catholics hoped to remain aloof from the fray. They were less than successful. Albert de Mun's earlier hesitancy gave way to his desire to stand by the anti-Dreyfusard army, and in spite of Leo XIII's call for neutrality, a number of bishops issued public statements against the Jewish community in France. They viewed Dreyfus's cause as a weapon against the church, because they reflected the long-held Catholic conviction that the Jews had been resolute enemies of Christ for 1,900 years.[8] This traditional anti-Semitism mixed with a mentality of religious defense guaranteed that even the more moderate Catholic leadership in France would be unsympathetic to the Dreyfusard campaigns.

Add this caution to the overt antipathies of *La Croix* and the other outbursts of Catholic virulence, and it is easy to see why the secular republicans judged the Ralliement to be a sham. For them, the Dreyfus affair had demonstrated that Catholicism was no friend of the republic; nor was it interested in the principles of justice and equality, especially if these values were applied to Jews. Having won a significant electoral victory, the anticlerical Radicals and Socialists formed a government of republican defense in 1899.

The premier of the anticlerical coalition was an aloof, dignified, and immaculately tailored lawyer named Pierre Marie René Waldeck-Rousseau. His credentials were impeccably republican, and his anticlericalism, though orthodox, was more moderate and balanced than that of many deputies within the government alliance. Under his ministry an associations bill was promulgated that was designed to weaken the influence of certain religious orders in French Catholic educational establishments. A Chamber of Deputies majority, more punitive than the prime minister, had expanded the initial proposal to include the stipulation that all unauthorized religious orders had to apply to the government for legal status. A refusal of such status to any order meant its dissolution and the legal right for the government to confiscate the order's property. The revised bill was passed into law on July 1, 1901, and although Waldeck-Rousseau had hoped for a moderate enforcement of the legislation, in 1902 his successor Emile Combes insisted on a literal and punitive administration of the law. Few orders were authorized, and police contingents were sent out to padlock religious houses and expel all monks and nuns who might be residing there.[9]

In the context of this anticlerical offensive, the public voices of the French church cried out with a nearly unanimous protest against the unjust treatment they felt they were receiving. From reactionary royalists to social democratic Catholic republicans there arose an outraged voice of religious defense. However, beneath that unanimity lay divisions that would only be detected with the passage of time and the deterioration of ecclesiastical fortunes.

+ 3 +

A Catholic Church Under Fire
(1899–1906)

*H*ostility *between the Third Republic* and the Catholic church was not a direct product of the Dreyfus affair and the government that emerged in its wake. Two decades earlier victorious republicanism had diverted its anticlericalism into a secular education program designed in part to undermine Catholic power and influence within the nation. The church's attempts to resist the new republic by negative policies of religious defense proved disastrous. Leo XIII's Ralliement, designed to reverse this discouraging trend, had been ignored politely by many influential sectors of French Catholicism. Only the Christian Democrats welcomed the papal appeal, but their minimal impact could not challenge seriously the Catholic majority's long-standing commitments against the French Revolution and its values. For almost a decade the Ralliement languished until the Dreyfus affair and the ensuing anticlerical legislation exposed its fragility. In the brief period from 1899 to 1906 Leo's policy would be crushed between the Scylla of anti-Catholic republicanism and the Charybdis of reactionary Catholicism.

With few exceptions, articulate French Catholics joined the ranks of the anti-Dreyfusards. Some like Albert de Mun did so for military and patriotic reasons, while others attacked Dreyfus for reasons similar to those employed by the Action Française.

Hostility toward the Jews was deep-rooted within sectors of French Catholicism. The notorious anti-Semitic press campaigns found in Edouard Drumont's *La Libre Parole* were subsidized largely by a Catholic readership. In some instances, priests would make direct contributions inspired by personal hatred of the Jews.[1]

Two of the more prominent religious orders in France joined Drumont in his hateful fulminations. The Jesuits, for the most part, remained aloof from the affair, but in their newspaper *Civiltà Cattolica* they had asserted that Dreyfus's guilt was proven by the fact that God had created the Jew to be a spy. Only the abrogation of their citizenship could resolve the problem of the Jews, the newspaper asserted.[2] However, it was the reactionary Assumptionists who campaigned most actively against the Dreyfusards in general and the Jews in particular. Their chief weapon was the most influential Catholic newspaper in all of France, the daily *La Croix* with its circulation of almost 200,000. Its popular format gave it mass appeal among Catholics, and its fraternal ties to the French hierarchy lent a quasi-official status to its utterances which was not shared by any other sector of the Catholic press. *La Croix* described itself as "the most anti-Jewish newspaper in France," because it believed that the sons of Abraham were both a grave danger to France and the natural enemy of the Christian faith. Consequently, when the Rennes verdict reaffirmed Dreyfus's condemnation, the newspaper uttered joyfully: "As Frenchmen, we rejoice! As Catholics, we thank God!"[3] From *La Croix*'s perspective, two Frances were in mortal combat, "Jewish, Protestant and so-called freethinking France" on the one hand, and "Catholic France," the defender of the army and nation on the other. Thus, for the Assumptionists, the counteroffensive against Dreyfus was a crusade "against the recognized enemies of Christ and the Church."[4]

Even the Ralliement's most unequivocal supporters, the Christian Democrats, joined the anti-Dreyfusards, and their reasons were usually a combination of patriotic militarism and anti-Semitism. Catholic republicanism's most influential daily *L'Ouest-Eclair* was a good case in point. Its owner and editor Emmanuel Desgrées du Loû was a nationalistic naval officer who embodied

The Catholic ultraright used the occasion to decry the republic itself and to urge a return to forms of society that predated the French Revolution. Canon Henry Delassus, editor of Cambrai's influential religious weekly and a most intransigent monarchist, spoke for those Catholic reactionaries who populated the Nord, one of the few remaining sections of France where the majority of inhabitants continued to practice its faith, even in some of the industrial areas. For him, the new anticlerical government meant that France was in captivity to a sinister triad: Jews, "who own the money and wish for the death of Jesus Christ's religion," socialists, who "lead the fatherland to revolution," and Freemasons, who "debase France and all which gives her honor."[10] This demonic elite was a natural by-product of the French Revolution with its "false dogmas of liberty, equality, popular sovereignty and the illegitimacy of property." Such doctrines of democracy and socialism were judged by Delassus to reflect what he called Rousseau's perverted dogma of "the immaculate conception of man." In contrast to this destructive France was the glorious France of throne and altar which bridled humankind's original sin through the "social inequality and social hierarchy" exemplified by Catholicism and the monarchy.[11] The Revolution reduced all this to chaos and opened the door to the tyrannous rule of the Masonic, socialistic, and Jewish triumvirate. Such opinions convinced Delassus and other leading Catholic reactionaries that the Christian Democrats were more comfortable with the church's enemies than with its friends. The reactionary canon continually harassed the *abbés démocrates* as well as the Sillon of Marc Sangnier.[12] Although they were not a majority among Catholic leaders, reactionary churchmen remained strident and influential voices in the most heavily populated Catholic regions of France. Their political ideology and violent rhetoric drew them closer to the Action Française than to their fellow believers among the Christian Democrats. The anticlerical offensive would be a bonanza for both these ultrarightist groups who discovered that their violent polemics were becoming increasingly credible to more moderate Catholics faced with mounting governmental assaults against the church. Anticlerical victories meant disillusionment with the Ralliement, isolation of the Christian Democrats, and growing hostility among Catholic moderates toward the Third Republic. All this signaled an evolution of the church toward the right end of the political spectrum. The reactionary Catholics and the Action Française would be the immediate beneficiaries of this process.

This growing intransigence of conservative *ralliés* against the government was a direct outgrowth of anticlerical legislation. Although the republic was not condemned per se and although the Christian Democrats were not included in these protests, the traditional Catholic centrists were using increasingly the hostile rhetoric of the reactionaries and were abandoning the papal language of Ralliement. Further, these conservatives were the bastions of Catholic power in France, embracing the most influential bishops, the pro-Catholic electoral coalition of the Action Libérale Populaire, and the daily newspaper *La Croix*.

France's powerful cardinals turned to the "two-France" rhetoric of the ultraright in their efforts to meet the anticlerical offensive. Episcopal voices were lifted against "the Masonic sects," "the Protestant Reformation," and "the revolutionary movement of 1789." Because of this subversion within the nation's body politic, France was "now divided in two, Christian France and anti-Christian France." The descriptions and symbols used by these prelates to describe Catholic France were drawn from the ancien régime and the Middle Ages. Love of nation and church were the twin pillars of the fatherland which was under the protection of Joan of Arc rather than Dame Liberty.[13] However, in spite of this reactionary language, France's leading bishops avoided anti-Semitic excesses and sought to use republican values to justify their protests. In a letter to Emile Loubet, the republic's president, Parisian archbishop François Richard sought to assure the republic's president that Catholics were simply protecting their "rights as citizens." "We do not demand privileges," he asserted, "but we do demand that Catholics not be deprived of those rights which belong to all the French."[14] For the most part, the powerful leaders of the French episcopate were divided among themselves. On the one hand, they longed for a prerevolutionary France in which the church retained privileges secure from internal enemies. In this respect, they were like reactionary Catholics and the

Action Française. On the other hand, they were prepared to abandon their ultra brothers if the republic could be rendered more conservative, more authoritarian and more pro-Catholic. Short of this, they would turn to the right in search of allies.

A similar combination of conservative politics and flexible tactics was also characteristic of Catholic electoral politics. *Ralliés* such as Albert de Mun and the provincial lawyer Jacques Piou decried "the masonic, Jacobin and socialist tyranny" that governed France, but they remained convinced that this coalition could be defeated at the polls via a strategy of electoral politics and constitutionality. Toward that end the Action Libérale Populaire was created on June 11, 1901. From the beginning, the ALP was a party of religious defense, indeed, almost a confessional party, though it claimed to be otherwise. Much like the hierarchy, it was caught between the siege mentality of "two-France" ideologies and the constitutional principles of the republic. Its dedication "to liberty with all its consequences" was offset by its subliminal clericalism.[15] Endorsement by both *La Croix* and the hierarchy served to further enhance the confessional image of the party. Before elections, bishops of the church would utilize both their diocesan weeklies and public appearances at ALP rallies to urge Catholic voters to cast their ballots for the party of de Mun and Piou. For its part, the Assumptionist daily softened its extremist language and appealed to French conservatives to adopt the ALP's program of "liberty for all" and "equality before the law" against "the sectarians and Jacobins." To be sure, the Action Libérale Populaire proclaimed a platform undergirded by republican values, but its confessional priorities, its ecclesiastical supporters, its funding sources, and the presence of numerous reactionaries within its ranks gave it the character of an organization of religious defense. Indeed, the ALP was a genuinely Ralliement party with a decidedly rightward drift.[16]

La Croix's overt support of the ALP, as well as its willingness to open its columns to selected Christian Democratic tribunes, demonstrated that French Catholicism's most influential newspaper was committed to a unity of all the nation's Catholics against the anticlerical government. In this respect, *La Croix* was at odds with church reactionaries.[17] However, at another level, it adopted and promulgated the shrill crusades of the Catholic ultraright. The French Revolution was described as a Protestant and German import which by 1789 had come to dominate France, that glorious "nation of Clovis, Charlemagne and Saint Louis." A virulent anti-Semitism continued to dominate the newspaper, and in this respect, it was no different from the Catholic reactionaries and the Action Française. *La Croix* was certain that the Jew was the revolutionary par excellence who had begun his long history of insurrection "at the foot of Calvary." Two desires dominated his thought: "to fight the religion of Jesus Christ and to dominate the world by the power of money."[18] Even Leo XIII's effort to moderate the paper by the appointment of the industrialist Paul Feron-Vrau to its directorship did not change significantly the tone of *La Croix*. Its vituperation against the Masonic, Protestant, Jewish triad and its rejection of the French Revolution in the name of medieval values pointed to its growing attraction to Catholicism's ultraright. Nevertheless, for the moment, *La Croix* joined with the Action Libérale Populaire and France's most prominent prelates in an attempt to preserve the increasingly fragile Ralliement in the face of anticlerical intransigence. Differing from both their reactionary and Christian Democratic confreres, they were prepared to adjust their very conservative values to Third Republican realities. Their ideology was more appealing to the former, but their tactics were more attractive to the latter. For a brief time, it appeared as if governmental hostility against the church would hold these disparate forces together.

However, it was the Christian Democrats who most openly undermined this hope for a grand union of all Catholics built upon the foundation of religious defense and constitutionality. Along with other Catholics, these republicans had been anti-Dreyfusard and had suffered persecution at the hands of anticlericals. As a result, they too initially attacked their foes in terms reminiscent of the Catholic right. Christian Democracy's influential daily *L'Ouest-Eclair* excoriated Freemasonry, Jewry and socialism, calling them grave dangers to the nation. The *abbés démocrates* were equally hostile. Father Naudet called the Dreyfusard government of Waldeck-Rousseau a victory for "the socialists, the Jews, the Genevan Protestants and the Freemasons," and Father Gayraud rose in the Chamber of Deputies to denounce the proposed legislation against the religious orders which he likened to Robespierre's Reign of Terror. Even the peacemaking Marc Sangnier bemoaned the "atheistic materialism" he saw underlying "the sectarian and Jacobin majority" that ruled France.[19]

Further, the Christian Democrats were prepared for a while to join with other Catholics in political ventures designed to defend the church against its governmental foes. For this reason, most of them entered the ranks of the Action Libérale Populaire. In Brittany, *L'Ouest-Eclair* opened its columns to the ALP leadership, and Desgrées du Loû sent Charles Bodin to be his newspaper's official representative in the party's Breton caucus. Bodin proclaimed publicly that the ALP was needed in France in order "to save those religious liberties currently trampled underfoot." Also cooperative efforts were established between Marc Sangnier and Jacques Piou. They encouraged each other's work, and Sangnier would speak occasionally at ALP rallies.[20] However, the sympathies and similarities which Catholic republicans shared with the Action Libérale Populaire and other Catholic conservatives had their limits.

Indeed, Christian Democracy's basic ideology necessitated a break even with those Catholics who were prepared to use the language of 1789 in the pursuit of ends many Catholic republicans believed were alien to the values of the French Revolution. Whereas Catholic conservatives could use republican means for nonrepublican ends, republican principles were values in their own right for the Christian Democrats. The French Revolution and its democratic tenets were axioms that could not be abandoned in the name of religious defense. Father Pierre Dabry, a Breton journalist, maintained that "the republic" was "the condition *sine qua non* of all advance" and "the necessary foundation of all healthy action and progress." *L'Ouest-Eclair* insisted that the Declaration of the Rights of Man and Citizen must remain the charter of the nation, and Marc Sangnier's disciples used their leader's notion of "the democratic excellence of Christianity" to define themselves as "convinced partisans of modern methods of republican government: universal suffrage, liberty, justice and fraternity."[21]

This firm commitment to the necessary amalgamation of republicanism and Catholicism led the Christian Democrats to break their alliance with the more pragmatic Action Libérale Populaire at the precise moment when the anticlerical campaign was gaining momentum. By 1903, *L'Ouest-Eclair* was publishing its suspicions that the ALP's allegiance to religious defense made it fertile soil for royalist infiltration. Emmanuel Desgrées du Loû made it clear that his newspaper would drop its support unless the ALP expelled all monarchists from its ranks. In the French Chamber of Deputies Father Gayraud broke with those Catholics "who wish to resist democratic progress." Sillon refused to be drawn into a confessional party in alliance with those whom it called "the interior enemies of Catholicism." For Father Paul Naudet, the ALP was a clerical, bourgeois, and royalist party which had turned the Ralliement into a lie. He was convinced that the only way "to safeguard the interests of religion" was to "break definitively with the conservatives" and to vote only for genuine republicans even if they were anticlericals.[22]

Beyond its dilution of Catholic commitment to the republic and beyond its invitation to royalist subversion, the ALP program of religious defense convinced the Christian Democrats that they could not count on Piou's party to press for basic social reform. Naudet bemoaned its lack of popular institutes, trade unions, cooperatives, and family banks, and he suggested that capitalism was "economically worse than socialism," since capitalism led to the ruin of both body and soul. Sillon's break with the ALP's social policy was less polemic but much more substantive. Convinced that economic democracy was necessary to preserve political democracy, the bourgeois followers of Marc Sangnier invited militant proletarians into their study circles and popular universities so that the two groups might prepare a future democracy worthy of that name. So convinced was the Sillon that democracy would fail without the grass-roots participation of the workers that it broke with the class collaborationism of traditional social Catholicism by advocating independent trade unions over against the factory owners.[23]

Therefore, although the Christian Democrats resisted the anticlericalism of the Dreyfusard coalition, they quickly became disenchanted with the methods and programs chosen by most Catholics to defend the church against its aggressive detractors. Eschewing all alliances with questionable republicans, overt royalists, and social conservatives, the Christian Democrats insisted that only unequivocal republicanism and vigorous social reform could win for the church a respected place in French society. Their refusal to adopt a program of religious defense alienated them from both the Catholic reactionaries and the church conservatives, hierarchical and lay. With the passage of time and with the intensification of governmental attacks against the church grew an increasing polarization which would shatter the Christian Democrats and work to the advantage of the reactionaries, including the Action Française.

This spreading atmosphere of civil war between church and state was exemplified by the rise to leadership of two intransigents, one to the premiership of France and the other to the papacy. Emile Combes, the ex-seminarian who replaced the retiring Waldeck-Rousseau as prime minister, was single-minded in his determination to reduce and circumscribe the power of the French church. The new premier was a provincial doctor and Mason, a small lonely man who had adopted his anticlericalism during the Bonapartist era and was now prepared to employ it through the bureaucracy of his government. His unflincing foe would be Guiseppe Sarto who was elected to the See of Peter after the death of Leo XIII in 1903. This new pope took the name of Pius X.

Immediately Combes intensified the anticlerical campaign against the French church. He enforced the existing antichurch legislation as strictly as possible and sought further occasions to use state machinery to control the church. Combes never intended an abrogation of the Napoleonic Concordat which he deemed to be a useful instrument to control the nation's clergy, but he put forward such a bill (1904) in the hope of rendering the French church more pliant to his wishes.²⁴

A proposed visit of the republic's moderate president Emile Loubet to the Kingdom of Italy was another occasion that inflamed church-government conflict. Such a visit would be viewed as an act of hostility against the Vatican, for since 1870 the pope had refused to recognize the new Italian government which had seized papal property and allowed the successor of Peter to retain only a small Vatican enclave. Not only did Combes refuse to negotiate the matter with the nuncio in Paris; but also he added insult to injury by his insistence that President Loubet not pay a conciliatory visit to the Vatican. French Catholicism responded to this diplomatic insult with outraged protest. Father Gayraud rose in the Chamber to chastize the government, and Albert de Mun expressed the indignation of Catholics in the pages of *La Croix*.²⁵ Pius X, in spite of the increasingly strained relations between the Vatican and France, expressed his formal protest in moderate language. However, those anticlericals more intransigent than Combes refused to be mollified. By a vote of 427 to 96 the deputies served notice on Piux X and French Catholics that the premier was free to recall the French ambassador to the Vatican and to close down the nuncio's office in Paris.²⁶ The government was one step away from obliterating French ties with the papacy.

Further strife involving interpretation of the Napoleonic Concordat was caused by the issue surrounding the power to name and invest bishops. According to the concordat, the French government would nominate candidates, and the papacy would grant canonical institution upon the governmental choices. Such a sensitive matter demanded diplomacy and tact. Emile Combes was not so inclined, and even less so were his own immoderate allies. Under their pressure he provoked the ire of the church by refusing to consult the nuncio with respect to episcopal nominations and by demanding the suppression of the word *nobis* from the Roman bulls of episcopal investiture that read *nobis nominavit* (named by us).²⁷ Although Pius X was prepared reluctantly to drop the offensive *nobis,* he would not relinquish the Vatican's ultimate control over who would or would not receive the bishop's mitre. The papal secretary of state summarized succinctly the papal position in a letter sent to the nuncio in Paris:

> It would be superfluous to repeat the necessity of reminding M. Combes several times that the Concordat, in conceding to the state the privilege of nomination to vacant churches in France, reserves for the Supreme Pontiff the right to examine the qualities of the governmental candidates and to turn them away if he does not judge them fit.[28]

This battle over ultimate control of the French hierarchy erupted in the controversy surrounding the bishops of Dijon and Laval. Msgr. le Nordez of Dijon and Msgr. Géay of Laval were among the few overtly republican bishops in France. As early as 1902, they had refused to sign an episcopal protest letter against the Waldeck-Rousseau legislation on the ground that the missive's language was too intransigent.[29] Such behavior angered the reactionary and royalist integrists within their dioceses, who furiously called for their removal. Rumors of scandal abounded against the bishops, public demonstrations were organized against them, and integrist protests were sent to Rome petitioning for their enforced retirement. By the late spring of 1904, Pius X called upon both bishops to resign. Géay and le Nordez appealed to the reigning anticlericals for a ruling on their behalf. In the name of the government, both Premier Combes and his foreign minister Théophile Delcassé protested that the papal action was a unilateral attack upon the Concordat.[30] The battle lines had been drawn. Neither side would budge, and the two bishops became pawns in the larger struggle between church and state. The pressure of the pope proved more persuasive to these republican prelates than government encouragement. Consequently, by September 1904 both men had resigned, and the sees of Dijon and Laval fell vacant. In retaliation, the government informed Merry del Val that France had decided to end its official relations with the Vatican. The French embassy to the Holy See was closed, and the nuncio was sent home.[31] Catholic protest erupted with a single voice as reactionary royalists joined with *ралlié*s and Christian Democrats to express their outrage against this humiliation to Catholic France.[32] But this fury only intensified the anticlericals' resolve to obliterate the Concordat. The Combes ministry was repudiated by its more anticlerical allies, and the new government which replaced it passed the Separation Law of December 1905.

The new law proved to be a watershed for church-state relations in France. With its passage, the drama of French political life shifted elsewhere in a number of directions. Increasing working-class pressures and growing military chauvinism in Germany divided the Dreyfusard coalition to the point where anticlericalism was no longer deemed a significant enough policy to hold Radicals and Socialists together. Consequently, the more moderate elements among the anticlericals came to dominate the government on ecclesiastical questions, and once the furor surrounding the Separation Law had died down, they were able to insure a less punitive enforcement of it. On the Catholic side, the loss of state support exposed some of the church's own internal weaknesses and problems. Religious vocations fell precipitously, the notable decline in religious practice became a growing concern, and the loss of the urban working class to Catholicism was increasingly apparent.[33] In the long run, such freedom from the state apparatus and the painful recognition of Catholicism's vulnerable status within French society would be grounds for numerous progressive Catholic experiments.

However, at that moment and in and of itself the law was a blatant effort to weaken the church within French society. Questions of church finances and property were all regulated to the detriment of the church. Most objectionable to the Catholics, however, was article 4 of the law which created governing bodies for the church called "cultic associations." It was not at all clear exactly how these organizations were to be structured, and it was feared by Catholics that they would be used by anti-Catholic republicans to democratize the church and erase episcopal and papal authority.[34] French churchmen suspected that the government had designed the "cultic associations" in order to undermine the traditional leadership of the hierarchy. The notion that bishops of the church might be elected by the laity and that laypersons and clergy alike might become joint managers of ecclesiastical property was profoundly offensive to the vast majority of French Catholics. Even before the passage of the law, the French cardinals had issued a public protest that warned Catholics that the proposed "cultic associations" would be independent "of all episcopal and priestly authority" and that they were designed to impose "a purely lay institution . . . upon the Catholic church."[35]

Within the church, no one challenged the cardinals. French Catholics were unanimously opposed to the separation legislation. Canon Delassus saw it as a Freemason plot designed to overthrow Christian civilization and establish Jewish "domination over the entire earth."[36] *La Croix* was certain that the law was created in an attempt to protestantize the Catholic Church via the "cultic associations," and the leadership of the Action Libérale Populaire felt that it was the significant weapon in a Freemason conspiracy designed to destroy Catholicism. Even the Christian Democrats condemned the law unanimously. For *L'Ouest-Eclair* it was a violation of "liberty and justice" and an invitation to perpetual church-state conflicts. Marc Sangnier viewed it as "an instrument of war against the Catholic church," and other Sillonists sensed that it was an attempt to dechristianize the nation.[37]

However, this Catholic unanimity did not extend beyond formal opposition to the law. Proposals for accommodation to the government bill were being advocated by republican Catholics as early as 1904. Paul Naudet suggested that there were a few advantages to the law, and Emmanuel Desgrées du Loû felt that passage of the bill might result in weakening the accusations of those who charged the church with political clericalism. Even after the bill became law, Christian Democrats like Jules Lemire were expressing public confidence that the "cultic associations" would be enforced with moderation.[38]

The more traditionally conservative prelates of the church were not so encouraged, but even they were prepared to make compromises. Their language of opposition had been vehement, but they continued to practice the tactics of Ralliement. When it became clear that church-state separation would soon become a reality, Cardinal François Richard of Paris commissioned his diocesan newspaper to prepare a series of articles designed to effect a working compromise between the proposed "cultic associations" and the hierarchical structure of the Catholic church.[39] After the law was passed, a number of conservative *rallié* laymen followed his example. An ad hoc committee of prominent Catholic intellectuals and political figures, led by the conservatives Ferdinand Brunetière and Denys Cochin, appealed publicly to the assembled bishops of France and urged them to adopt a *modus vivendi* with the legislation. They argued that the "cultic associations" could be adapted to Catholic structures because the law stated that these bodies must "conform 'to the general organizational rules of that cult whose exercise they propose to assure.'" For this reason, these "green cardinals," as they came to be called, because they were entitled to wear the green regalia of the Académie Française, urged the bishops to create "cultic associations" which they could define and control.[40]

The Gallican episcopacy responded favorably to this request. Although they condemned the law as "false and pernicious" by an overwhelming vote of 72 to 2, a substantial majority of them invested Msgr. Fulbert Petit, the archbishop of Besançon, with the task of creating a model "cultic association" which would be acceptable to Catholic doctrine and practice. The document he presented to the episcopal assembly, in due time, insured that authority over the faithful and control of ecclesiastical goods and property would remain vested in the traditional hierarchy of the church. After some heated discussion, the bishops voted his model "cultic association" by the wide margin of 56 to 18. Fully three-quarters of the nation's prelates were prepared to live with the law.[41]

Catholic democrats throughout the land were elated. The Sillon and Jules Lemire had been urging acceptance of the new legislation, and Emmanuel Desgrées du Loû applauded the efforts of the "green cardinals."[42] Even the continued opposition of Albert de Mun and the shrill accusation of Henri Delassus that article 4 would "transform the monarchical Church instituted by

... Christ into a democracy and a republic" could not hide the fact that the French hierarchy had upheld the *ralliement* by a substantial majority.[43] The voices of restraint and religious peace had been endorsed by the official church at precisely the moment when the moderate secularist Aristide Briand began to divert the government from its harsh anticlerical practices. Apparently the storm had passed. Antichurch vehemence had subsided, the Catholic reactionaries had not been heeded by the assembled bishops, and the Action Française had gone unnoticed. Christian Democracy was emerging slowly from its former isolation and seemed to be vindicated by the episcopal vote.

Piux X shattered all that with the publication of his encyclical *Gravissimo Officii* on August 10, 1906. For three years he had attempted to negotiate his differences with the Third Republic and had watched each effort fail. As late as the first months of 1906, he refrained from insisting upon a single tactical line for the French church to follow with respect to the offensive law.[44] The August encyclical was a reversal of that previous policy, and from that moment, the pope adopted a hard-line strategy. In the letter, he assured the French hierarchy that he had searched carefully for possible areas of compromise but had discovered none. His chief concern was the "cultic associations" which he found to be the very antithesis of the church's divinely ordained hierarchical nature. Under no circumstances could the church of France abide by the Separation Law.[45] *Gravissimo Officii* baptized the position taken by the Catholic reactionaries in France, and the policy of compromise with and accommodation to the republic, advocated by the Christian Democrats, was rejected definitively by the pope.

Thus, what the secular republicans had failed to accomplish on their own was brought to fruition by Piux X. The Ralliement, though undermined seriously by certain Catholics' anti-Dreyfusard behavior, had survived the full weight of the anticlerical campaign. In spite of the increasing shrillness of the Catholic reactionaries, most traditional church leaders softened their vehement protests by a willingness to compromise with their aggressive foes. The harsh legislation against the religious orders, the Loubet visit to Rome, the bishops' affair, the closing of the Vatican embassy, and even the Separation Law had crippled the Ralliement seriously but had not destroyed it. To be sure, more and more traditional conservatives within the church began to employ the reactionaries' language with growing frequency, and the success of the harsh anticlerical program had weakened the moderates and Christian Democrats within the church. Divisions among Catholics were being accentuated to the advantage of the reactionaries. Nevertheless, the hierarchy did not allow its vocal anger to override diplomatic prudence. In spite of the increasingly harsh language of *La Croix,* Albert de Mun, and the Action Libérale Populaire, the bishops sought to make peace with the law and its hated "cultic associations." This effort may have halted the rightward drift of traditional Catholics toward the integrists and away from the republic, had it not been for the intervention of Piux X in August of 1906. His encyclical buried the beleaguered Ralliement and paved the way for a counterrevolutionary offensive within the French church. From the moment of the letter's appearance until the outbreak of the Great War in 1914, the balance of power within Catholicism would be held by the ultraconservative integrists. The church would declare war against the Christian Democrats, moderates would become suspect, and a friendship would be forged between the Action Française and the Catholic church.

✣ 4 ✣

Catholic Integrists Purge the Church
(1906–1914)

Although the successful anticlerical campaign had not destroyed the French church's capacity for compromise, it had undermined it seriously. Divisions between Catholics had been accentuated by the republic's hostility. However, in spite of the increasing rhetoric of civil war, the bishops had been prepared to adopt a modus vivendi with the hated separation legislation of 1905. Pius X refused to permit such a compromise. His *Gravissimo Officii* was a call for massive Catholic civil disobedience in France. This policy reversal gave Catholic reactionaries the leverage they needed to settle scores with their more moderate enemies and to go over to the offensive. The new papal program came to be called "integrism" by its friends, for it was felt that the pontiff's policies were dedicated to that which was most integral or basic to the church. In reality his shift marked a decisive end to the Ralliement policy of his predecessor and a return to the counterrevolutionary *Syllabus* mentality of Piux IX. From 1907 until his death in 1914, Pius X sought to purify the church of all those elements that he labeled "modernism." In a word, this meant that he would align himself with the church's intransigent reactionaries and that he would persecute Christian Democrats and other moderates who sought to make peace with a post–French Revolutionary world.

Gravissimo Officii had announced the papal shift with respect to the French government. *Lamentabili Sane* (July 3, 1907) and *Pascendi Dominici Gregis* (September 8, 1907) inaugurated his purge of unwelcome forces within the church. Initially, these two encyclicals were directed against the books and ideas of liberal intellectuals within ecclesiastical institutions, such as the New Testament professor Alfred Loisy. However, within a few years steps were taken to weed out all suspect persons and ideas from the educational apparatus of the church. In Rome, Pius X created the Pontifical Biblical Institute (1909) to insure the promotion and promulgation of orthodoxy in the field of scriptural studies, and throughout the Catholic world he ordered the construction of organizations designed to protect Catholic doctrine against modernist infiltrations. Bishops and the superiors of religious orders were ordered "to exercise the greatest vigilance" over seminary professors, and every diocese was expected to set up committees with the express task of censoring all dangerous literature. Only the most orthodox of seminary professors were hired, and these were forbidden to take courses at public universities. Candidates for the priesthood had to be examined rigorously in an effort to muzzle all "spirit of novelty," and both professors and students of Catholic institutions were required to take antimodernist oaths.[1]

This growing atmosphere of suspicion and hatred toward new ideas was welcomed by integrist and reactionary Catholics throughout France. Father Emmanuel Barbier, a noted anti-Sillonist theologian, welcomed the papal campaign, and the royalist Henri Delassus attempted to link his Christian Democratic foes with the heresy of modernism. Most important, however, was the support given to the pontiff by prominent French cardinals. Léon-Adolphe Amette, François Richard's prointegrist successor to the archdiocesan see of Paris, and August Dubourg of Rennes were instrumental in constructing and overseeing antimodernist organizations and crusades in their respective archdioceses.[2]

To guarantee that his program of purification and clerical homogenization was successful, the Holy Father took measures to insure that his hierarchy in France would be as integrist as possible. In some few instances, republican bishops, who had sought to make peace with the anticlerical government, were forced to resign. Such had been the case with Msgrs. Géay of Laval and le Nordez of Dijon. The prodemocratic bishop of Tarentaise, Msgr. Lucien-Léon Lacroix, was forced to step down from his diocesan post shortly after his attempt to create a "cultic association" that could be found acceptable to both church and state.[3] These papal actions do not suggest necessarily that the pontiff had rejected republicanism per se. His chief concern seems to have been the desire to curtail potential rebellion and independent behavior within the French hierarchy. The insistence that all bishops pursue his integrist program with unequivocal obedience indicated a clearly authoritarian vision of the church rather than an explicitly counterrevolutionary one. Nevertheless, these two notions could not be separated so easily. Shortly after the publication of *Pascendi* it became increasingly apparent that his integrist program was an amalgamation of hierarchical and antidemocratic convictions.

This was manifest in the papal appointment of fourteen new bishops to empty sees within France. At one level, the pontiff abandoned the practice of episcopal collegiality by naming these prelates without consulting any other members of the French hierarchy. The ardent royalist François Marty was assigned the vacant see of Montauban against the candidate whom the region's bishops had suggested to the pope. Even a minimum of episcopal democracy was not acceptable to His Holiness. At another level, these appointments were given to militant reactionaries within the French church. In addition to the promotion of Msgr. Marty, Pius X awarded a cardinal's hat to Msgr. de Cabrières, the monarchist bishop of Montpellier. The naming of the counterrevolutionaries Léon-Adolphe Amette and August Dubourg to the archdioceses of Paris and Rennes, respectively, not only guaranteed the cardinalate for these churchmen, but also meant that reactionary policies would dominate the two most important sees in France. Finally, at Lyon the more moderate Cardinal Coullié was replaced by the integrist Msgr. Sevin, and the reactionary Canon Delassus was exalted to the rank of Monseigneur. All of these prelates were royalists and would become in time open supporters of the Action Française.[4] Thus had Pius X taken steps to insure that the French church's administrative machinery would respond with uniformity to his hard-line program. Rigid oversight of the church's institution's required rigid overseers. Toward that end the pontiff had made a concerted effort to intensify his direct control over the French hierarchy both by the removal of moderate republican bishops and by the promotion of integrist churchmen to the most influential ecclesiastical positions in the land.

At the Vatican itself, the pope inaugurated measures designed to assure that a counterrevolutionary atmosphere would pervade the papal bureaucracy. Leo XIII's moderate secretary of state, Cardinal Rampolla, was replaced by the Spanish reactionary Merry del Val, and the monarchist Jesuit Louis Billot, one of the pope's chief advisors, was made a cardinal in 1912. Other integrist promotions at the Vatican included Cardinal de Laï, the secretary of the Consistorial Congregation, and Father Pie de Langogne, the head of the Capuchin order. However, most notorious of all the papal ultras was Msgr. Umberto Benigni, the creator of the *Sodalitium Pianum*. This organization was an integrist espionage unit which used its newspaper the *Correspondance de Rome* and other machinery to purge the church of "modernist" undesirables. Although it is not entirely clear to what depth this sodality had papal support, evidence indicates that Benigni's campaigns had the blessings, albeit noncanonical, of both Pius X and Merry del Val.[5] Thus, from the inauguration of the antimodernist campaign until the outbreak of war in 1914, the Holy See had embarked on a rigid crusade designed to return the church to the counterrevolutionary position it had upheld at the First Vatican Council of 1870. To facilitate this campaign, Pius X had tightened ecclesiastical machinery, purged the hierarchy of questionable men and promoted those clergy most attuned to his siege mentality.[6]

In addition, he sought to purify and control the political activities and organizations of French Catholics, lay and clerical alike. The extent of this campaign reached the public through what the French secular press called the Montagnini affair. In 1907, the French government expelled the former nuncio's auditor Msgr. Montagnini from France but not before his private papers were confiscated. These documents revealed that Vatican figures were attempting to discredit moderate prorepublican bishops, such as Msgrs. Fuzet, Mignot, and Petit, as well as the Christian Democratic leadership of France, which included Marc Sangnier and the *abbés démocrates* Fathers Gayraud, Lemire, Dabry, and Naudet. The angry response to this by prominent Catholic republicans could not hide the ominous reality that a campaign was under way in high places to destroy Christian Democracy in France.[7] The success of such a campaign would remove from French Catholicism the most significant roadblock to Action Française influence within the church.

Christian Democrats had never been secure within the French church. Even the tenacious survival of Ralliement tactics by the hierarchy until 1906 did not prevent the reactionaries from relentlessly assaulting the leading republican Catholics. Nevertheless, until the Separation Law of 1905 Catholic democrats were more or less welcome within some larger Catholic groups such as the Action Libérale Populaire. Even most bishops tolerated their activity and ideas, and in some instances, a few were even favorable toward them. Marc Sangnier's Christian mysticism and youthful zeal for the church won the support of a handful of influential prelates, and even popes Leo XIII and Pius X had blessed his work. These endorsements assisted Sillonist recruitment among Catholic students to the extent that the future of the organization promised to be a bright one.[8] In spite of these successes, both the Sillon and the other Christian Democrats were harassed at every turn by the ultrarightists. Sangnier's disciples were assaulted continually in the articles of *L'Action Française*, in Delassus's *Semaine Religieuse de Cambrai*, and in the books written by Emmanuel Barbier. The priest deputies Gayraud and Lemire were constant targets for the barbs of Henri Delassus, while the journalist democratic priests Dabry and Naudet found their newspapers under frequent episcopal censure throughout Brittany and the Nord. From its birth, *L'Ouest-Eclair* had faced the opposition of virtually all the Catholic elites in Brittany. The influential cardinals of Rennes endorsed publicly the newspaper's reactionary competitors, and Dubourg's predecessor Cardinal Labouré promised that he would punish any priest who read *L'Ouest-Eclair*.[9] Even the Vatican did not remain aloof from antidemocratic crusades. Although his language was more moderate than that of the French Catholic ultras, Leo XIII had warned American and Italian Christian Democrats against excesses in his encyclicals *Testem Benevolentiae* (1899) and *Graves de Communi* (1901). Pius X, even during the earlier more moderate phase of his pontificate, had cautioned Catholic republicans "never to meddle in politics" and never to deviate from hierarchical control.[10]

Certainly the last vestiges of the Ralliement had protected the French Christian Democrats from destruction. As long as they could retain a toehold in the camp of the pragmatic conservatives, they could avoid that isolation which would guarantee their destruction. However, that process of segregation had begun even prior to *Gravissimo Officii* by virtue of both the reactionaries' indictments and the Christian Democrats' public break with the Action Libérale Populaire. When it became clear that the Vatican had abandoned its internal and external moderation for a consistent integrist policy, the French Catholic ultrarightists sensed correctly that the fate of the Christian Democrats had been sealed. Building upon their past tactics, these integrists manipulated the growing defensive mentality within the church in order to gain the support of powerful prelates and lay leaders who were abandoning their former *rallié* tactics under the pressure of the Vatican. The reactionaries singled out the forces of Christian Democracy one by one for ostracism and destruction. Initially, they intensified their press campaigns against these vulnerable Catholics; next they were able to inspire episcopal censures against them; and finally, the Vatican would intervene to pronounce the decisive condemnation. By 1914, Christian Democracy in France had been wounded mortally.[11]

First to feel the weight of ecclesiastical censure were those *abbés démocrates* involved actively in newspaper work. The decisive action took place in Brittany, and the initial casualties were *La Vie Catholique* of Father Pierre Dabry and *La Justice Sociale* of Father Paul Naudet. By 1906 these priests had offended traditional Catholic conservatives by bold attacks against their clerical foes and by their refusal to join a confessional electoral coalition which was not exclusively republican. Father Dabry broke blatantly with both conservatives and reactionaries by advocating a coalition of all republican parties in France against the forces of religious reaction. His insistence that even Radicals and Socialists were worthy allies in the struggle against "the atheist Charles Maurras, the clericalist Feron-Vrau and the hybrid Piou" incensed the Breton Catholic leadership. Local bishops refused to tolerate such direct attacks against the director of *La Croix* and the chief of the ALP. Encouraged by his fellow reactionaries, Cardinal Auguste Dubourg of Rennes utilized earlier episcopal reprimands to turn on the two newspapers. The archbishop reminded the two democratic priests that they had violated the papal requirement in *Pascendi* which commanded all clerical journalists to receive diocesan authorization for their publications. In virtue of this, Dubourg forbade the reading of the two papers by priests and laity alike. On February 13, 1908, three months later, the Vatican condemned *La Vie Catholique* and *La Justice Sociale* and instructed their editors to engage in no further journalistic activities. The contributions of Father Naudet and Dabry to Christian Democracy were ended abruptly and decisively.[12]

The destruction of *L'Ouest-Eclair* was not so easy. Although its origins in 1899 were inauspicious, its directors the superpatriotic Emmanuel Desgrées du Loû and the pro-Sillonist *abbé démocrate* Félix Trochu used their business and journalistic skills to good advantage. Further, Desgrées du Loû's legitimist family origins, his long-term ties with de Mun's social Catholicism and his reputation as a devout Catholic throughout his beloved Brittany made him less vulnerable to integrist attacks. Consequently, in less than five years he was able to win the financial and moral support of other important French Catholics, both moderate and Christian Democratic. Finally, the newspaper itself was able to outdistance both *Le Nouvelliste de Bretagne* and *Le Journal de Rennes*, its reactionary competitors who had the material and ideological endorsement of the archdiocese. However, *L'Ouest-Eclair*'s most significant backing came from the Breton populace itself. In the face of urbanization and modernization, royalism was weakening rapidly in Brittany and giving way to the views of a mass citizenry that could be characterized as socially conservative, religiously Catholic, and resolutely republican. *L'Ouest-Eclair* was attuned consciously to this rising majority, and the decision to be these citizens' voice made it the most important Christian Democratic newspaper in France.[13]

Nevertheless, declining monarchism and clericalism fought a stiff resistance against ascending Christian Democracy in Brittany. For its part, *L'Ouest-Eclair* was cautious. Its break with the ALP had been cordial, and it refused to engage in vehement polemics with the church hierarchy. Further, its Catholic credentials and conservative republicanism made it almost impervious to attack. Consequently, the reactionaries turned to the weapon of scandal. In 1910 Albert Monniot, a friend of Edouard Drumont and the Action Française, published a libelous pamphlet against the newspaper and its directors, but Desgrées du Loû and Trochu brought the matter to court and had no trouble winning their case. At this point the enemies of *L'Ouest-Eclair* found its Achilles heel, Father Félix Trochu. If the newspaper itself could not be destroyed, at least its staunchly political and priestly editor could be silenced by archepiscopal fiat. Cardinal Dubourg rose to the occasion. He insisted that Trochu forgive the debt which the court had imposed upon Monniot in the libel case. The priest regretted his archbishop's intervention but expressed privately a willingness to comply if Dubourg would publish an official communication stating that the personal charges made against him by Drumont's friends were indeed slanderous. The cardinal's response, published in local reactionary newspapers, was a direct injunction for Trochu to drop all charges against his foe without further comment. The *abbé démocrate* agreed reluctantly, but this was not enough for Dubourg. He formed an archdiocesan commission of inquiry designed to recommend the prompt retirement of Felix Trochu from *L'Ouest-Eclair*. When the committee proffered its predictable suggestion, Cardinal Dubourg acted upon it immediately. Trochu was ordered to resign from his newspaper, and all protest of injustice was in vain. The cardinal's forced expulsion of the journalistic priest was upheld in an official letter by Pius X.[14]

Father Trochu attempted to retain a discreet relationship with the newspaper, but Dubourg would not tolerate what he felt to be blatant insubordination. From time to time until the outbreak of the Great War, Trochu would be forced to attend disciplinary audiences at those moments when *L'Ouest-Eclair*'s support of republican candidates contradicted the preferences of the Breton hierarchy.[15] That the *abbé démocrate* no longer worked for the newspaper did not minimize the harassment heaped upon him by angry reactionaries and local prelates. If they could not stop *L'Ouest-Eclair*'s advances in republican politics, at least they could weaken the paper by removing its talented Christian Democratic priest. In this latter goal, they were successful.

The two democratic priests in the Chamber of Deputies were made to feel the weight of the reactionary shift in Catholic politics as well. Hippolyte Gayraud, a politically active priest from Maritime Brittany, had experienced massive ultrarightist opposition well before the Separation Law. His articles in *L'Univers*, defending a Christian Democratic political program, met stiff opposition from the newspaper's readership. Even the Vatican's *L'Osservatore Romano* called his position negative, contradictory, and divisive to Catholicism. In addition, the integrists among his constituents never forgave him for defeating their candidate. Consequently, in 1902 they united with his bishop to organize a campaign to replace him. Their effort failed miserably, but they continued to attack his prorepublican speeches in the Chamber of Deputies. Only an early death spared him from the integrist crusade that crushed his colleague in the legislature.[16]

Jules Lemire, a priest deputy from the industrialized Catholic Nord, was a devout Catholic, a zealous republican, and a committed social reformer. Of peasant origins, this young legitimist priest moved into the Christian Democratic camp via a sensitivity for the poor and marginal which had led him first into social Catholicism and from there to republicanism. From his first election to the Chamber of Deputies in 1893 until the Great European War, he defended publicly the values and programs of his newly adopted Christian Democracy. However, in spite of his immense popularity among Catholics and non-Catholics, he was the recipient of sharp attacks from influential reactionaries for over twenty years. The integrists were unable to unseat him at the polls, so they tried to remove him by attacking his behavior as a priest and as a Catholic. This strategy was made plausible with the passage of the Separation Bill and the papal rejoinder to it. Rather than responding intransigently to the law, Lemire advocated a stance of accommodation to it and urged French Catholics to convert Pius X to the idea of "cultic associations" in France. Henri Delassus used Lemire's position to mount a campaign against him. He accused the democratic priest of dividing Catholics and of violating his priestly vows by scandalous public behavior and by political actions contrary to the wishes of the church. Delassus convinced the archdiocesan leadership of Cambrai to send these protests to Rome, and Merry del Val's response upheld the judgments of the reactionary canon. Further, the Holy See insisted that no priest could seek political office without the prior authorization of his bishop.[17]

Matters languished for a number of years until 1910, and once again Delassus, now a monseigneur, opened the attack. Lemire's behavior, he argued, had not only vitiated his priestly character, but also placed him beyond the pale of the church among the excommunicated. In retaliation for this and other public insults, Father Lemire brought charges before the diocesan court against Delassus and another integrist priest. Both of the accused were exonerated, and the courtroom became the scene for further polemics against the democratic priest.[18]

The harassment against Lemire peaked in the last two years before the war, just prior to a legislative election. The integrists were determined to make one final effort to defeat him decisively; they hoped to force the withdrawal of his candidacy. First of all, the archdiocese condemned the Lemirist newspaper *Cri de Flandres*. Next, pressure was put upon the priest-deputy to register his candidacy with the proper ecclesiastical authorities, but Lemire avoided what he knew would be a certain repudiation of his political life by official sources. The new assistant bishop of Cambrai, Alexis-Armand Charost, was an avid integrist who had won his antimodernist credentials in the anti-Trochu campaign. It was he who took charge of the anti-Lemirist offensive. Using Cardinal de Laï's Vatican decree which required diocesan approval of all priestly politicans, Charost demanded that Father Lemire renounce his own candidacy. The priest refused in the name of personal liberty. Msgr. Charost's response was unequivocal. Jules Lemire was suspended from his priestly duties, and the people of Flanders were told that "no Catholic in good conscience" could vote for him. The bishop's injunctions were futile. The Catholic voters of Flanders, with some help from the leftist parties, sent the suspended priest back to the Chamber of Deputies by a clear majority. Charost's outrage could not hide the fact that large sections of the Catholic voting public were refusing to uphold the politics of clerical reaction. Nevertheless, Father Lemire had been disciplined severely, making him another significant victim of the counterrevolutionary purge against Christian Democracy.[19]

Of all the condemnations leveled against Catholic republicans, none was as important as the one which fell upon the Sillon and its charismatic leader in August 1910. As the sole Christian Democratic organization of note, the Sillon had passed through a brief period of expansion, experimentation, and even episcopal good will. That trend was reversed in the last five years of its life. From *Gravissimo Officii* to the late summer of 1910, the Sillon sustained blow after blow of opposition until it was obliterated successfully. Its rapid plummet can be explained by a number of factors.

First of all, it was becoming increasingly apparent that Sangnier's brand of mystical Christian Democracy was crystallizing in such a way as to draw attention to its affinities with international pacifism and socialism. The Sillon was questioning social Catholic values upholding private property and was becoming less circumspect about its independence from the church's hierarchy. Coupled with this ideological drift was its growing participation in the political arena in support of those positions found so condemnable in the *abbés démocrates*. Sangnier's break with the Action Libérale Populaire, his public criticism of *La Croix* and his independent candidacy at Sceaux in 1909 alienated him further from mainline Catholicism. His openly social democratic platform shocked even his friends.[20]

Finally, the reactionary campaign against the Sillonists had never abated. Emmanuel Barbier's books had begun to have their effect among a growing number of bishops. As early as 1906, the ultra bishop of Quimper, Msgr. Dubillard forbade all his clergy and seminarians to attend the proposed Sillonist congress at Brest. In addition, he urged Catholic lay associations to boycott the assembly. His condemnation of Sillonist ideology and independence from ecclesiastical authority was employed by other bishops in the years to come. Dubillard was soon joined by Msgr. Lemmonier of Bayeux, Msgr. Delamaire of Cambrai, Cardinal Dubourg of Rennes, and Cardinal de Cabrières of Montpellier. By 1910, the trickle of bishops which opposed the Sillon had become a torrent. Sources of recruitment were drying up under episcopal pressure, and the handful of pro-Sillonist prelates could not prevent the deluge which was overwhelming Sangnier and his organization.[21]

On August 25, 1910, Pius X published the definitive anathema against the Sillon. The pontiff believed that Sangnier and his followers had violated both church principles and authority. He charged that the Sillon had made "blasphemous alliances between the Gospel and the Revolution" by suggesting that Catholicism, with its eighteen centuries of "great bishops and monarchs," did not understand correctly "the social notions of authority, liberty, equality, fraternity and human dignity." His Holiness added that Sangnier's disciples divided Catholics by pursuing political programs independent of the church's hierarchy. For these reasons, the Sillon was ordered to disband, and its former members were instructed to join those diocesan groups to which their respective bishops would direct them. Marc Sangnier responded with an immediate submission. He dismantled the Sillon and spent the last years before the war laying the groundwork for a rebirth of Christian Democracy.[22]

Thus, by 1914 the Catholic integrists had won massive victories against their most formidable foes within the church. One by one, the leading Christian Democrats had been isolated and smashed. Episcopal moderation, so apparent in the earlier efforts to construct an acceptable "cultic association," had dissipated with the papal decision to abandon the Ralliement. Marching behind the reactionaries, the princes of the church turned upon the Christian Democrats and disciplined them. In every instance the Vatican had entered the fray to make definitive the condemnations already inaugurated by the ultrarightists and upheld by the bishops.

Integrism had come to dominate both the Vatican and French churches to such an extent that even leading Catholic conservatives and pragmatists were distrusted and harassed from time to time. The Montagnini papers had cast suspicion upon such well-known figures as Albert de Mun and Msgr. Fulbert Petit, and domestic integrists were not satisfied with the values and practices of some of their influential conservative allies. Emmanuel Barbier attacked the constitutional strategy of the Action Libérale Populaire and *La Croix,* and his charges were echoed by Henri Delassus in the *Semaine Religieuse de Cambrai.* Most significant, however, was the integrist hierarchy's growing dissatisfaction with the ALP. By 1909, Jacques Piou and the conservative republican rhetoric of his party were criticized increasingly by Rome and the French episcopate. Instead, the bishops preferred a confessional party of religious defense which would unite all Catholics under the jurisdiction of the hierarchy and the diocesan bureaucracies. Toward that end, the prelates endorsed the Union Catholique of Colonel Emile Keller, a reactionary army officer. Rapidly the royalist Keller won the vital sanction of France's cardinals Amette of Paris, Dubourg of Rennes, and Couillé of Lyon. These and other archbishops presided regularly over the congresses and rallies of the Union Catholique and urged Catholics everywhere to stand behind Keller's efforts. Merry del Val communicated the papal blessing and hopes for success to this ultrarightist organization. Decidedly reactionary, antimodern in ideology and dependent upon diocesan machinery, Keller's Catholic group was an ideal instrument for the integrists, French and papal. It lacked both the autonomy and the ambivalence of the ALP. In program and structure it was the natural product of the new counterrevolutionary mood which had come to prevail at the Vatican.[23]

Events in France and Rome had radically altered the perspective of Gallican Catholicism. In one decade, the political forces of the church had abandoned the Ralliement of Leo XIII only to adopt the integrist program of Pius X. Until the anticlerical offensive and the passage of the Separation Bill, royalists and reactionaries had been a powerful but minority voice within French Catholicism. Meanwhile most of the bishops and lay leaders pursued a strategy of pragmatic compromise with the anticlerical republic, a program which allowed the Christian Democrats some room for maneuvering. The papal refusal to come to terms with the law of 1905 signaled an end to the shaky entente between Catholic republicans and tactical *ralliés*. Pius X's thoroughgoing integrism at the Vatican and in France spelled doom for the Christian Democrats. Within seven years of the publication of *Pascendi*, they had been destroyed almost completely.

The most significant beneficiary of this reactionary atmosphere was the struggling Action Française. Its earlier enthusiasm for Catholicism had not included the Ralliement, and it felt a continuing antipathy for the Christian Democrats. In short, the Catholicism loved so deeply by the royalist league was that which had won the day in the wake of *Gravissimo Officii*. No wonder, then, that the expanding army of reactionaries within the church would become attracted to the Action Française. This siege mentality of Catholicism shortly before the outbreak of the European conflagration was the soil in which the alliance between Catholicism and the Action Française would be nourished.

+ 5 +

The Birth of a Friendship
(1906–1914)

Why would *French and Vatican Catholicism* find the Action Française so appealing at this time? To be sure, the royalist league had eulogized the Catholic church for a number of reasons, but this praise had been limited and conditional. It had not been the universal or divine character of Catholicism which inspired the admiration of Charles Maurras. Instead he heralded the church as one vital symbol of his narrowly patriotic nationalism and as an important bastion of classical Latin civilization. In effect, Catholicism was only one laudatory means to a loftier end, one corollary of the higher principle embodied in the *pays réel*. As a further embarrassment, the league's leading philosopher was an agnostic dedicated to the positivism of Auguste Comte. Finally, there was the matter of Action Française violence; yet sadly, its physical and verbal attacks against Jews, Masons, Protestants, and socialists could be tolerated, even accepted, by most Catholics in France who viewed these groups as enemies. Anti-Semitism and anti-Protestantism were interwoven in the very fabric of traditional Catholicism, and Masons and socialists had a long history of active anticlericalism. However, how could Catholics permit a political league to malign other Catholics, especially members of the hierarchy? How could Catholics allow the Action Française to turn them against fellow believers simply because these latter did not accept royalist integral nationalism?

In spite of all these obstacles, such a bizarre relationship between the two did come to pass. This accord, best described as a mutual admiration society, was informal rather than official. Nevertheless, its impact should not be underestimated. Within an eight-year period, from 1906 to 1914, the Action Française came to exercise a profound influence over French Catholics, an influence that reached into the very chambers of the Vatican itself. By 1914 important ties between prominent Catholics and the royalist league had been established, while at the same time its impact upon French Christians continued to augment.

For one thing, the Action Française had become a prominent political actor at the extreme right of French national life. Institutionally, its organizational life was adapted to appeal to any and all groups hostile to the republic. Even the syndicalist working class was not ignored.[1] Within a few years after its creation, *L'Action Française* had supplanted the former royalist newspaper *Le Gaulois,* and in June of 1911 the royalist pretender made the Maurrasian daily the official monarchist newspaper in place of the *Correspondance Nationale*. Finally, the Camelots du Roi were frequently in the streets and at church doors to assault their enemies and sell their newspaper. To the extent that the Action Française came to dominate much of the French ultraright, so also would it provide an inspiration or home for those politically active Catholics imbued with royalist and reactionary values.[2]

At the same time, this growing power of the league had been assisted by Catholics themselves. From the very beginning, membership had included a large number of practicing Catholics, and several of them held leadership positions in the organization. Even some priests began to join. As the league began to expand rapidly in size, so too did its number of Catholics and clerics increase. Non-Catholic members were the exception rather than the rule. Consequently, when membership increased to almost 40,000, it was duly noted that the vast number of new partisans were Catholic by conviction. Indeed, it has been estimated that a full 10 percent of new recruits were clergymen. The chief sources of new members were priests, seminarians, and Catholic students who had been attracted first by the Sillon and Christian Democracy. Priestly candidates were convinced increasingly "that the liberty of the Catholic church and the prosperity of the French fatherland" demanded allegiance to "the monarchy and the program of the Action Française." Even Catholic high schools formed chapters of the league, and seminary professors were publishing more and more their conversions from Christian Democracy to reactionary monarchism. Thus, at precisely the moment when integrism was being adopted at Rome and in France, the Action Française was coming to benefit from this new mood in the educational institutions of Catholic France. These vital sources of recruitment were beginning to dry up for the Sillon at the very instant they were opening up for the Action Française. Christian Democracy's losses had become the Maurrasians' gains.[3]

As time passed, the royalist league penetrated other influential sectors within the French church. A number of prominent French clergymen came to be avid devotees of Charles Maurras. This was especially true in the Dominican order where such well-known figures as Georges de Pascal, Jacques Vallée, and Garrigou-Lagrange eulogized the integral monarchists. The celebrated preaching friar Father Janvier, named cathedral canon at Rennes by the reactionary Cardinal Dubourg, remained an ardent admirer of the royalists for years. Father J.-M.Besse, a renowned Benedictine, was a most outspoken defender of the integral nationalists. He called Maurras's celebrated commentary on Pius IX's *Syllabus of Errors* a masterpiece "of impeccable orthodoxy." In addition, the Action Française benefited from its contacts with lay persons and lay organizations. Even prior to the war, a number of noted intellectuals were attracted to Maurrasian ideas. Among them were leaders of the Catholic renaissance in France, notably the literary figures Georges Bernanons and Henri Massis as well as the philosophers Jacques Maritain and his wife Raïssa. Further, the league made serious inroads into the Association Catholique de la Jeunesse Française, the largest Catholic youth group in France, and a number of Colonel Keller's Union Catholique units were dominated by the integral nationalists. The specifically Catholic press was not immune to Maurrasian influence either. A number of *La Croix*'s readers were attracted to the royalist league through the parallel views they read in the Assumptionist daily, and the financial troubles of *L'Univers* were a direct benefit to the integral nationalists. This celebrated Catholic daily had evolved into a moderate *rallié* newspaper, but declining fortunes put it upon the auction block in 1912. Royalist friends of the Action Française bought it and thus ended its brief flirtation with more progressive Catholics. Finally, before the war fraternal ties were established between the league and provincial Catholic reactionary newspapers. One such case in point was its links with *Le Nouvelliste de Bretagne* at Rennes.[4]

Most important, however, was the approbation of a growing number of French bishops toward the Action Française. With the Vatican's policy shift toward ecclesiastical reaction and with the appointment of more integrist prelates, the French hierarchy was evolving rapidly toward an ultrarightist perspective. A number of these new princes of the church were overt royalists or, at least, intransigent reactionaries. To them the Action Française seemed very attractive indeed. Msgr. Touchet, the bishop of Orléans, found within its ranks the most ardent defenders of the Joan of Arc he cherished. In 1913 he telegraphed words of gratitude to Maxime Réal del Sarte, the sculptor leader of the Camelots du Roi, for the punitive raid into the streets that he had ordered for Joan of Arc's defense. For Touchet, the public violence of the Action Française was not a scandal, especially when performed in the name of the heroine who had restored the throne to France centuries before. When Christian Democrats in the heavily Catholic Lorraine mounted a campaign against the Maurrasian royalists, they encountered the resolute opposition of Charles Turinaz, the reactionary bishop of Nancy. He praised the integral nationalists for their defense of the church and accused the Christian Democrats of treason and false Catholicism. Msgr. François Marty, whom Pius X had appointed to the vacant see of Montauban, was an avid partisan of the Action Française, as was the monarchist archbishop of Montpellier, Cardinal de Cabrières. This last prelate paid an honorary visit to the Institut d'Action Française. There he pronounced the blessing of his archdiocese upon the integral nationalists. The high point of his speech was the terse assertion: "I am very Action Française." Finally, in Paris Cardinal Amette was known to work cooperatively with the Maurrasians, and in Lyon Cardinal Sevin proved to be one of their ardent defenders.[5]

Cardinal Auguste Dubourg, archbishop of Rennes, was the integral nationalists' most fervent episcopal partisan in Brittany. He endorsed those royalist and reactionary newspapers which had fraternal ties with the Action Française, and he tolerated the outbursts of Maurrasians against the Sillon at local press conferences. The diocesan apparatus he constructed against modernist ideas was not employed against the integral nationalists. When Dubourg appointed Father Janvier as honorary cathedral canon, it meant that an ardent devotee of the league had personal access to the archbishop. The cardinal's active crusade against *L'Ouest-Eclair* in general and Father Félix Trochu in particular was of immediate benefit to the Maurrasians. By intervening directly in the Monniot affair, Dubourg had sanctioned the Camelots' participation in this scandal and had taken sides with the Action Française against its most serious journalistic foe in Brittany.[6]

Unsurprisingly, one of the most outspoken advocates of the Action Française was Msgr. Henri Delassus, the newly promoted reactionary prelate of the Nord. In striking contrast to his frenzied hatred of the Christian Democrats was his deep affection for Charles Maurras and the royalist league. On a number of occasions he utilized his religious weekly to sing their praises and to defend them against their detractors. He cited the league's creation of study institutes to defend the integrist doctrine as certain proof that these royalists recognized that "there is no better salvation for society than a return to that integral verity preached only by the Catholic church." His praise knew no bounds. The Action Française's dedication to "the Catholic idea and the monarchist principle" would be the source of the nation's rebirth, and Maurras's *Syllabus* commentary was called "one of the most succinct, most clear and most orthodox that has ever been written." In addition, Delassus used his polemical skills to defend the royalist league against its detractors. He acknowledged the unbelief of some of its members, but he pointed out that the most "declared adversaries of the *Action Française*" were the Christian Democrats and the Sillon, both of whom had been condemned by the church's hierarchy. He concluded with this blunt contrast: "No bishop, even now, has spoken publicly against the *Action Française;* the Holy See has never said anything against the *Action Française* in spite of its adversaries' insistence." For Delassus, the twofold loyalty of integral nationalism to "Catholicism and royalty"made the Action Française France's vital antidote to the poison of the French Revolution.[7]

In many instances, the French hierarchy applauded gains made by all direct allies of the Maurrasian royalists even when the Action Française was not mentioned specifically. For example, the ownership transfer of *L'Univers* to reactionary monarchists was acclaimed by Cardinal de Cabrières, Cardinal Dubillard, Msgr. Oury, and the bishops of Aire, Angers, Cahors, Coutances, Montauban, Pamiers, and Verdun. Thus by 1914 the most important elements within the French hierarchy had come to accept the Action Française. In some cases, this involved simply a benevolent neutrality, but quite often it took the form of public and effusive admiration.[8]

Such esteem, in time, came to penetrate the walls of the Vatican itself. Cardinal Louis Billot, one of the pope's prominent theologians, applauded the Action Française openly, and Father Le Floch, the rector of Rome's French seminary, shared similar sentiments. Both men were monarchical integrists, and both were passionate partisans of the papal counterrevolutionary strategy. Finally, it was a scarcely guarded secret that the pontiff himself sympathized with the Action Française. In a private audience granted to Charles Maurras's mother, Pius X spoke highly of the royalist philosopher. "I bless his work" were the concluding words of His Holiness.[9]

This rapid augmentation of Action Française influence among Catholics had manifested itself during a period of marked strategical change within the church. Maurrasian attraction to and defense of Catholicism at this critical time made it most appealing to the more ultrarightist elements within prominent ecclesiastical circles. Its violence was overlooked, and its narrow patriotism was characteristic of many French Catholics as well. Even the agnosticism of Maurras was explained away. In a church where a siege mentality prevailed, alliances were formed on the basis of rhetorical and tactical uniformity. Assaulted by anticlericals from the outside and questioned by experimental Christian Democrats from the inside, the Catholic church was in the process of searching for powerful comrades who would pay homage to her strategic intransigence. That the Action Française was prepared to do just that seemed sufficient to most traditional and reactionary Catholics. It is in this context that one can find an explanation for the ambivalent friendship between the Action Française and the Catholic church.

Of course, defense of Catholicism was not sufficient in and of itself. Action Française popularity with leading churchmen was predicated upon the brand of Catholicism that the integral nationalists heralded. On one level, these superpatriots retained their rigid nationalism but offset it by appeals to France's Catholic heritage. The league continued to affirm that "the religious policy of . . . France . . . was necessarily Catholic," because this sacred tradition was opposed by its very nature "to a regime of banal equality." At another level, its xenophobic devotion to France was softened by its dediction to Latin Catholic civilization. Indeed, with the advent of Pius X to the Holy See, the Action Française more and more identified its brand of universalism with the changed strategy at the Vatican. The first issue of the royalist daily called its "integral nationalism . . . the triumph of the *Syllabus*," because "the Catholic church" was the only force capable of resisting both "anarchic individualism" and the Jewish "dream of universal domination." Thus was stringent patriotism combined with an equally rigid internationalism, and both were linked by a reactionary species of Catholicism. Action Française Catholicism was, at one and the same time, nationalistic and papal. The integrist atmosphere at Rome was amenable to such a position, and the Maurrasians credited Pius X for this happy state of affairs. Because of him and his ultrarightist strategy, the royalist league presented itself as a legitimate organ of religious defense against both the external anticlericals and the internal modernists.[10]

First of all, the disciples of Maurras displayed these newly earned credentials by shrill polemics leveled against the enemies of reactionary Catholicism found within the governmental parties. In both rhetoric and policy, the Action Française vilified the persons and programs regularly attacked by the bishops, *La Croix* and the Union Catholique of Colonel Keller. *L'Action Française* continued to publish blasts against the federation of Jews, Protestants, Masons, and foreigners who were plotting the destruction of the Catholic church. The devout Louis Dimier lauded the church's "war of religion" against the Jews, arguing that Christ's injunction to love one's neighbor did not apply to Hebrews. [11]

In addition, the Maurrasians took up the gauntlet with Catholic ultras against the step-by-step anticlericalism of the republican government. They defended Pius X's decision to remove the republican bishops of Dijon and Laval, and they were certain that the closure of the Vatican embassy was further proof that "the spirit of the Revolution" was attempting "to build a new civilization" upon the bones of a martyred Catholicism. By the time of the Separation Bill's passage, the outrage of the Action Française had reached a fevered pitch. Not only did the law ravage the church's property rights; it was also a violation of natural law and the Ten Commandments. As a result, one could not be expected to obey it.[12] *L'Action Française* was calling for that same civil disobedience mandated by Pius X in *Gravissimo Officii*. In further support of this policy, the royalist newspaper would report regularly all the arrests and court proceedings of those priests and bishops charged with resisting the separation legislation. These clergy were viewed by the Maurrasians as martyrs inspired by the pope to combat "the Jacobin tyranny." The league's daily published a column called "Livre d'Or de l'Action Française" which it described as "lists of our wounded, arrested and condemned members who have defended the church." Often these leaguers were Camelots du Roi who had been incarcerated after street fights or for resisting government entry into the churches for the purpose of taking inventory of ecclesiastical goods. The arrested militants would use the courts as public podiums for continuing the church-state conflicts.[13] To integrist and traditional Catholics, these activities contrasted favorably with the compromising and confusing behavior of the Christian Democrats. Their embarrassing silence or their suggestions for peace with the government seemed treasonous when compared with the pro-Catholic militancy of the Action Française.

The Maurrasian league employed similar ardor when it dealt with the internal enemies of Catholic counterrevolutionaries. It became a fervent advocate of the antimodernist crusade by lauding the papal condemnation of Alfred Loisy and by commending the integrist promotions and machinery which the Vatican had inspired. *La Croix* was praised for its defense of the pope; Louis Billot was congratulated for his promotion to the cardinalate; and the campaigns of Msgr. Umberto Benigni were applauded with great fervor. The church's reactionary crusade against its own modernists was linked by the Action Française to the growing pressure to beatify the French heroine Joan of Arc. Camelot du Roi demonstrations in her honor were directed against the Sillon and all those who wished to deprive the land of its "national lady." The league's review was singularly unembarrassed by the disclosure of Msgr. Montagnini's espionage activities; in fact, the campaign against conservative *ralliés* and Christian Democrats in France was welcomed with great joy by the Action Française.[14]

From the start, the integral nationalists had voiced sharp criticism of those conservatives and traditionalists who were loath to abandon the tactics of the Ralliement. The *ralliés'* attraction to constitutional means and their hesitancy to adopt a strictly confessional party angered the Action Française. Consequently it continued to fire rather frequent broadsides against the Action Libérale Populaire and the moderate social Catholic Semaines Sociales. However, most of its disdain for flexible conservatives was reserved for *rallié* bishops. Msgr. Fuzet, the archbishop of Rouen, was accused of pacifist sympathies, and Cardinal Lecot was stigmatized as a liberal who abandoned the "cultic associations" only when compelled by the pope. Even public outbursts against bishops by the league were tolerated if integrist Catholics felt that a particular prelate was sympathetic to the republic. At a Catholic youth rally in the diocese of Nice, Msgr. Chapon was forced to intervene to restore order when a Maurrasian monarchist named Robert Pelletier continued to harass the speaker Marc Sangnier. When the bishop informed the heckler that the republic could be reformed, Pelletier snapped back, "The republic is based upon the Rights of Man, and His Holiness Pius IX has condemned the Rights of Man."[15]

However, most Action Française rage was directed toward the Christian Democrats. Because integral nationalism rejected republicanism in principle, it could not tolerate any Catholic who cherished the values of 1789. These hatreds had been axiomatic with the royalist organization since its birth, but they were becoming increasingly fashionable within Catholic circles during the period of the Ralliement's eclipse. The league activist Louis Dimier was willing to admit the possibility that an honest Catholic might be seduced by republican ideas, but he added that retention of these convictions in the face of anti-Catholic excesses was a mortal danger "to the profession of the Catholic faith." With the passage of time, even this minimal moderation was abandoned. Everywhere the Christian Democrats were maligned with the most violent language. Even the use of defamation and slander were not alien to the league. Félix Trochu's experiences bore testimony to that.[16]

Nevertheless, the Action Française's most vilified enemy was the Sillon of Marc Sangnier. Charles Maurras's "Le Dilemme de Marc Sangnier" was the league's philosophical edifice against this foe, and it would provide the ideological rationale of integrist opposition against Christian Democracy for the next thirty-five years. When the pope repudiated every compromise with the separation legislation and instructed all Catholics to do the same, the Action Française intensified its crusade against the Sillon and its leader. They were accused of giving aid and comfort "to the enemies of religion and the fatherland," and Sangnier's disciples were numbered among Joan of Arc's detractors. The league's review published articles by Emmanuel Barbier against the Sillon and had its own series on the subject by Nel Arlès. Finally, Sangnier himself could expect to be heckled by Camelots du Roi at any public rally where Catholics were present.[17] When the wheels of fortune began to turn against the Sillon, the Action Française was overjoyed. With great relish its daily published the episcopal censures against Sangnier one by one, and it printed the papal condemnation in full. This anathema was declared to be "an intellectual and moral event" of the greatest magnitude and "an incomparable model of critical analysis." The newspaper's concluding editorial remarks were effusive: "Never, since the *Syllabus* of Pius IX, have the revolutionary doctrines been condemned with such precision and clarity." In the days which followed, *L'Action Française* also reproduced in their entirety both the Sillon's official submission and the personal letter of Marc Sangnier to Pius X, in which the democratic tribune assured the Holy Father of his total obedience to the papal directives. Although the integral nationalists expressed gratification over Sangnier's act of loyalty to the church, they continued to be skeptical. They saw in his newly created daily newspaper *La Démocratie* a disguised resurrection of the heretical Sillon.[18]

With the Sillon's condemnation, the Action Française reached the pinnacle of its success against the Christian Democrats. Its archenemy within the French church had been discredited and disbanded. The Maurrasians were now free to expand their influence among French Catholics, and they did so with continued advantage for the next fifteen years. Nevertheless, the shadow of Marc Sangnier continued to fall upon the monarchists. His resilience was remarkable, and he would rise again to challenge the political and Catholic credentials of his victorious royalist foes. In 1926 and 1927 the Action Française would be commanded by the pope to make a sacrifice similar to the one made by Sangnier years earlier. That it refused to do so makes a striking contrast with those whose devotion to Catholicism it had challenged so glibly in 1910. Meanwhile it appeared as if the Action Française's Catholic reputation was impregnable. Such was not the case. In spite of its support of the Vatican's integrist program and in spite of its growing number of influential friends in high places, the royalists were also accumulating adversaries at an alarming rate.

A number of these foes were veterans in the campaign against Maurrasian counterrevolution. Chief among them were the Sillonists and the team of Christian Democrats who owned and operated *L'Ouest-Eclair*.

For about a decade the Catholic republicans had been spawning the ideological apparatus which they would use to cast doubts on the professed Catholicism of the Action Française. As early as 1901 Marc Sangnier was warning Catholics that the philosophy of Charles Maurras was excessively authoritarian and that his "integral monarchical nationalism" was a repudiation of that traditional French patriotism which involved "working for the reign of justice and love in the world." For Sillon, royalty belonged exclusively to God, whereas secular democracy could achieve its crowning glory by uniting the principles of 1789 with the moral force of Catholicism.[19]

In the arena of political struggle the most successful foe of the Action Française was *L'Ouest-Eclair*. Even before the Separation Bill had become law, Brittany's Christian Democratic daily had campaigned actively to prevent the election of royalists to the Chamber of Deputies. So dedicated was it to this task that it broke with the Action Libérale Populaire or any other party that might decide to base its platform solely on religious defense. It castigated the Action Française and those *ralliés* "who would rather see Catholicism perish" than have the church abandon their personal reactionary programs. Against the political coalitions sponsored by the Breton hierarchy, *L'Ouest-Eclair* used its pages to endorse conservative republicans who, on occasion, were able to defeat those confessional candidates chosen by the bishops and esteemed by the Action Française. Even personal vendettas against Desgrées du Loû and Trochu by the royalists did not halt the advance of *L'Ouest-Eclair*. Its response to the Monniot charges was evidence of that.[20] In its struggles with the integral nationalists, the newspaper's directors had learned some important lessons. On the one hand, they were becoming increasingly aware that the Maurrasians could be defeated at the polls and challenged successfully in the courts. On the other hand, they knew that Father Félix Trochu would remain vulnerable to Action Française

The Birth of a Friendship   +   75

hate crusades as long as integrist prelates dominated Breton Catholicism. *L'Ouest-Eclair* and its *abbé démocrate* would experience this dual reality for the next two decades.

For the time being, however, the Christian Democrats were everywhere thrown on the defensive, and the Action Française had established itself as an ardent defender of the Catholic faith. In spite of this seemingly hopeless situation, the Catholic republicans began to regroup their forces in order to build a solid case against the Maurrasian royalists which would appeal to moderate and traditional Catholics. By 1912 they had constructed a fourfold apologetic.

First of all, they charged the league with disrespect for divinely established authority. Desgrées du Loû accused it of encouraging revolution by its blatant disdain for the established governing powers. In addition, the Christian Democrats were able to illustrate a number of occasions when royalist leaguers displayed public scorn for nonreactionary bishops. However, these arguments could not find fertile soil in which to grow before the war. Anticlerical successes rendered useless the Catholic doctrine of required obedience to the state, and the church's counterrevolutionary crusade was not concerned with insults directed toward pro-Sillonist bishops. The Christian Democrats' second argument was more effective. Integral nationalism was accused of being too narrow in theory and too violent in practice. It was felt that the Maurrasian axiom "by any means" was blatantly immoral and that the royalists' idea of patriotism was "an idolatrous conception of the fatherland." France was not "an end in itself," argued a former Sillonist. He concluded: "As for us, we put God above all else, and we believe that humanity, redeemed by the blood of Christ, is superior to every fatherland. We are Catholics before we are French."[21] It was upon this issue of the Action Française's Catholic credentials that the Christian Democrats sought to make their third point. In fact, they argued that the royalist league placed "religion at the service of politics," a direct reference to the slogan "politics above all else" (*politique d'abord*). Integral nationalism was attracted only to those aspects of Catholicism that conformed with monarchism, and Maurras defended the church, "not according to religious convictions but uniquely because of his royalist needs." These Sillonist indictments were based upon the conviction that the Action Française had been drawn only to a few external realities of ecclesiastical structure. The church's "inner beauties" and divine realities escaped the Maurrasians totally.[22] This reference to the politicizing of Catholicism by Maurras led naturally to the Christian Democrats' final accusation. The royalist reactionaries and their philosopher were stigmatized as heretics and unbelievers who exercised a "pernicious influence" in "certain ecclesiastical circles." It was felt that their ideas undermined "basic Catholic doctrine." Charles Maurras was a natural target for these charges. The *abbés démocrates* and *L'Ouest-Eclair* referred frequently to his acknowledged agnosticism, and the Sillon suggested that Catholics could learn nothing from "a positivist and atheistic monarchist."[23] Although these Christian Democrats had been isolated from mainline Catholicism and had found their own orthodoxy called into question, the polemics they constructed against the integral nationalists began to produce some desired results.

Soon others, equally chagrined by the Action Française's growing influence among Catholics, developed and expanded the Christian Democrats' arguments into a campaign designed to bring Maurrasian heterodoxy to the attention of traditional Catholics and the Holy Father himself. At Lyon, the Christian Democratic social Catholic Joseph Vialatoux employed a similar logic against the integrists, and in his *Avec Nietzsche à l'assaut du christianisme* (1910) the prorepublican theologian Father Jules Pierre portrayed Charles Maurras as a philosopher who exploited Christ's church for base ends. Within the next four years he published two other works against the integral nationalists and their leader, *Les Nouveaux Défis de l'Action Française à la conscience chrétienne* (1912) and *Réponse à M. Maurras, L'Action Française et ses directeurs païennes* (1914). In 1911 the noted philosopher Father Lucien Laberthonnière wrote his *Positivisme et catholicisme à propos de l'Action Française,* a study designed to expose the non-Catholic convictions of Charles Maurras and his followers.[24]

However, most frightening to the integral nationalists was the restive behavior of the pro-Sillonist bishops. Msgrs. Péchenard of Soissons, Mignot of Albi, Catteau of Luçon, and Chapon of Nice had all expressed public disapproval of the Action Française, its leaders, and its activities. The critique of Msgr. Guillibert of Fréjus, Maurras's former teacher and a traditionalist of repute, was especially damning. His accusations could not be denounced as tainted with Christian Democracy. He praised the books of Father Pierre, and he denounced the royalist league to Rome because it formed a haven for "detestable doctrines of the most brutal paganism, or the most subtle modernism, under the immaculate attire of a highly proclaimed confidence in the Catholic church." Guillibert was not the only prominent Catholic to pressure Rome to investigate the orthodoxy of the Action Française and its leadership. The other moderate bishops followed his lead, and the growing number of publications against Maurras and the league in the final years before the war began to have a cumulative effect. Building upon the critical points developed by the Christian Democrats, these works refined and emphasized those arguments which stigmatized the Maurrasians as heretical, modernist, agnostic, and non-Catholic. The seemingly impregnable Action Française found itself suddenly vulnerable in the face of charges similar to the ones that it had leveled so recently against its own enemies within the Catholic church.[25]

Friends of the Action Française rallied to its defense. The Sillon's archfoe Emmanuel Barbier sent word to Rome commending the royalist league, and Msgr. Henri Delassus published detailed arguments in support of a Catholic-Maurrasian alliance. The prominent Jesuit theologian Yves de la Brière used the pages of *Etudes* to construct a case designed to acquit Charles Maurras of the anti-Catholic charges being laid at his feet. Although he did not deny that Maurras's positivism was open to serious criticism, he went on to add that the royalist philosopher was an able defender of the church who promulgated a notion of Catholicism as orthodox as Pius IX's *Syllabus of Errors*.[26]

Charles Maurras himself recognized the gravity of the situation. He sensed that his personal convictions could threaten the recently acquired relationship that the Action Française enjoyed with integrist and traditional Catholics in high places. The organization could ill afford to alienate such powerful friends. To avert this danger, the royalist leader answered the objections of his foes in a new book, *L'Action Française et la religion catholique,* which appeared in 1913. In this volume, he barely addressed himself to charges of disobedience to proper authorities. His support of papal integrism and religious defense made such an apologetic superfluous. The other charges against him could not be dismissed so easily. He informed his readers that the Christian Democrats were more prone to excess and violence than the Action Française, and he pointed out that the league's slogan "by any means" (*par tous les moyens*) was used by many important Catholic leaders as well.[27]

Not surprisingly, Maurras spent most of the book trying to dispel those charges which called the Catholic loyalty of the Action Française into question. He insisted that the league's *politique d'abord* involved merely a tactical priority and not a definitional primacy. His conviction that the French Revolution had destroyed all forces capable of confronting its demonic anarchy led him to adopt a strategy of political power seizure. He contended that control and transformation of the state was vitally necessary before Catholicism could be restored to its proper glory within French society. Without *politique d'abord* there could be no effective religious defense. In a word, the royalist leader sought to assure Catholics that his league's notion of political priority was temporal and chronological rather than doctrinal and philosophical. The stigma of Maurras's agnosticism and its potential danger to the faith of traditional Catholics had to be treated with the utmost delicacy. First of all, the royalist philosopher assured his Catholic readers that his suspect and offensive earlier writings were kept deliberately independent of his Action Française connections. He pointed out that his questionable *Anthinéa* did not appear in any league publications and that its heterodox material had been excised from the book's more recent editions. Further, Maurras did not deny his religious skepticism but added quickly that a Catholic-positivist alliance was necessary to defeat "Protestantism, Masonry and the Jewish world." Finally, he denied emphatically that his agnosticism posed any danger for believing Catholics. To the contrary, the league's unbelievers continued to be inspired personally by "examples of Catholic piety and practice."[28]

So intent was Maurras on identifying himself with the Catholic church that he concluded his book by appending to it a long letter of deferential respect to Pius X. In this communication, the royalist leader alluded to his agnosticism but hastened to add that the pontificate of His Holiness was a profound inspiration to all the league's members, believer and unbeliever alike. He assured the pontiff that the integral nationalists had always upheld "Catholicism in its entirety. . . . This is *because we are Catholic,*" Maurras concluded, "and not *although we are Catholic.*"[29] The apologetic efforts by the monarchist philosopher in 1913 were by no means fruitless. Pressures from enemies had forced him to formulate some definitive answers to potentially embarrassing questions about the nature of what some were describing as a very bizarre relationship. In addition, the book's publication was an act of skillfull diplomacy. Its relative moderation, its forthright qualities, and its spirit of respect for and submission to the pope all helped to diffuse the Christian Democratic case against the integral royalists.

Nevertheless, on January 16, 1914, the Congregation of the Index condemned seven works by Charles Maurras and the league's review, because it was felt that the points of view expressed therein were especially dangerous to Catholic youth. The pope did not countermand this decision; neither did he enforce it. Instead, he reserved for himself the right to publish this decree of condemnation at a time that he deemed appropriate.[30] In such a way Pius X both preserved his deeply traditional theology and protected one of the most powerful defenders of his policies in France. In a letter to the integrist bishop of Lille, Alexis-Armand Charost, the pontiff stated that he had enough data to condemn Maurras, but he added that the royalists' detractors were motivated more "by hatred of the political doctrines of the Action Française" than by "love and zeal for holy religion." The pope confided to Charost: "Also, as long as I live, the Action Française will never be condemned. It has done much good. It defends the principle of authority. It defends order." So attracted was the pontiff to Maurras and his pro-Catholic writings that he did not hesitate to give him a blessing by proxy when the honorary Papal Chamberlain Camille Bellaigue made such a request on the royalist leader's behalf. "Our benediction! Yes, all our benedictions!" announced the pope to Bellaigue. "And tell him that he is a good defender of the faith."[31] The pro-Catholic credentials of Charles Maurras and the Action Française had been vindicated by the direct intervention of Pius X against a condemnation promulgated by his own antimodernist machinery. This was in striking contrast to the action that he had taken against Sillon almost four years earlier.

In eight short years the Action Française had made a profound impact upon both French and Vatican Catholicism. Utilizing the defensive mentality engendered among Catholics and identifying with the integrist program adopted by the church's leadership, the royalist league posed successfully as a loyal advocate of the faith against both its external and internal foes. Its support was welcomed by the church's reactionaries and an increasing number of bishops, while its own membership ranks were swelled by an influx of Catholics. A desperate Christian Democratic rearguard action against the royalists had inaugurated a campaign designed to expose the Maurrasians as false Catholics. The failure of this offensive was the direct result of papal intervention. Pius X had refused to let the Index publish its condemnation of Maurras and his league. His Holiness put the decree in a drawer. There it would lie, available for future use should the need arise. For Pius X that moment never came. In less than a year his mortal remains lay in state in Saint Peter's basilica, and Europe had been plunged into total war. The presence of German armies on French soil prompted Catholics to put aside their partisan quarrels with each other and with the anticlerical republic. The Action Française would use this newly found national unity to entrench itself further among Catholics and to enhance its patriotic credentials within the nation as a whole.

✢ 6 ✢

The Apogee of a Friendship
(1914–1925)

*P*ius X had intervened to rescue the Action Française from a disastrous condemnation, but in a very real sense, the royalist league's savior was the Great European War. The presence of the hated *boche* on French soil catapulted previous domestic foes into a patriotic alliance constructed to repel the foreign invader. Former quarrels were suspended in an atmosphere of national emergency. The anterior church-state conflicts and inter-Catholic divisions gave way to a mood of unity which was called the Union Sacrée. A complete sacrificial loyalty to the nation was demanded of all its parts, and anything that suggested discord in this wartime coalition was viewed with grave suspicion.

In such an environment the Action Française thrived. Its anti-Germanism seemed vindicated by harsh military realities, and it was able to take advantage of its ultranationalist reputation in the midst of a France involved in total war. Throughout the conflict and during the immediate postwar period, France displayed a military patriotic face to the world. Chauvinistic fervor against Germany, social conservatism, and anticommunism dominated the war governments and the Bloc National that followed. Such a setting provided a comfortable meeting ground for the Action Française and the most politically active French Catholics. During this period the royalists continued to display their

Catholic credentials along with their patriotic ones. The brief anticlerical revival of the Cartel des Gauches in 1924 provided further opportunities for the integral nationalists to pose as defenders of the church against an anti-Christian republic. Thus from the outbreak of war to the Herriot government, the Action Française entered fully into the political life of the nation and was viewed as a respectable expression of French patriotism. Its newspaper columns had been directed more against the Germans than the republic, and its qualified support for the Bloc Nationale enhanced its patriotic repute and increased its Catholic support. In fact, this decade marked the zenith of the league's popularity and influence among Catholics.

The German invasion in August 1914 had halted abruptly the Christian Democratic counteroffensive against the Maurrasians. Union Sacrée demanded a moratorium on such secondary quarrels. Meanwhile, the very fact of wartime unity served to solidify the already strong accord between the Action Française and prominent French Catholics. The language, symbols, and values used by these two groups in defense of patriotic solidarity were reactionary and alien to republican values. Union Sacrée was viewed by the ecclesiastical authorities as a religious crusade based upon France's ancient religious traditions. Beyond the expected appeals for peace and national unity in the name of the Virgin Mary, large numbers of the French episcopate resorted to the vision of the throne and altar society of pre–French Revolutionary days. Cardinal Luçon, the dean of French prelates, summed up the feelings of the country's reactionary churchmen by reciting God's favor toward the nation of "Clovis, Joan of Arc and Christ, the friend of the Francs." His appeal was that his beloved country would renounce its "public irreligion" and "return to the path of its Christian tradition." Luçon's call for an end to governmental anticlericalism and the restoration of a monarchical and Catholic France demonstrated that the two-France mentality of the integrists had survived the wartime national unity. Such imagery was medieval, as was the hierarchy's raison d'être for the armed conflict. Germany, who was the aggressor, was Protestant Germany nurtured on the ideas of Luther. Against this invasion stood France, the eldest daughter of the church.[1]

La Croix adopted a similar chauvinism toward the Germans, but this did not prevent it from retaining its prewar suspicions toward the republic. Its confidence was in the army which had "reconciled the French" rather than in "the divisions of parliament" which had been "the cause of France's feebleness." The newspaper's unwavering conviction was that France's weakness in the face of German military might was due to the Revolution's expulsion of God in the name of the Rights of Man. Parallel notions of *union sacrée* were promulgated by right-wing Catholic intellectuals. The Catholic-inspired *Revue des Deux Mondes* identified the military with the nation by calling the army "the living fatherland." In fact, stated the review, national unity had been "the patient work of royalty." The king had been "the redresser of wrongs, the guardian of the right, the protector of the weak, the great chaplain, the universal refuge" and "the Lord's anointed" until revolutionary regicide changed all that. The pro-Maurrasian Henri Massis deplored Prussian militarism which he viewed as the murderous and criminal spirit of Martin Luther, and Jacques Maritain used the columns of *La Croix* to describe wartime French unity in the terminology of counterreformation and counterrevolution. He perceived that a direct line extended from Luther and Calvin through Rousseau and Robespierre to the Prussian *guerre à outrance* of his own day. The German Reformation's "egocentrism" was one principal cause of the French Revolution's "absolute democratic individualism."[2]

Finally, reactionary and traditional French Catholics used the language of martyrdom to describe the war. Cardinal Désiré-Joseph Mercier, the patriarch of German-occupied Belgium, became a paradigm of passive resistance to the godless invader, and the shelling of the ancient cathedral at Reims, the church of Clovis and Joan of Arc, was an affront to "the French soul, as well as to the Christian soul." The sacrificial war effort demanded of the French was linked to the Sacred Heart piety, symbolized by the almost completed basilica on the heights of Montmartre. In her hour of trial, France could rely upon Joan of Arc to deliver her not only from the ravages of German imperialism but also from the treasonous anticlericalism which had been her Calvary for so long.[3]

Not surprisingly, the Action Française entered the fray with similar perceptions of the Union Sacrée. Rabid nationalism, combined with a reactionary pro-Catholicism, enabled the royalist league to identify fully with the language and values of most influential Catholics who supported the war effort. In 1917 Charles Maurras wrote a book called *Le Pape, la guerre et la paix*. Included in its contents were contrasts of Latin Catholicism and German Lutheranism which paralleled those drawn by Jacques Maritain and others. The royalist philosopher was convinced that the spirit of Martin Luther would destroy civilization unless it was faced in battle by Catholicism and Latin ideals. For Maurras the Great War was a titanic clash between Germanism and Christianity. Much like the traditional Catholics, the integral nationalists eulogized the resistance symbolism illustrated by Cardinal Mercier in Belgium. Also, Joan of Arc and Sacred Heart imagery were given frequent attention in the columns of *L'Action Française*. The saint of the fatherland was described as the foremost enemy of the nation's anticlericals, and Louis Dimier called the Montmartre basilica "the immortal hope of the fatherland." Shortly after the armistice, the royalist newspaper published the discourse of its friend Msgr. Touchet in honor of Saint Joan's canonization and the Sacred Heart. In these ways the Action Française identified with the language, values, and symbols used by traditional and reactionary Catholics throughout the war period.[4]

A similar judgment may be rendered with respect to Catholic political practice throughout the duration of the armed conflict. Both Maurrasians and Catholics viewed themselves as public watchdogs over the Union Sacrée, and in the name of this task, they continued to attack their former enemies. This became clear in their assaults upon what they deemed to be a traitorous mood of pacifism found among some government figures. *L'Action Française* was incensed by the efforts of Louis-Jean Malvy, the minister of the interior, and ex-premier Joseph Caillaux to promote a compromise peace with Germany. Integral nationalists and most public Catholics attacked the "defeatism" of these Radicals in the name of punitive peace advocated by Georges Clemenceau. A number of bishops joined with *La Croix* in welcoming the trials of Malvy and Caillaux as "the just punishment of a party" built upon "base passions and vulgar appetites." Even the Christian Democratic *L'Ouest-Eclair* feared what it called that "obsession for peace" that was undermining France's "duty to conquer."[5] In addition, most Catholics and integral nationalists were hostile toward any expressions of internationalism beyond the ecclesiastical variety represented by Rome. Their punitive understanding of peace and their narrow patriotism rendered them fearful of any new order beyond the tradition of separate nations mutually interrelating on the basis of a balance of power. Even more dangerous than pacifism was international socialism and its Bolshevik counterpart which had seized power in Russia toward the end of the war. *La Croix* insisted that communism's "profound hatred of the Catholic church" required an official rechristianization of France. Only this decisive step would give the nation enough moral fiber to join the anti-Bolshevik crusade. For its part, *L'Ouest-Eclair* insisted that the red flag could never replace the tricolor. Socialism and class struggle were hateful German imports which would be vanquished by the benevolent French traditions of love and class cooperation exemplified by social Catholicism. The Breton daily castigated the Bolsheviks as "Jews or Jew-sympathizers" bent on destroying Western civilization. *L'Action Française* echoed these opinions in its own denunciations of the Marxists. Revolution was a German notion in direct opposition to the social corporatism of Tour du Pin. Unlike papal internationalism, bolshevism was constructed upon utopian fantasies. For the Maurrasians the choice was simple, either "internationalism and revolution" or "social order, the rights of the fatherland and the Catholic church."[6]

However, it was the continuation of earlier religious conflicts that most strikingly forged enduring bonds between the integral nationalists and traditional French Catholics. Prewar values and hostilities were not obliterated as much as they were sidestepped. Consequently, these former battles erupted again under the stresses of war. Due to rather frequent attacks by Radical newspapers and the Socialist *L'Humanité,* Catholics felt compelled to defend their patriotic credentials and to counterattack. Books were written by leading Catholic intellectuals pointing out the priestly sacrifices made in the name of the war effort. Bishops echoed these sentiments, and the rector of the Institut Catholique in Paris, Alfred Baudrillart, lamented the fact that "no monarchical regime" had been able to take root "since the deplorable rupture of our national traditions during the epoch of the Revolution." For him, the lack of a king explained France's current divisions even in the face of a foreign enemy. Nevertheless, it was *La Croix* that countered the anticlerical charges most relentlessly. *L'Humanité* and the Radical *La Dépêche de Toulouse* were accused of politicizing the trenches against Catholics. Such offensives in violation of basic religious freedoms were crimes of "treason against the front and the fatherland." The Action Française joined *La Croix*'s press campaign against the anticlericals. Maurras castigated the same newspapers and lauded those priests who rendered sacrificial service to the fatherland in the military hospitals and on the battlefield.[7]

Finally, both *La Croix* and *Action Française* upheld the reputation of the pope when the anticlericals accused him of anti-French and pro-German behavior. The Assumptionist editor of *La Croix* Father Bertoye responded to these charges by pointing out that anti-Catholic legislation and the rupture of diplomatic relations had alienated the Vatican from the Third Republic. Maurrasians joined with Bertoye in calling for a reopening of the embassy to the Holy See. Further, the Action Française insisted that Benedict XV, the successor of Pius X, was no ally of Germany against France. In the midst of these polemics, Charles Maurras wrote his definitive defense of the papacy's wartime activities. *Le Pape, la guerre et la paix* was a resounding affirmation of the Vatican's legitimate universality against the "onslaught of international hate" advocated by the competing socialists. The royalist philosopher insisted that the pope's autonomy made him the arbiter of international law, "the legislator of the war, and the founder of the peace." Although the Action Française was devoted to a rigorous patriotism, Maurras concluded that this conviction did not prevent him from asserting that the Holy Father was the incarnation of legitimate internationalism.[8]

However, this defense of the pontiff was tested sorely when Benedict XV published his *To the Belligerent Peoples and to Their Leaders* (August 1, 1917) in the hope that a negotiated peace could be arranged. The pope pleaded for a cease-fire, a return to prewar boundaries, and a peaceful arbitration of all territorial disputes. His appeal was stillborn not only among the warring nations but also among French Catholics who insisted upon the return of Alsace-Lorraine. The French hierarchy showed diplomatic prudence by hiding behind a wall of silence. For example, Cardinal Dubourg sent a personal letter of gratitude to His Holiness but did not publish the encyclical in his own religious weekly. *La Croix* questioned the pope's right to judge territorial questions and suggested that his desire for peace would be brought to fruition by the armies of France. *L'Action Française* was no less critical. Louis Dimier called the date of the encyclical's publication that "day when the Holy See took a step contrary to our [French] interests." For the first time since the Ralliement, the Action Française had found itself in conflict with the Vatican's wishes, but it was careful to voice its opposition in diplomatic language. Even this break with papal policy did not harm its pro-Catholic credentials, for few among French Catholics welcomed Benedict's initiatives.[9]

In its customary fashion, the Maurrasian league aggravated its assaults against the Christian Democrats, especially the former Sillonists. Even though Marc Sangnier had enlisted in the army and closed down the offices of *La Démocratie* temporarily, the royalists still viewed Catholic republicanism as a "public enemy" both of traditional France and the church. Louis Dimier was convinced that Sangnier's followers were pursuing a personal vendetta against the royalists "under the cloak of Catholic piety." These polemics versus the Christian Democrats contrasted sharply with the more pacifistic stance of Catholic traditionals toward their prodemocratic comrades. Nevertheless, the nation's Catholic integrists aligned themselves with the more militant Action Française. Cardinal Dubourg and his Breton allies continued to attack *L'Ouest-Eclair* and Félix Trochu. *Le Nouvelliste de Bretagne* called its competitor unpatriotic and pro-German, and Rennes's archbishop tried to force Father Trochu to resign from the director's post of the republican newspaper, a position which he had accepted when Desgrées du Loû was mobilized at Brest. A compromise was worked out between the two protagonists, but this breach of the Union Sacrée by Dubourg was indicative of the problems that Christian Democracy continued to face in Brittany.[10]

All in all, the war years had been good to the Maurrasian royalists. Their patriotic reputation had soared, and their Catholic credentials had been vindicated by their shared language and practice with a substantial and important number of the nation's Catholics. Forgotten were the more questionable elements of Action Française philosophy and behavior. Its reactionary and pro-Catholic brand of patriotism squared well with that expressed by most influential Catholics in the land. It joined with these same ecclesiastical circles in defense of the church against persistent anticlerical attacks and socialist dreams. Even when it criticized the papal encyclical on a negotiated peace and condemned the Christian Democrats, the league did not break with the mood of official Catholicism in France. No wonder, then, that by the time the hostilities ceased in 1918, the Action Française had enhanced its reputation as a defender of the faith and had expanded its influence among French-speaking Catholics.[11]

This was especially true with respect to the prelates of the French church. The old and faithful Cardinal de Cabrières maintained his openly supportive relationship with both Charles Maurras and the Action Française. On the occasion of his eighty-seventh birthday, the aging prelate praised the royalists and Camelots du Roi for their loyalty and courage during the war. Msgr. Penon, raised to the episcopal see of Moulins during the pontificate of Pius X, was another devotee of integral nationalism. He referred to Maurras's defense of the church as the "source of an immense ideological movement in favor of tradition." The bishop of Orléans retained his public affection for the royalist league, and cardinals Mercier of Belgium and Sevin of Lyon eulogized Maurrasian virtues. Finally, Charles Maurras himself won an important ally in the person of Cardinal Paulin Andrieu, the archbishop of Bordeaux. Andrieu was convinced that Maurras defended the father-

The Apogee of a Friendship ✦ 89

land "with a pen equally as valuable as any sword," but the cardinal was most impressed by the brand of counterrevolutionary Catholicism that the monarchical organization upheld.[12]

Expansion of hierarchical support did not exhaust the growing influence of the Action Française among domestic Catholics. Important sectors of the Catholic press became increasingly attracted to the patriotic and propapal arguments of the Maurrasians. Surprisingly enough, even the Christian Democratic *L'Ouest-Eclair* was affected positively. Its polemics against the league ceased for the duration of the war, and Emmanuel Desgrées du Loû went so far as to commend the intelligence found in Maurras's and Daudet's apologetics. *La Croix*'s praise was even more effusive. It lauded the league's campaign against the "defeatist press" and defended the royalist daily against governmental efforts to suppress it. Daudet was called "a good patriot," and his newspaper was commended as "a valiant organ." Father Bertoye expressed satisfaction that Louis Dimier had aligned himself with *La Croix* against the papal peace proposals, and he acclaimed Maurras's *Le Pape, la guerre et la paix*. To be sure, he stated his reservations concerning Daudet's language and Maurras's unbelief, but this did not prevent him from rendering homage to them.[13] In spite of Maurras's agnosticism, the reactionary Assumptionist did not hesitate to conclude:

> Much that is Catholic is found deeply within him! What deep sentiment of tradition and religious interest in the nation! What a cult of admiration for Catholic institutions, for the church and for the pope! What irresistible logic in defense of their rights! He has left no stone unturned, and on all points of attack, he has been with us in the breach.[14]

During the war the Action Française had augmented its status as a recognized defender of the Catholic church and papacy. Its enemies within the church had been diverted from their anti-Maurrasian campaigns for *raisons de guerre*, and its growing reputation among the bishops seemed assured. The league's patriotic credentials were lauded by some Christian Democrats, and *La Croix* had recognized it as an ally in the crusade of religious defense. The future appeared bright for the integral nationalists, and the immediate postwar years seemed to justify such an assessment.

From the armistice of 1918 until the emergence of the Locarno spirit, the Action Française flourished. By virtue of its patriotic zeal for the Union Sacrée, it had entered the mainstream of French political life and would remain there for the duration of the Bloc National government. This coalition of rightist parties, led initially by the now superpatriotic Georges Clemenceau, governed France in the negative spirit of anti-Germanism and antibolshevism until its defensive program was rejected by the electorate in 1924. Such an atmosphere proved conducive to the Action Française which sent its sole deputy Léon Daudet to the Chamber of Deputies under the umbrella of the Bloc National.

Immediately after the war, French Catholics rallied also to the conservative Bloc National. For them this coalition of rightist parties meant a continuation of national pride, suspicion of the League of Nations, and territorial gains against the defeated Germans. They stood resolutely behind the Carthaginian peace advocated by the old "tiger" Georges Clemenceau. The collective letter of the French hierarchy, published early in 1924, reflected a patriotic ideology designed to warm the heart of any devoted integral nationalist. All loyal citizens were urged to beware of internationalist doctrines contrary to both "nature and religion," likely a reference to both bolshevism and the Wilsonian ideas embodied in the new League of Nations. Further, these prelates echoed the Maurrasians by advocating a hard-line enforcement of the Treaty of Versailles. Individual bishops made similar assessments. One described the Wilsonian league as a utopian creation "inspired by the theories of J.-J. Rousseau and the Declaration of the Rights of Man," while others insisted upon a relentless bellicosity toward Germany. Some prelates went so far as to criticize the papal condemnation of Poincaré's Ruhr invasion, arguing that God and justice demanded "the reparation of wrong done to another."[15] The most popular sectors of the Catholic press, including both *La Croix* and *L'Ouest-Eclair,* echoed the shrill patriotism of the French prelates. Both papers had little confidence in the League of Nations, and both advocated a program of justice vis-à-vis Germany. *La Croix* defended the Ruhr incursion, and *L'Ouest-Eclair* argued that Poincaré's occupation forces must be maintained against the communists, cosmopolitan banking interests, and the internationalist humanitarians.[16]

Most important, the Catholic church hoped that the Bloc National would become the political instrument it could utilize to reverse the republic's anticlerical legislation. For this reason the hierarchy appealed to the Catholic electors in 1919 to vote for the rightist parties. From the monarchist Cardinal de Cabrières to the republican Msgr. Chapon of Nice, the bishops deplored the religious disunity which they felt the Reformation and French Revolution had imposed upon France, and they insisted upon a return of state aid to Catholic schools, a reversal of the most offensive elements in the separation legislation and a reinstitution of the Vatican embassy. In a public letter addressed by the entire French hierarchy to the French electorate, the nation's higher clergy expressed a willingness to live with the despised law of 1905 as long as the state would remain, at the very least, benevolently neutral toward the institutions and programs of the church.[17]

Too much, however, should not be made of this timid overture to the republic. On the one hand, the anticlericals were not a strong element within the Bloc National. Most of their firebrands were candidates in the opposition parties. Consequently, the Catholics were able to count on the support of conservative republicans with whom they had forged patriotic ties during the Union Sacrée. On the other hand, the individual bishops adopted more intransigent positions when they made electoral appeals within their own diocesan boundaries. Cardinal Dubourg's instructions to the Breton voters were framed in the language of prewar church-state conflicts. He told Catholics that they were forbidden to cast their ballots for Freemasons or "fomenters of anarchy, social destruction and socialism." He concluded his injunctions with the assertion that no government would be acceptable to the church unless it first repudiated the "impious legislation . . . condemned by the popes Leo XIII and Pius X." Similar directives were printed in other diocesan weeklies throughout France. For example, Cardinal Paulin Andrieu of Bordeaux used a catechetical format to excoriate the anticlerical laws. Their very presence was an invitation to the kind of social disorder exemplified by the Bolshevik disaster in Russia.[18] Standing resolutely behind the bishops were the two prominent Catholic dailies. Father Bertoye of *La Croix* demanded "a permanent statute for the church," "parity of the schools," and the reestablishment of official relations with the Vatican. *L'Ouest-Eclair* reiterated these claims.[19]

Once the Bloc National was in power, influential Catholics began to press for specific adjustments of the prewar legislation they despised. Their campaigns centered on the restoration of diplomatic relations with the Holy See and the removal of the statutory vagueness surrounding the "cultic associations." Of the two, the reinstatement of the Vatican was the easier task to achieve. In spite of anticlerical intransigence in some quarters, many important secular leaders, such as Raymond Poincaré, Alexandre Millerand, and Artistide Briand, recognized that religious peace at home and abroad would aid their conservative ambitions. Catholics would be useful allies in those foreign and domestic policies which deemed antibolshevism to be a top priority. In due time, the embassy was reopened, and Catholic affection for the Bloc National was solidified. The issue of the "cultic associations" was far more difficult to resolve. The law of 1905 was deeply repugnant to most influential Catholics. Nevertheless, a few bishops, the government, and the pope sought a compromise with the controversial "cultic associations" which could salvage the Separation Law while ending opposition to it. Most of the French ecclesiastical dignitaries were not so flexible. Over 75 percent of the bishops were hesitant and hostile to compromise. A number of these prelates expressed their opposition to the pontiff himself in audiences granted at Rome; most of the others used their diocesan publications to undermine all concession to what they felt was "heresy and schism." They feared that the hated associations would enforce a democratization of the church's hierarchy. Even when Pope Pius XI was able to negotiate an acceptable interpretation of the law, the episcopate responded with less than enthusiasm. Hostility to the secular republic was deeply rooted in the French hierarchy and long survived the new pope's gestures of *ralliement*.[20]

In spite of the continuing tension between Catholics and secular republicans, both forces remained united because of the mutually perceived threat of communism. The successful Bolshevik Revolution, the eruption of serious work stoppages in France and the victory for the Third International at Tours in 1920 combined to frighten conservatives throughout France. Catholics were not immune to such anxieties, and with very few exceptions they contributed to the anti-Red hysteria that was growing in France. Toward the end of the war, *L'Ouest-Eclair* and *La Croix* were uttering warnings against the Russian Bolsheviks, a pattern that continued in the years that followed. A crusade mentality developed rapidly among French Catholics to the point where the eradication of communism was viewed as a necessary corollary to the preservation of "Roman civilization."[21]

Quite naturally, the hierarchy formed the backbone of French Catholic anticommunism. The joint episcopal statement published in the spring of 1919 warned that "class struggle would be disastrous for everybody." In its place the bishops advocated employer-employee collaboration in the name of Catholic social doctrine. The more reactionary prelates lumped together all the traditional enemies of the church into the common vat of bolshevism. In the opinion of Cardinal Andrieu, the Russian Revolution had been unleashed by Germany with the connivance of "Judaism, Freemasonry, Protestantism and socialism." According to him, the republic's laicist laws were the direct "application of Bolshevik theories" because they overturned the three bastions of social order, "property, liberty and authority." Even the more moderate bishops, who were prepared to make peace with a conservative republic, would not compromise with Marxism in any form. Msgr. Eugène Louis Ernest Julien, bishop of Arras and a personal friend of Marc Sangnier, declared that socialism was "in formal opposition to Catholic teaching" and a complete violation of "nature, good sense and the facts." For the episcopate, communism was the most frightful enemy of the church because it sought to reduce authority to "the lowest common denominator."[22]

Finally, the French church looked to the Bloc National to protect it against the reviving anti-Catholicism represented by the Cartel des Gauches, an alliance of Radicals and Socialists determined to win the elections of 1924. This coalition sought a reversal of the chauvinistic platforms of the governing rightists via a rapprochement with Germany, resolute support of the League of Nations, and possible diplomatic recognition of the Soviet Union. Domestically, the cartel advocated mild social reforms. However, no real bond could be formed securely around the delicate questions involved in a common domestic program. As a result, the two parties fell back upon the prewar tradition of anticlericalism. In the face of such a danger the bishops once again instructed the Catholic voters about their electoral duties. The prelates called for a platform of religious and social defense against the twin horrors of laicism and communism, and toward this end, they exhorted their constituents to cast their ballots for right-wing candidates of the Bloc National. The mass Catholic press stood behind the church's ecclesiastical leadership. *La Croix* demanded a war against the Masons, and *L'Ouest-Eclair* warned that support of the leftist coalition meant "permanent revolution."[23]

Much to the Catholics' chagrin, the rightist bloc was defeated, and the Cartel des Gauches formed a government around the figure of Edouard Herriot. The premier, himself a devout laicist, was pressured to inaugurate anew a militant anticlerical program. He did so by committing his ruling coalition to closing the Vatican embassy and the imposition of secular legislation upon the educational system of Alsace-Lorraine. Catholics rallied to defend their beleaguered church, and their strategical unity proved effective. Opposition to the destruction of diplomatic relations with the Holy See was voiced by reactionaries, traditionals, and Christian Democrats. In his newly formed *Vie Catholique* the prorepublican publisher Francisque Gay made the angry accusation that Herriot's government had abandoned "the white pope" of Christian charity in order to court "the red pope" of Moscow. In spite of this impressive show of Catholic unity the Chamber voted to close the embassy. However, the hesitancy of the Senate and the fall of the Herriot government prevented any action in the matter. This issue became a dead letter for the duration of the republic.[24]

Notably more impressive was the organized opposition of Catholics to the laicization of Alsace-Lorraine. The recovered provinces were heavily Catholic and had learned to resist secularization of their school system while they were under German rule. Therefore, when Herriot's cartel tried to break the live-and-let-live understanding which the Bloc National had respected in Alsace and Lorraine, the bishops of Metz and Strasbourg rang the tocsin of antigovernmental resistance. They demanded that all citizens join a Catholic league which would organize mass rallies designed to collect signatures for protest petitions. Over half a million names were collected. Catholic Alsace-Lorraine had stood behind its confessional school system unequivocally.[25]

However, resistance was not limited to these regions alone. Within a brief period, Catholic opposition had produced a national network. From the reactionary fulminations of Jean Guiraud at *La Croix* to the moderate critiques of Marc Sangnier, the Catholic press united behind the angry Alsatians. Beyond this, the most decisive action against the anticlericals was the massive protest campaign mounted by the newly organized Fédération Nationale Catholique. Much like the earlier Union Catholique of Colonel Keller, the new federation was sponsored by the hierarchy and was instituted as an organ of religious defense by a devoutly reactionary military officer, General Edouard de Curières de Castelnau. This integral royalist, with his blend of ultra Catholicism and rabid patriotism, organized his units for the express purpose of stemming the cartel's anticlerical tide. By the time of its first national congress in February 1925, the FNC had over two million members scattered throughout the eighty-two dioceses of France. At its mass rallies, the integrist general and local members of the hierarchy railed against the anti-Catholic government. Jean Guiraud used the columns of *La Croix* to advertise de Castelnau's public meetings, and he united his own antilaicist league, the Associations Catholiques de Chefs de Famille, with the general's federation for the duration of the counter-offensive against the cartel. He even suggested that the FNC should form a Catholic political party. Meanwhile, the de Castelnau campaign increased in tempo. Rallies were followed by demonstrations in the major cities. In the heavily Catholic areas, some of them reached nearly 100,000, with the more dechristianized regions still supplying a few thousand activists for these anticartel parades. The campaign was climaxed by a public declaration of the French cardinals and archbishops calling upon the nation's Catholics to adopt "a more militant and energetic attitude" in defense of the church's rights. They were told to "declare war upon laicism and its principles" until the iniquitous anti-Catholic laws were swept from the land.[26]

Catholic strength asserted itself throughout the nation, forcing the Cartel des Gauches to back down. Alsace-Lorraine retained its confessional schools, and the nation returned to the compromise settlements which the church had worked out with the Bloc National. Anticlericalism had proven to be an anachronism; it would no longer serve as the mortar to seal electoral coalitions. Nor could the church use religious defense effectively beyond support of the status quo which had emerged in the early 1920s. The law of 1905 was in France to stay, and all the skill of Catholic mass pressure was unable to change that. When the dust of the conflict had settled in 1925, it became clear that the religious passions of both sides had resulted in a stalemate. The Vatican embassy and the Alsatian schools had survived, but so had the Separation Law of 1905. Like it or not, French Catholicism was compelled to coexist with a secular republican state, and it did so, with some reluctance, until the "divine miracle" of Philippe Pétain.

Where was the Action Française in all of this? It was aligning itself with former Catholic friends and earning new ones. It continued to trumpet its xenophobic nationalism in language much like that of the most chauvinistic bishops. *L'Action Française* praised the 1924 episcopal letter on patriotism and concluded that the prelates' doctrine had always been practiced loyally by the royalist league. Hatred of Germany persisted even after the signing of the peace. From the podium of the French legislative chamber Léon Daudet raised his voice periodically for the enforcement of a Carthaginian peace. He defended Poincaré's invasion of the Ruhr much as the nation's conservative Catholics had done, arguing that Germany remained the cradle of Protestantism's "Luther . . . and his Jewish bankers." Indeed, the integral nationalists feared that the League of Nations would be utilized to resurrect the hated *boche* and to convince France's Radicals to abandon the justice embodied in the Treaty of Versailles. The Maurrasians joined the more reactionary bishops in denouncing all Wilsonian ideas and remained intransigent foes of the Locarno spirit throughout the 1920s. In fact, they believed that there were striking ideological ties between the League of Nations and bolshevism. For them, Catholicism and order were diametrically opposed to socialism and collectivism. By its militant anti-Germanism, its suspicions toward the Wilsonian league and its sainted horror of communism, the Action Française was able to strengthen its ties with reactionary and traditional Catholics in the years immediately following the war.[27]

Nevertheless, the royalist organization's chief merit in church circles was its unrelenting defense of ecclesiastical interests as they were perceived by most influential French Catholics. Article after article appeared in its daily advocating a speedy reopening of the Vatican embassy. On the matter of the "cultic associations," the integral nationalists allied themselves with the nation's most reactionary prelates. All compromise with the demonic law of 1905 was rejected because it promulgated a notion of the church which was democratic and antihierarchical. With the rise to power of the Cartel des Gauches, the Action Française was able both to intensify its attacks upon the republic and to pose once again as an unequivocal defender of the Catholic faith. Léon Daudet argued that anticlericalism was a Protestant import from Germany that the republic was using to undermine the deeply rooted Catholic morality of France. In fact, the cartel government was living proof that "the democratic republic" was "in its very essence the enemy of Catholicism." In every respect, the integral nationalists eulogized the struggle of the Alsatian people to retain their confessional school system against Herriot's offensive. Throughout the crisis, *L'Action Française* published the outraged protests of reactionary and proroyalist bishops. Joint episcopal statements were given front-page coverage, as were the massive demonstrations launched by Catholics against the government. The royalist newspaper published the antilaicist program of the Alsatian bishops and followed favorably the crusade of the Fédération Nationale Catholique and its reactionary general. So sympathetic was the Action Française to de Castelnau that its Camelots du Roi would serve as his bodyguard at FNC rallies.[28]

In all of these ways, the Action Française found itself allied with the mainstream of French Catholicism after the war. It echoed a xenophobia similar to that espoused by *L'Ouest-Eclair* and *La Croix,* and it shared the domestic hierarchy's devotion to the harsh Versailles peace against Germany, the bishops' suspicion of the League of Nations, and the church's crusading anticommunism. Most important, the royalist league used its resources in defense of Catholic interests. The laicist campaign of the Herriot government had enhanced the Catholic credentials of the Maurrasians. Indeed, the integral nationalists had always thrived in an atmosphere of religious civil war, for in such moments they were able to combine effectively Catholic defense and integral nationalism.

Within the church's camp, only the Christian Democrats remained immune to Maurrasian seductions. Consequently, the royalist militants continued to assault Catholic republicanism with harsh polemics. Most hated by the Action Française was Marc Sangnier and his new league, the Jeune République. Charges of resurrected Sillonist heresies were leveled against Sangnier's disciples, and the royalist leadership suggested that its old enemy had succumbed to German idealism, Wilsonian internationalism, and communism. Finally, the Christian Democratic tribune was accused of aligning himself with the anticlerical Cartel des Gauches. When these verbal tirades did not suffice to deter Sangnier from his programs of religious and international peace, the Action Française unleashed the violent Camelots du Roi against him, and he was beaten in the streets. The Christian Democrats of *L'Ouest-Eclair* were also the target of a royalist counteroffensive shortly after the war. For the fourth time in two decades the reactionaries united to remove Father Félix Trochu from his journalistic post. The battle lines were drawn around the electoral campaign which brought the Bloc National to power. Both the local Action Française and its ally *Le Nouvelliste de Bretagne* accused *L'Ouest-Eclair* of supporting the anticlerical Radical party. Emmanuel Desgrées du Loû responded that his newspaper was solidly behind the Bloc National and only supported a handful of pro-Catholic Radicals rather than the royalist choices of the integral nationalists. When the conservative republican candidates proved victorious, the Christian Democrats were elated, but their joy was short-lived. The Action Française was bent on revenge, and it found assistance in the person of the ultraconservative senator Jenouvrier who turned to Cardinal Dubourg for help. The reactionary archbishop retaliated against *L'Ouest-Eclair* by once again insisting that Father Trochu resign from the newspaper's directorship. The *abbé démocrate* promised immediate obedience but begged his spiritual father not to publish the matter. Trochu's wishes went unheeded, for Dubourg printed the entire condemnation with editorial commentary in his diocesan review. Desgrées du Loû's insistence that Trochu had been the victim of antirepublican forces could not hide the fact that the Action Française had scored another victory over its democratic foes within the church.[29]

Everywhere the Action Française had been successful in demonstrating its loyalty to the Catholic cause. The French church had emerged from the Union Sacrée with newly won patriotic credentials, but it had neither abandoned its defensive mentality nor its commitment to the abolition of prewar anticlerical victories. Such entrenched reactionary dreams made French Catholicism increasingly susceptible to the appeals of the Action Française. As long as the Christian Democrats could be isolated effectively and as long as an atmosphere of religious civil war could prevail, then the Maurrasians could look forward to a strengthened alliance with Catholicism. That mood of religious defense against the Third Republic was able to unite all Catholics, save the tiny cadres of Catholic republicans, until the collapse of the Cartel des Gauches. In a brief period of seven years, the Action Française had taken advantage of this siege mentality not only to entrench itself in ecclesiastical circles but also to expand its influence among French-speaking Catholics. The decade that began with the guns of August 1914 and ended with the collapse of the Third Republic's last anticlerical offensive in 1925 marked the apogee of the ambivalent friendship between the integral nationalists and the Catholic Church.

By the mid-1920s the Action Française had penetrated every significant arena of Catholic public life in France and Belgium. The league's influence in Catholic intellectual circles had reached an all-time high. Charles Maurras's reactionary ideology dominated the fashionable salons of the French Catholic right, while leading devout literary figures of the Catholic renaissance like Jacques Maritain, Georges Bernanos, and Henri Massis, the editor of the review *Rome,* looked to the monarchist philosopher for inspiration.[30]

However, it was the royalists' influence over the church's leadership, the Catholic press, and the mass organizations of the newly emerging Catholic Action that was most decisive. Hierarchical support remained solid for the royalist league in the immediate postwar years. Cardinal Dubourg and his successor Cardinal Alexis-Armand Charost printed articles from *L'Action Française* in their diocesan weekly and stood behind the local royalists in their political activities. Old episcopal supporters of the integral nationalists remained loyal, such as Msgr. Penon of Moulins, Msgr. Marty of Montauban, and the aged Cardinal de Cabrières of Montpellier. When Charles Maurras's mother died, Msgr. Guillibert of Fréjus sent his sympathies, and Msgrs. Penon and Rivière of Aix were present in the funeral procession. Cardinal Mercier, the primate of Belgium and the symbol of the neo-Thomist revival there, continued to be sympathetic to Action Française influence in his land. Msgr. Ernest Richard, the archbishop of Auch, recruited actively for the league, and Msgr. Jean-Victor Chesnelong, the archbishop of Sens, called himself a Maurrasian royalist. Most of the French cardinals and all resident archbishops could be classified as friendly to the royalist league. In addition, the Dominican orator Father Janvier, who was held in esteem by the French hierarchy, remained a loyal friend of the Action Française.[31]

Maurrasian influence increased in the Catholic-dominated right-wing press as well. The royalist league expanded its own publications by creating a regionally oriented Sunday paper called *L'Action Française du Dimanche* and a rural periodical named *L'Action Française Agricole*. The daily *L'Univers* remained in the hands of the league's allies, and in 1923 Drumont's former anti-Semitic paper was sold to friends of the Action Française. In addition, the hierarchy-supported *Le Nouvelliste de Bretagne*, Brittany's leading integrist newspaper, was operated by Eugène Delahaye, an avid royalist and open advocate of the Action Française. The powerful regional daily *L'Express du Midi*, with a circulation of nearly 900,000, frequently published articles by two prominent royalist members of the league, the historian Jacques Bainville and Robert Havard de la Montagne. This paper's inspiration was decidedly Maurrasian. Even *La Croix* continued its wartime praise of the Action Française. Jean Guiraud added his eulogies to those of Father Bertoye by lauding the intelligence of Maurras in spite of his unbelief and by assuring devout readers that this agnosticism was offset by an influential Catholic presence in the league. Against such formidable support from most of the Catholic press, the Christian Democratic newspapers had little effect. The Action Française had retained the sympathy of most of the Catholic press. Indeed, its own newspaper was considered to be a Catholic publication.[32]

The friendly and cooperative ties between the leaders of the Fédération Nationale Catholique and the Action Française insured that the latter would have a profound influence on this new organ of mass Catholic Action. De Castelnau himself was a reactionary royalist and sympathetic to the followers of Maurras. In one instance, he even appeared in court as an advocate of some Camelots du Roi who had been indicted for acts of street violence against Marc Sangnier. In addition, the league's lawyer Xavier Vallat was an active orator of the FNC. The federation's chaplain was none other than Father Janvier, a long-time friend of the Action Française. Often the leading personalities of both groups appeared in public together. Both Léon Daudet and General de Castelnau were seen fraternizing at the funeral of Cardinal Mercier, and on other occasions both organizations cooperated publicly. In one instance the FNC held a rally at Rouen which was disrupted by some local communists. The Camelots du Roi, who were in charge of keeping order, turned their canes on the communists when "the Reds" began to heckle the departing de Castelnau. Certainly, parallel ideologies account in part for the fraternal ties between the two groups. Although its royalism was most often implied, there can be no doubt that the Fédération Nationale Catholique was an organ of reactionary religious defense which yearned for a Catholic France predating the French Revolution. Freemasonry was the essential enemy, because it was "of necessity anti-Catholic." It was nurtured in the womb of the Protestant Reformation, was imported into France with the *philosophes* and was unleashed on the great Gallic nation with the French Revolution. Since that tragic event, the vain illusions of "liberty, equality, fraternity," have wreaked havoc upon France by destroying the monarchy and undermining religion. By these values the Masons and the Grand Revolution had opened the door to the "egalitarian rage of socialism" and had tried to sweep out "all moral forces, religion and fatherland" from the soil of France. Such were the principles of the Fédération Nationale Catholique, and they were in every way identical to those of the Action Française. In many cases joint ideologies prompted joint memberships, and in some instances local units of the FNC were dominated by Maurrasian leaguers. This was apparent in the Ligue des Catholiques de l'Anjou, a Breton unit of the federation, which was persuaded to support Léon Daudet's candidacy for the Senate in 1925. The presence of Action Française members and ideas at every level in the Fédération Nationale Catholique was most impressive. It meant that the royalist league was having an impact upon that Catholic group in France which was exceedingly powerful both in terms of numerical strength and episcopal sponsorship.[33]

A similar influence was making itself felt in the Catholic youth federations of both France and Belgium. The royalist league was making serious inroads into Catholic schools and using these for aggressive recruitment campaigns. Its ideological hold on the Association Catholique de la Jeunesse Française was so strong that the youth league's more progressive leaders expressed the fear that the Maurrasians would soon control their federation. The extent of this impact upon Catholic youth became apparent when the Association Catholique de la Jeunesse Belge published the results of a popularity poll it had taken among the readership of its *Cahiers de la Jeunesse Belge*. The following question was asked: "Among the writers of the last twenty-five years, whom do you consider to be your master?" Out of 443 votes, 174 were cast for Charles Maurras. The runner-up was fifty votes behind him, and the primate of Belgium, Cardinal Mercier, received only a dismal six votes. Beyond the shadow of a doubt, the Action Française and its philosophy had penetrated deeply into the midst of French-speaking Catholic youth groups and was a more pervasive influence there than the hierarchy itself.[34]

From its humble origins as a fringe organization on the extreme right, the Action Française had become the undisputed voice of ultrarightist French politics in barely two decades. Parallel to this success was its growing ties with the nation's Catholics. By the time the Herriot government collapsed, the Maurrasian league had reached the apogee of its ambivalent alliance with the Catholic church. However, this good fortune blinded integral nationalism to its own vulnerability. It seemed incapable of perceiving that the times had altered since the prewar period. Anticlericalism had spent itself as a serious political force, and without it the Action Française could no longer be an effective ally of Catholicism. The future belonged to more moderate forces within the church which were willing to make peace with both the French republic and modern pluralistic society. This shift in direction by Vatican and French Catholics has been called the Second Ralliement. From below, it meant the rise of a great variety of religious publications and organizations after the war, a reality which rendered a monolithic church increasingly impossible. From above, it signified the Holy See's willingness to achieve old goals by the altered tactics of compromise. The new pope, Pius XI, expected the French church to close its ranks loyally behind him. These events did not bode well for the Action Française. Its very success would be its Achilles' heel. Winds of change had begun to blow within Catholicism, and the Action Française was not supple enough to adapt to them.

♦ 7 ♦

The Winds of Change
(1914–1925)

*B*y 1925 the Action Française had attained the apex of its repute among Catholics. It had won the sympathy of the French hierarchy and the most popular sectors of the Catholic press. Its influence in the mass organizations of Catholic Action was pervasive. The praises of Charles Maurras were sung by Catholics everywhere in France and Belgium. The royalist league's entrenchment in French-speaking ecclesiastical circles seemed assured. Such, however, was not the case. The times were changing both in France and at the Vatican, and the Action Française did not seem prepared to make the proper adjustments. Indeed, the league appeared to be oblivious to the growing strength of the forces for change within the church and French society at large. War and the harsh peace which followed strengthened the conservative republicans within the nation. Militarism, anti-Germanism, and anticommunism were hardly the monopoly of royalists. Victory on the battlefield had enhanced the republic's patriotic image to the point where the political right was becoming increasingly comfortable with a republic in the image of Georges Clemenceau, Alexandre Millerand, Raymond Poincaré, and even Aristide Briand. More and more the church was becoming aware that these men and their conservative republic were prepared to make peace with Catholicism at home and abroad. However, principled royalism did not allow the Action Française to evolve with this changing mood.

In addition, the Catholic church was much less monolithic and more pragmatic than it had been for decades. From the highest levels of its leadership down to its grass-roots cadres, the Vatican and French Catholicism were taking steps to adjust to postwar changes in France. Even before the guns on the western front had fallen silent, the winds of change had begun to blow quietly within the church. Understandably, the voices for religious peace were first heard from the Christian Democrats. *L'Ouest-Eclair* insisted that the Union Sacrée demanded a sincere rallying to the republic, and Marc Sangnier led his prodemocratic Jeune République into the Bloc National where it served as the coalition's left wing.[1]

Change was brewing also at the Vatican. Benedict XV, the pope who had replaced Pius X, was no integrist. Behind the scenes he was inaugurating a quiet campaign to undermine this ultrarightist influence both in Rome and in France. Shortly after the outbreak of war, the bishop of Albi, Msgr. Mignot, addressed a letter to the pope's new secretary of state, the more moderate Pietro Gasparri, warning him of "the occult activity" of Msgr. Benigni's *Sodalitium Pianum*. Why, Mignot pleaded, should "the great majority of French Catholics" be labeled "with suspicion" by such an organization without authority? Within a month, the new pontiff had responded to his bishop's appeal by publishing the encyclical *Ad Beatissimi*. In it he bemoaned Catholic divisions and called for an end to extremist language that violated Christian charity. Although the integrists were not named, they were aware that the pope was referring to them. Meanwhile, Benedict XV continued his anti-integrist gestures. In the early spring of 1917 he received Marc Sangnier in a personal audience and urged him to take up a religious and social program in France. A year before the Holy Father died in 1922, he dismantled the *Sodalitium Pianum* completely.[2]

After the negotiating of the Versailles settlement, the Catholic forces for change began to assert themselves more and more. Within France a new Catholic pluralism was emerging and making itself felt in religious milieus. Most of these manifestations were Christian Democratic in inspiration, but unlike the prewar examples, they were more numerous, more varied, and had wide support among those portions of the Catholic population who endorsed accommodation to post-French Revolutionary values. At the Vatican, both Benedict XV and his successor Pius XI were employing new methods to pursue the rights and privileges of the church and to combat the new Bolshevik menace which appeared to be threatening the old order everywhere. Toward these ends, the postwar pontiffs were committed to a strategy of negotiated settlement with all the noncommunist powers of Europe. Where the church had problems with a particular nation, like France for example, it would try to resolve these by compromise and diplomacy. It was the church's standard program of religious defense in more moderate dress. The end was the same, but the tactics had changed. Any government form, short of bolshevism, was acceptable to the Holy See as long as the rights and privileges of Catholics were upheld. In a word, the papacy had returned to the pragmatic program of Leo XIII, the policy of using constitutional means to achieve ecclesiastical ends. This combination of high-level clerical pragmatism and grass-roots Catholic pluralism opened the door in France to what has been called the Second Ralliement.[3]

The growing mood for religious peace at Rome, supported by the traditional Christian Democrats and coupled with the proliferation of novel Catholic groups, would prove fatal to the Action Française's influence among Catholics. The church's republicans had never abandoned their enmity toward the Maurrasians, and given the gradual thaw of past religious quarrels, these democrats were able to challenge their old foes from a more advantageous position. Building upon their prewar polemics, they continued to accuse the integral nationalists of extremism and reactionary values which hurt the reputation of French Catholicism. Both Emmanuel Desgrées du Loû and Marc Sangnier deplored the royalists' violence, and both were convinced that Maurrasian politics intensified religious passions to the detriment of the French church. Consequently, these two democrats made every effort to demonstrate that the Action Française spoke for itself only and not for the Catholic Church.[4]

This Christian Democratic opposition to integrism and the Action Française was carried beyond ideological bouts into the arenas of public life. In Paris the battle was undertaken almost exclusively by the Jeune République. In general, the former Sillonists sought to break decisively with all reactionary and conservative politics in order to pursue a program of international and domestic peace built upon more advanced forms of democracy and inspired by the tenets of Christianity. By separating themselves from their more conservative religious brothers, they stood alone among Catholics on almost every major political issue confronting the nation. Although Sangnier was elected to the Chamber of Deputies on the Bloc National ticket, he broke frequently with its anticommunistic social conservatism and its ultrapatriotic foreign policy. Specifically, he advocated industrial democracy and factory comanagement in place of anti-Red vendettas, condemned the Ruhr invasion, called for sending food supplies to the famine-beleaguered Soviet Union and appealed for an international peace program more democratic than the League of Nations. Sangnier guided his Jeune République to pursue pan-European peace efforts with such zeal that the Vatican instructed its nuncio to France, Msgr. Cerretti, to express its approval of this work to the democratic tribune. Nevertheless, Sangnier's successes were minimal. He felt compelled to abandon the Bloc National in 1924 and to appeal to the electorate without coalition support. His proworker and international disarmament programs were rejected by his constituency. That his defeat was so decisive indicated how fragile were these first Catholic efforts in the arena of leftist politics. Nevertheless, a precedent had been set. Some elements of French Catholicism had begun their evolution toward the democratic left.[5]

More particularly, the Jeune République opposed the Action Française directly in the same political forums. In the Chamber of Deputies, Sangnier argued that the republican character of the Bloc National demanded the exclusion of Léon Daudet from the coalition. Both men would often rise in parliament for the express purpose of criticizing the other. After the Camelots had attacked Sangnier in the streets of Paris, the former Sillonist used the legislature's podium to excoriate his royalist enemies. He appealed to his fellow deputies to be done with the Action Française and to rally against it "for the honor of both France and the Republic." When this happens, he prophesied, "the evil scum of the Action Française will soon be swept away, and true patriotism, the human patriotism of France will shine resplendent throughout the world." Sangnier's speeches were not able to remove Daudet from the Bloc National, but the point had been made. The defeat of the rightist coalition in 1924 would accomplish what Sangnier's words had been unable to achieve. Léon Daudet was not reelected, and the Action Française's brief and limited success with parliamentary politics came to an end.[6] Interestingly enough, the royalists' return to antidemocratic opposition would coincide with the increasing commitment of the Vatican to rightist constitutional politics within the framework of the Third Republic. Unequivocal resistance and Ralliement were not a good mix.

Sangnier's opposition to the royalists and the defeat of Daudet at the polls in 1924 were compounded by three decisive victories for *L'Ouest-Eclair* in its continuing war with the Action Française. Two of these occurred in elections, and the third was won in the courts. First of all, the Christian Democratic daily had endorsed a few Radicals in the 1919 elections who were prepared to support the negotiation of church-state differences. This policy was a direct attempt to undermine Catholic candidates who were monarchists. Their defeat infuriated the Action Française so much that once again it was able to influence Cardinal Dubourg to compel Father Trochu to resign from his newspaper. This victory, however, was only a Pyrrhic one for the royalists. The election had demonstrated that the Catholic population of Brittany was turning away from monarchism toward the republic. Integral nationalism was giving way to conservative republicanism in the most Catholic region of France. *L'Ouest-Eclair* would gain by this trend, and the Action Française would lose. Maurrasianism's powers of retaliation were limited increasingly to the willingness of Rennes' reactionary archbishops to punish the *abbé démocrate* Félix Trochu.[7]

This growing influence of *L'Ouest-Eclair* in election campaigns against its royalist foes was nowhere demonstrated more strikingly than in its role in the defeat of Léon Daudet's bid for a Senate seat in June 1925. When the reactionary Jules Delahaye died earlier that year, Daudet announced his candidacy for the vacated position, and he solicited and won the support of the Ligue Catholique d'Anjou, an affiliate of the Fédération Nationale Catholique. With the help of de Castelnau's federation, the Daudet campaign appealed to the Catholics in the Maine-et-Loire department under the rubric of unity and religious defense. Meanwhile, *L'Ouest-Eclair* mounted a counteroffensive of its own. Articles began to appear regularly against the Daudet candidacy and in support of the conservative republicans who opposed him. Further, Emmanuel Desgrées du Loû protested the entry of the FNC into the election on the ground that it had violated its nonpolitical status, and this critique was upheld by Msgr. Duparc, the bishop of Quimper. His intervention forced de Castelnau to demand the withdrawal of the Breton affiliate. Even the entry of *La Croix* into the fray in support of Daudet did not stop the Christian Democrats' momentum. When the royalist failed to achieve a majority on the first ballot, Desgrées du Loû and Trochu were able to convince the Radical candidate to withdraw from the race and thus assure the victory for the Catholic republican Manceau.[8] For *L'Ouest-Eclair,* it had been a victory of no mean importance. Coupled with Daudet's defeat in the elections of 1924, this setback forever removed the Action Française from French electoral life, and it did so in that part of France where reactionary Catholics were strongest.

Even the attempt on the part of the royalists to avenge themselves against this defeat was a miserable failure. Daudet sought to bring suit against Father Trochu in civil court in the midst of a mud-slinging press campaign. *L'Ouest-Eclair* had been accused of contracting for a series of postcards which included some pornographic scenes and had responded by assuring its readers that this scandal was just another example of *L'Action Française*'s yellow journalism. Cardinal Alexis-Armand Charost, Dubourg's successor, gave Daudet the necessary authorization to bring Trochu to court. At this point, the Vatican ordered its French nuncio to intervene. Msgr. Cerretti pressured Charost to revoke his previous authorization and forced him to permit the *abbé démocrate* to pursue his journalistic career in peace. Reluctantly the archbishop complied. The Breton daily's court victories a year later in this postcard scandal were anticlimactic to its larger political and ecclesiastical triumphs.[9] Through all of this, *L'Ouest-Eclair* had done its part to isolate the Action Française further from the Catholic mainstream, and in so doing, it had made its contribution to the league's approaching condemnation by the church.

The prewar Christian Democrats of *L'Ouest-Eclair* and the Jeune République had managed to survive through some very difficult times. Their royalist and integrist foes had wounded them sorely but had been unable to crush them decisively. Indeed, these Catholic republicans had begun to reverse their earlier losses and were assisted in their revival by the birth of numerous Catholic groups prepared to accept the values of 1789 and social reforms. This emergence of grassroots Catholic pluralism in the early 1920s was one more sign that the winds of change within Catholicism were blowing against the Action Française. Some of these novel Catholic forms were inspired directly by Christian Democratic values. These included the Parti Démocrate Populaire, the Catholic weekly *Vie Catholique,* and the Confédération Française des Travailleurs Chrétiens.

Until the postwar decades, Catholic republicans had been unable to create a viable political party. However, in spite of these initial organizational failures, Catholics committed to republican government had never abandoned their dream of creating an effective party to implement their convictions in the field of electoral politics. The mood of "sacred union" assisted this task. Divisions gave way to cooperation until, by 1924, groundwork had been laid for the birth of their party. Earlier discussions by the Jeune République, members of the Semaines Sociales, the Association Catholique de la Jeunesse Française, Catholic trade unionists, and numerous Christian Democratic federations had ironed out the preliminary difficulties that had prevented the culmination of this political vision. Only Sangnier's group remained outside the new party which fielded candidates for the first time in 1924. The fledgling Parti Démocrate Populaire (PDP) was able to elect only thirteen deputies, but this was sufficient to form a parliamentary faction, an unprecedented step for the French Christian Democrats. In the west, where it received a significant percentage of its electoral support, it had the endorsement of *L'Ouest-Eclair,* and in Paris, its semiofficial weekly *Le Petit Démocrate* retained a modest circulation of about 20,000.[10] However, without the contribution of the more progressive followers of Marc Sangnier, the Popular Democrats were doomed to become a party of religious defense and social conservatism. To be sure, they were devoted to republicanism, but this was colored by their commitment to *liberté d'enseignement,* the church's slogan for state aid to religious schools. Added to this confessional aura was a deep strain of anticommunism. The party's support of the League of Nations was viewed within this framework, and it employed social Catholic language in the battle against Marxist "class struggle." In spite of its left-liberal vocabulary, the Parti Démocrate Populaire was locked into a right-centrist and conservative position. Its electoral constituents resided chiefly in Brittany and Alsace, and the majority of PDP deputies came from these areas. The Catholic voters of these regions had turned to the republic, but they had not abandoned their political and social conservatism. In the Chamber itself the PDP was often linked inevitably to the rightist and right-center coalitions where it practised conservative politics still further. After the early 1930s its brief fortunes declined, but it managed to limp along until 1940 when several of its deputies voted the suicide of the Third Republic via the offering of full powers to Philippe Pétain.[11] Nevertheless, its existence in France after 1924 was living testimony that Christian Democracy had become a respectable expression of Catholic political life. The performance of the Popular Democrats demonstrated that Catholic republicanism could be used to uphold the social order and to defend the vested interests of the church. This kind of realization would render the Action Française more and more superfluous to Catholics.

The years immediately following the war saw the rise to prominence of the talented Christian Democratic journalist Francisque Gay. As codirector of the Parisian publication firm of Bloud and Gay, he had the means to inaugurate a weekly of religious information in 1924. Although its subscription list included only 16,000, its reading public numbered occasionally in excess of 50,000 people. *Vie Catholique,* though inclined toward Christian Democracy by virtue of its creator and editor, was not dedicated to a single political line. Rather, it was characterized as "an organ of unity between all the Catholics of France and a collective instrument of their propaganda and apostolate." Gay promised never to deviate from this joint purpose of supporting both Catholic pluralism and religious defense, and he assured his readers that *Vie Catholique* would be loyally obedient to the church's hierarchy. On specific political and social issues, Gay's weekly espoused the moderately conservative positions of the PDP. It called for massive popular resistance to the anticlericalism of the Cartel des Gauches and its endorsement of Catholic trade unionism and the League of Nations reflected its staunch commitment to anticommunism. Its homage to confessional labor unions was based upon these organizations' dedication to the destruction of the "communist menace" in order "to save civilization" from "Bolshevik aggression." This loyalty to religious defense and the preservation of the social order, along with its pledge to await the hierarchy's marching orders, won for *Vie Catholique* the esteem of a number of influential prelates. Cardinal Louis-Ernest Dubois, the archbishop of Paris, and Pius XI himself are two cases in point. In addition, it appealed to the more liberal sectors of the Catholic intelligentsia, and by so doing it created a vital alternative to Maurrasian ideology for those scholars and political leaders who had joined the Second Ralliement.[12]

The last important manifestation of prorepublican Catholicism to emerge in the immediate postwar period was the Confédération Française des Travailleurs Chrétiens (CFTC). This Catholic trade union federation was inaugurated in November 1919 by the amalgamation of several disparate Catholic working-class organizations. The new federation had over 150,000 members, but its 43,000 clerical workers were the largest single group in the fledgling union. Nevertheless, there were substantial numbers of proletarians in its ranks, especially among the textile workers and miners of the heavily Catholic Nord. Its growth rate was considerable. Within less than twenty years, its membership numbered half a million in 2,384 different units. Structurally the CFTC was a contradiction. Decision making was decentralized at a local level, making mass action extremely difficult, while the control of finances and administration was highly centralized along the same organizational lines as France's ecclesiastical geography. This very bureaucratic mixture would give to the CFTC an image of confessionalism and class collaborationism which was anathema to any organization seeking to woo industrial workers. Its ideology seemed to warrant such suspicions. Although the union leadership declared its loyalty to the republican principles of 1789, it refused to adopt much of the value system that dominated the French proletariat. Its social doctrine was built upon the paternalism of Leo XIII's *Rerum Novarum,* and it opposed the celebration of Labor Day, May first. To be sure, it criticized capitalism sharply, but its harshest rhetoric was reserved for socialism and communism. The CFTC's espousal of social reform was described as "a work of . . . social pacification" and "the most efficacious force of resistance . . . against the tenets of class struggle." Christian trade unionism was deemed to be the most effective bulwark against Marxism. In practice, the CFTC advocated class cooperation between owners and workers along the lines suggested years before by Albert de Mun, and collaboration with those of other ideological persuasions would be tolerated only if it involved "the struggle against socialism." Under the pressure of its own proletarian membership, the CFTC would evolve slowly toward more social democratic positions, but throughout the interwar period, its leadership and ideology served as a more conservative brake to these progressive impulses. Thus, throughout the 1920s and 1930s, it functioned as an extension into the proletariat of a confessional program dedicated to religious defense and social conservatism.[13]

These three manifestations of emerging Catholic pluralism in France intensified the optimism of the forces for change within the French church. The prewar *L'Ouest-Eclair* and Marc Sangnier were no longer isolated. By 1925 the proliferation of Catholic groups sympathetic to republicanism and social reform served to assist the removal of the pariah status given to Christian Democrats before the war. By their combination of resolute republicanism and social timidity, these new forces would demonstrate to many influential and conservative Catholics that the vested interests of their church could use new means for old ends. Ecclesiastics in high places were beginning to ascertain that new tools were more amenable to their goals than the inflexible tactics of the Action Française. In a very real sense, this discovery by the church's hierarchy was the essence of the Second Ralliement.

This was certainly true from the Vatican's point of view. Nowhere was this more apparent than in the reign of Pope Pius XI, who sat in Saint Peter's chair from 1922 until his death in 1939. *Ubi Arcano Dei* (December 23, 1922) was his inaugural encyclical, and in many ways, it outlined the program that he would pursue throughout his lengthy pontificate. In it the pope expressed his deep concerns about the continuing European conflicts which the First World War had unleashed. He feared that Western civilization remained under the constant threat of future wars which could be fueled easily by the "spirit of violence and hatred" inspired by "extreme nationalism." To pacify such a volatile situation, the pontiff instructed the faithful to support reputable international organizations such as the League of Nations which he felt to be a twentieth-century embodiment of Thomistic teachings on justice and international law. Thus it would seem that the papacy had exchanged an integrist vision of the world for a philosophy akin to that of the Jeune République. Such was not the case. In spite of the nuncio's friendly visit to Marc Sangnier in 1922, the new pope was neither a democrat nor an advocate of international egalitarianism at any level. His esteem for the League of Nations and international peace was a corollary of a more ultraconservative policy. Underlying all his Ralliement language was his basic devotion to a consistent program of religious defense and anti-Marxism. *Ubi Arcano Dei* indicated that as well. For the pope, only the institutional Catholic church could accomplish successfully what the League of Nations hoped to achieve. Indeed, the church's prestigious tradition and its divine status were the two characteristics that would enable it "to lead mankind" on this road of peace and social order. Of course, this did not mean that the church would intervene in "purely civil affairs." Nevertheless, it could not "permit nor tolerate" the state's use "of certain laws or unjust regulations to interfere with the constitution given to the church by Christ," nor would the church allow national governments "to violate the rights of God Himself over civil society." Without this support of Catholicism and its divinely appointed leadership, Western civilization would become the victim of bolshevism. Domestic discord and "the war between the classes" were felt to be "a much more dangerous and lamentable evil" than military conflict and extreme nationalism. Revolution and social conflict were the demons most necessary to exorcize by an alliance between Catholicism and the forces of order.[14] This horror of bolshevism explains, to a great extent, Pius XI's consistent preference for authoritarian governments throughout the interwar period. *Ubi Arcano Dei* developed the ideology of his program. The next eighteen years would demonstrate exactly how the pontiff decided to interpret and implement his so-called Second Ralliement.

In practice the papal plan revealed itself in two immediate ways. At the diplomatic level it involved the resolution of differences between church and state via treaty agreements. Pius XI was the pope of concordats who sought pacts governing church-state relations with every major European state. On another level he sought to recatholicize society by massive domestic missionary movements designed to recover the ground which the church had lost since the French Revolution. This effort was called Catholic Action, and it necessitated control of these groups by either the pope or the bishops. Influential autonomous Catholic groups were looked upon with disfavor by the pontiff, and whenever he could, he engineered their replacement by organizations under the direction of the hierarchy.

Both manifestations of this Ralliement emerged in France in the mid-1920s. First of all, the Holy See made peace with the

Third Republic, After the Bloc National government had engineered the restoration of the Vatican embassy, the road was opened to negotiate some kind of compromise with the separation legislation. Since the end of the war, a handful of moderate bishops had been pressing for some adaptation to the "cultic associations." Chief among them was Msgr. Gibier, the bishop of Versailles. Feeling the need for religious peace and legal protection for the church, Gibier reorganized his diocese along much the same lines as Msgr. Fulbert Petit had recommended in 1906. On May 15, 1923, the pope wrote a letter to the bishop of Versailles congratulating him on the diocesan reorganization, and Cardinal Gasparri expressed the hope that all French dioceses would follow the patterns set at Versailles. Pius XI's direct intervention in support of the moderate bishops arrived in France less than a year later in the form of the encyclical *Maximam Gravissimamque*. His Holiness mixed harsh language with pragmatic and moderate means to resolve the impasse on the "cultic associations." He reiterated Pius X's condemnation "of the iniquitous Separation Law," but he urged the French clergy to come to terms with the bill if the new governmental "diocesan associations" met two criteria. First, they had "to be in accord . . . with the divine constitution and laws of the church," and second, they had to protect the church legally against a resurgence of anticlericalism. Leaving nothing to chance, the pontiff published his own set of model statutes which he required for all acceptable "diocesan associations." In every instance, these articles insured that the bishops and the Holy See remained in control of the church and that its hierarchical structure was preserved in every respect.[15] By such gestures Pius XI effected a religious peace with the French state and a legal compromise with the Separation Law which guaranteed episcopal rule over the faithful and papal control over the French hierarchy. The issues had not changed since the time of Pius X. Only the times and protagonists were different. Religious defense and the preservation of the church's authoritarian structure remained at the heart of the Vatican's program. In this respect Pius X and Pius XI advocated parallel programs; only the personalities and the means employed were not identical. Gone was the intransigence of Emile Combes and Pius X. In its place was the suppleness of Aristide Briand and the diplomatic pragmatism of Pius XI. The Vatican had maintained the religious defense program of Pius X but had resorted to the tactics of Leo XIII. Both the vested interests of the church and the crusade against communism demanded a rallying to the French Third Republic.

However, the uniqueness of Pius XI lay chiefly in his effort to enlist large cadres of the Catholic laity into an army of religious defense commanded by the hierachy. This program, usually called Catholic Action, took different forms in different lands, but in every case the strategy was to activate and mobilize the laity to advance the interests of the church in temporal society. In France Catholic Action was expected to rechristianize the nation and to fight the domestic battles of the church under the banner of the episcopate. Pluralism was quite acceptable as long as it did not violate this essential format. For this reason, the church's leadership could advance the cause of such divergent expressions as *Vie Catholique* and the Fédération Nationale Catholique. Support for the former did not indicate a hierarchical preference for Christian Democracy. Rather, it displayed the bishops' espousal of a newspaper dedicated to religious defense, anticommunism, and obedience to the ecclesiastical heads of the church.

Similar reasons account for the esteem enjoyed by the Fédération Nationale Catholique. The defensive and ultrarightist character of de Castelnau's organization made it a reincarnation of the prewar Union Catholique, but unlike Keller's earlier efforts, the FNC was much larger and more successful. Its mass mobilization against the anticlerical cartel had won the admiration of all conservative Catholics. Further, its ideology paralleled that of the Action Française in almost every instance. Only the monarchical preferences of some of its leaders and its anti-Semitism were more subdued than those of its Maurrasian ally. Extreme nationalism, love of a pre-1789 nation and church, rejection of political democracy, and hatred of the Masons were all well-published tenets of the FNC. Its crusade mentality against Marxism was united with a social Catholicism of the most right-wing variety which combined a medieval corporatism with social charity. Although elements of its philosophy, namely its lack of enthusiasm for the League of Nations, proved too stringent for some moderate bishops and Pius XI, its social conservatism, anticommunism, and capacity to resist anti-Catholic forces aroused the hierarchy's positive interest more than any other Catholic organization in France was able to do.[16]

One chief reason for this was the federation's structure, which was designed with the theory of Catholic Action in mind. First of all, the framework of the federation was organized along the same hierarchical lines as the church itself. The national committee, under Castelnau's presidency, was linked to the Assembly of French Cardinals and Archbishops by the FNC national chaplain Father Janvier. Secondly, at every diocesan and parish level the federation had a section which included a liaison delegated by the church's clerical leadership. The chart used by the diocese of Lille portrays this interrelationship which was standard fare for the FNC throughout the nation. (See figure 1.) *Credo*, the federation's monthly, described Lille's organizational plan as a graph "which shows clearly the relationship of lay initiative and ecclesiastical authority, as well as the system of relationships between the work and piety programs of the Fédération Nationale Catholique within the diocese, the parish, and the parish unions." De Castelnau himself called his organization a "Catholic entente" which had been "established in absolute accord with the ecclesiastical authorities."[17]

Such ideological affinities with the papal program and structural links with the church's hierarchy made the Fédération Nationale Catholique an ideal instrument of Catholic Action, much as the pope had conceived it. For these reasons de Castelnau's federation had the overwhelming support of the French episcopate and the Vatican. Public declarations of hierarchical esteem were always forthcoming at FNC rallies and national assemblies where the nation's cardinals would share the podium with the reactionary general and where a papal benediction of the organization would be read. By letter Pius XI praised the federation's "defense of religious interests" and its obedience to hierarchical

Figure 1. Organizational Plan of the Diocese of Lille, 1925

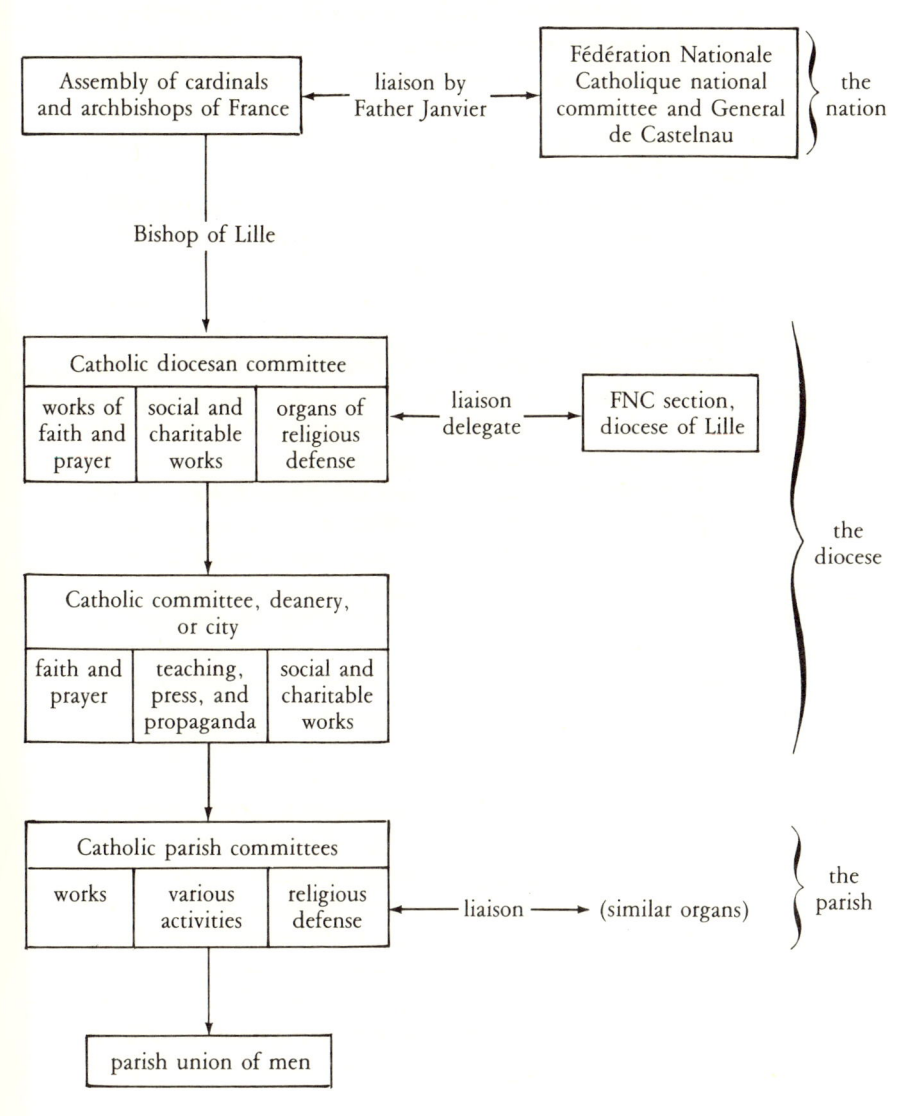

```
┌─────────────────────┐                    ┌──────────────────────┐
│ Assembly of cardinals│   liaison by      │ Fédération Nationale │  ⎫
│ and archbishops of   │◄─ Father Janvier ─►│ Catholique national │  ⎬ the
│      France         │                    │ committee and General│  ⎪ nation
└─────────────────────┘                    │    de Castelnau      │  ⎭
                                           └──────────────────────┘
            │
            ▼
    Bishop of Lille
            │
            ▼
┌──────────────────────────────────────┐
│     Catholic diocesan committee      │
├──────────┬───────────┬───────────────┤        ┌──────────────────┐
│ works of │ social and│   organs of   │ liaison│  FNC section,    │
│ faith and│ charitable│   religious   │◄delegate►│ diocese of Lille│
│  prayer  │   works   │    defense    │        │                  │
└──────────┴───────────┴───────────────┘        └──────────────────┘
            │                                                        ⎫
            ▼                                                        ⎪
┌──────────────────────────────────────┐                             ⎪
│  Catholic committee, deanery,        │                             ⎬ the
│          or city                     │                             ⎪ diocese
├──────────┬───────────┬───────────────┤                             ⎪
│ faith and│ teaching, │  social and   │                             ⎭
│  prayer  │ press, and│  charitable   │
│          │ propaganda│    works      │
└──────────┴───────────┴───────────────┘
            │
            ▼
┌──────────────────────────────────────┐
│      Catholic parish committees      │
├──────────┬───────────┬───────────────┤                             ⎫
│  works   │  various  │   religious   │                             ⎬ the
│          │ activities│    defense    │◄── liaison ──► (similar organs) parish
└──────────┴───────────┴───────────────┘                             ⎭
            │
            ▼
┌──────────────────────────┐
│  parish union of men     │
└──────────────────────────┘
```

Source: "La F.N.C. dans le diocèse de Lille," *Credo,* Sept. 25, 1925, p. 10. Translated by Oscar L. Arnal.

control according to the Holy See's set patterns for Catholic Action.[18] Indeed, the fledgling FNC was proving ideal for the program envisioned by *Ubi Arcano Dei* and Catholic Action. It would be the papal favorite in France because it contained every element deemed essential by the Vatican. First of all, it was a mass organization that had demonstrated its capacity to fight the temporal enemies of the church. It was indeed an army of militant laity prepared to penetrate secular society in the name of and for ecclesiastical interests as defined by the clergy. Second, it coupled this massive religious defense program with a deep commitment to the crusade against the Bolshevik menace. In line with *Ubi Arcano Dei,* it saw Catholicism as the defender of the social order and Western civilization. Finally, it was linked structurally to the upper echelons of the church. This meant that organizationally the federation was under the auspices of the hierarchy in both direct and indirect ways. Pius XI was wary of lay autonomy, although his pragmatism compelled him to recognize that the day of the laity and Catholic pluralism was at hand. Catholic Action was his strategy to marry this growing reality to the clerical and authoritarian character of his church. In these new Catholic groups the laity were to be the infantry and the bishops were to be the generals. As long as Catholic personalities and organizations were in line with papal values or programs, these pluralistic forces would be endorsed or at least tolerated. However, as soon as Pius XI felt that clergy or laity were undermining his authority, he would exercise the disciplinary forces of the Vatican against such disobedient subversives. It is in this context that one can discover the primary reasons for the papal condemnation of the Action Française in 1926.

After all, the Fédération Nationale Catholique had the same ideology as the Action Française, but it did not have its autonomy. In addition, the FNC had been much more useful to the church than its royalist ally. *L'Action Française* could vilify the republic and anticlericalism with as much venom as it could muster, but it was de Castelnau's organization that had mobilized the successful Catholic campaign against the Herriot offensive. The Maurrasians were too autonomous and too ineffective for the

Vatican's taste, and in spite of the solidarity between de Castelnau and the royalist league, His Holiness was preparing to choose the former at the expense of the latter.

Although the Union Sacrée and the Bloc National had enhanced the Catholic prestige of the Action Française, it was fast becoming a liability to the Vatican. The rigidity of its program was coming into increasing conflict with the changing atmosphere at Rome. On too many occasions it had endorsed policies that did not have the support of the Holy See. During the war Louis Dimier and other royalists had rejected Benedict XV's peace proposals, a grim reminder to nonintegrists at Rome that Action Française loyalty to the papacy was less than perfect. The Vatican could not and would not accept the facile Maurrasian distinction between the pope as unquestioned spiritual authority and the pope as one temporal leader among many. After the war the Action Française continued to object to papal peace policies within both France and Europe. Contrary to the Holy See's convictions, the integral nationalists welcomed Poincaré's invasion of the Ruhr, and they resisted all compromise with the Separation Law of 1905. *L'Action Française* responded to the papal acceptance of the "dioceasan associations" with an injudicious article entitled "The Pope at Canossa." Its position on this issue was a direct slap at *Maximam Gravissimamque*.[19]

These serious breaks with papal policy were compounded by direct attacks upon the successors of Pius X. The Action Française was reverting to the anti-ralliement tactics it had practised in the last years of Leo XIII's reign. Only this time the popes themselves were not spared, and the language used against them bordered on the abusive. The papal hero of the integral royalists remained Pius X throughout the Third Republic and beyond. His integrism was used by the monarchical league to chastise the less stringent strategies of the two popes who succeeded him. This became most apparent when Benedict XV died and when the conclave began which would elect the new pope. *L'Action Française* stated bluntly: "Certainly the political ideas of Benedict XV, his particular traditions, and his bureaucratic structure rendered him scarcely favorable to our political hopes." The newspaper's

Roman correspondent supported the candidacy of either Cardinal de Laï or Merry del Val, both active integrists from the Pius X pontificate. Moreover, the royalist daily had only critical words for Cardinal Pietro Gasparri, who was described as infected with "very Wilsonian ideas." Its harshest words, however, were reserved for Achille Ratti, the prelate who would become Pope Pius XI: "This cardinal belongs to the liberal clan," and "he is a partisan of collaboration between Italy, Germany, and Bolshevist Russia."[20]

With Ratti's elevation to Peter's chair and with the retention of Cardinal Gasparri at the Vatican's state secretariat, the Action Française could be assured of ecclesiastical opposition at the highest levels of church leadership. The Vatican would not long tolerate the disobedient autonomy exercised by the royalist league. Maurrasianism's very popularity and success with French-speaking Catholics would necessitate speedy and decisive action by the Holy See against its erstwhile friend. Intoxicated by its own Catholic reputation, the Action Française refused to consider that postwar changes within the church could lay the groundwork for its own condemnation. This blindness would prove fatal for the royalists.

+ 8 +

The Church Condemns the Action Française
(1925-1929)

Basking in the glory of its Catholic credentials, the Action Française was totally unprepared for the deluge that overwhelmed it less than a year after it had reached the zenith of its ecclesiastical prestige. It had won the applause of bishops, the friendship of *La Croix,* and the hearts of Catholic Action militants. However, the royalist league had lost touch with Rome and was losing ground slowly in France. It had been driven from its tiny parliamentary redoubt by aggressive Christian Democrats, and mass Catholic Action forces were proving more effective against the church's enemies than the Maurrasians. Finally, the integral monarchists were becoming increasingly a source of Catholic division in France, and their disrespect for the pope and his program was becoming manifest at an alarming rate. As long as Pius XI hoped to organize French Catholics under his and the hierarchy's leadership, he would be forced to act decisively against the integral nationalists. If he intended to field an effective Catholic Action program, the pope would be compelled to condemn the Action Française.

The final campaign to dislodge the royalist league from its prestigious pinnacle dawned in the wake of the Belgian popularity poll that had so exalted Charles Maurras. Many of that nation's Catholics were appalled at its results. Consequently, they mounted a counteroffensive against the integral nationalists. The Christian Democrat Fernand Passelecq inaugurated a series of articles against Maurras in *La Libre Belgique,* and he employed the arguments which had been constructed before the war by his fellow Catholic republicans. He added nothing novel to the case against the Action Française, but he was able to set the stage for subsequent developments.[1]

From Belgium the drama shifted to the Vatican where Pius XI was preparing to launch his own offensive against the Action Française. Rumors began to circulate in France that the nuncio Msgr. Cerretti was advising the pope to draft a leading French integrist prelate to launch the campaign against the royalist league. When Cardinals Luçon of Reims, Charost of Rennes, Maurin of Lyon and Msgr. Touchet of Orléans turned down the papal appeal, the lot fell to the pro-Maurrasian Cardinal Paulin Andrieu of Bordeaux. Sensing a mood change at Rome, the pragmatic papalist Andrieu was prepared to disengage himself from the royalists. Under the guise of a rejoinder to Catholic youth, who were supposedly asking what influence the Action Française should have upon their ideas, the aging prelate took up the attack and drew upon the arguments of Passelecq. His ostensible response, published in the archdiocesan weekly *L'Acquitaine,* began with the assertion that Catholics had full freedom to espouse the governmental form of their choice. However, he pointed out that the Action Française presumed to usurp religious and doctrinal authority which belonged only to the pope and his bishops. Finally, he accused the league of "atheism, agnosticism, . . . anti-Catholicism, amorality," subversion, paganism, injustice, and violence. For these reasons, the archbishop concluded that the Action Française should be shunned ruthlessly.[2]

Soon it became clear that Andrieu's article was not an isolated act. In less than a month, Pius XI sent a letter of gratitude to the archbishop of Bordeaux which was published in the Vatican's newspaper *L'Osservatore Romano.* Shortly thereafter the pontiff told members of the Franciscan order that Andrieu's letter was authoritative and apostolic and not simply the personal gesture of one prelate. By the end of the year, the pope was ready to announce his definitive condemnation of the Action Française, and he did so via the famous consistorial allocution of December 20, 1926. His first words were a command that forbade all Catholics to belong "to a school which puts the interests of political parties above religion and causes the latter to serve the former." He feared that Catholic youth would be susceptible to Maurrasian "dangerous doctrines or influences"; therefore, he insisted that "Catholics are not permitted to support, encourage or read newspapers published by men whose writings deviate from our dogma and our morals." Then, the Holy Father turned to issues which might be called questions of Catholic Action. He deplored religious divisions in France and called for a resolute union of all Catholics "in the defense of the church's divine rights." Such solidarity would lead also to a social stability within the nation at large. Finally, the pope reminded his audience of his own supreme authority and assured them that religious duty rather than political partisanship had prompted the condemnation.[3] Throughout the discourse the Holy Father had shown no inclination toward either Christian Democracy or any other form of government. To be sure, he employed a few arguments that had been developed by Catholic republicans years before, but these points had been designed to turn traditional Catholics against the integral nationalists rather than toward more progressive alternatives. However, he added to these objections personal anxieties about Action Française threats to his own authority over French believers and Catholic Action. His decision to muzzle the Action Française was essentially a decisive effort to break the independence of French Catholics and place them under the direction of the church's hierarchy. To insure that his allocution would be taken seriously, he promulgated the earlier condemnation of the Holy Office on December 29, 1926, and added the daily *L'Action Française* to the list of Charles Maurras's forbidden books.[4] Pius XI had acted unequivocally against the Maurrasians. They were forced into a position of either submission or revolt. The same two choices were being offered to the French church. Would Catholics in France uphold the papal decision, or would they rally to the harassed Maurrasians?

Understandably, the Christian Democrats received the news

with great joy. *Le Petit Démocrate,* the weekly organ of the Parti Démocrate Populaire, defended the papal decision and charged *La Croix*'s Jean Guiraud with offering public sympathy to the condemned royalists.[5] *L'Ouest-Eclair* called the pontifical condemnation a decisive action "for the safeguard of principles which are basic to civilization," and Marc Sangnier insisted that the Vatican's actions had removed the scandal whereby many Catholics had identified with this anti-Gospel organization. However, neither the Rennes daily nor the *Jeune République* gave much space to the condemnation. They mentioned it with enthusiasm in a few articles and then moved on to other concerns.[6] Nevertheless, a number of Christian Democrats played an active role in the drama caused by the papal anathema against the Action Française. They were led by Francisque Gay and publicized their views in his weekly *Vie Catholique*. Beginning with the appearance of Cardinal Andrieu's letter and continuing until the end of 1928, Gay committed his newspaper to the pontiff's campaign. Much of what he had to say had been developed by earlier Christian Democrats. He made reference to the royalists' subordination of religion to politics, he warned believers against Maurras's agnosticism and pagan devotion to classical culture, and he decried the excessive violence that he felt characterized the league. However, his chief accusation was the Action Française's "insubordination against pontifical authority," that single stark reality of its "refusal to obey the pope."[7]

Further, *La Vie Catholique* took upon itself the task of forming a press crusade against the Action Française. In order to encourage this effort, the Bloud and Gay firm published a special brochure entitled *Non, L'Action Française n'a bien servi ni l'église ni la France,* and Francisque Gay himself wrote the book *Comment j'ai défendu le pape.* However, by mid-1927 he was coming to the sad realization that his endorsement of the Vatican's condemnation was eliciting little enthusiasm among the major forces of French Catholicism. Therefore, he felt compelled to criticize those who seemed less than enthusiastic about the pontiff's anti-Maurrasian judgments. Consequently he chastized the silence and hesitancy of *Le Nouvelliste de Bretagne,* noting that there could be no neutrality between the disobedient royalists and the Holy See. However, it was *La Croix*'s sympathy for the Action Française that most galled Francisque Gay. He berated its editors for printing letters directed against *La Vie Catholique*, but most of all he condemned the daily's shameful silence in the whole affair. His appeal was for *La Croix* to join *La Vie Catholique* in this campaign of Catholic unity and "in defense of the Roman directives and teachings." Finally, the Christian Democratic editor wrote several articles criticizing the Maurrasian sympathies of the FNC's Xavier Vallat who was serving as an Action Française lawyer. Beyond the columns of *La Vie Catholique* Gay and his colleagues organized financial campaigns to assist the Vatican's program, created a youth group called the Volunteers of the Pope to counteract the Camelots du Roi and led a propapal pilgrimage to Rome in 1929 as a fitting climax to their long offensive against the integral nationalists.[8]

All these activities in support of the Vatican were personally costly to Francisque Gay and his friends. The Bloud and Gay publishing company lost significant sums of money because of the pro-Roman policy of *La Vie Catholique*. Prominent Catholic prelates refused to write books for the firm, and numerous Catholic schools in western France canceled sizeable orders for textbooks. Francisque Gay himself was vilified unmercifully, and a number of threats were made on his life. All in all, it was a long and difficult campaign, but Gay could and did console himself with the honor of having led the only significant and unequivocal press battle against the Action Française.[9] To be sure, the other Christian Democrats had welcomed the papal condemnation, but none were willing to serve the Vatican's anti-Maurrasian offensive with the zeal and tenacity of Francisque Gay and his *Vie Catholique*.

Beyond the Christian Democrats, Pius XI made little headway in his search for allies. He did manage to make some inroads among the French Catholic intellectuals, and those who came to his support published a study against the Action Française called *Pourquoi Rome a parlé*. These authors, including a seminary professor, two Dominican theologians, a Jesuit priest, and a lay philosopher, heightened the Christian Democrats' arguments by their more sophisticated theological analyses. In this sense, they represented the mainstream of the church more significantly than their openly democratic colleagues. They chose to emphasize those matters that had been singled out by Cardinal Andrieu and the Holy Father, namely the questions of church authority and the agnosticism of Charles Maurras. Most important among these Catholic thinkers was the neo-Thomist Jacques Maritain. His reputation, combined with his former Maurrasianism, made his conversion to the papal cause especially significant. In 1927 he published his *Primauté du spirituel* in response to the disobedience of the Action Française. In it he expressed his deep sorrow over Maurras's tragic dilemma, a love for the church's authority and order without an awareness "of its essential nature and inspiration." Maritain sought to assure his readers that the papal decision was religious, not political, and as such, he demanded of Catholics full and unequivocal obedience. The neo-Thomist warned believers against excessive nationalism which he called a direct threat to Catholic universalism. Maritain's book was an important turning point in the conflict. The young scholar had unassailable scholastic and Catholic credentials. As part of the neo-Thomist revival, he was one of the most prominent theologians in France, and as a former devotee of Maurrasian philosophical reaction, he was not tainted with Christian Democratic connections. His theology was unquestionably conservative and impeccably orthodox. The shift of his intellectual skills to the Vatican camp constituted a serious blow to the Action Française and marked his emergence as the leading papal theologian in France.[10]

At this point Pius XI had exhausted his supply of significant allies. Elsewhere he encountered lukewarm support at best, and often he was faced with quiet, yet resolute, resistance. The most powerful sectors of the French church were either sympathetic or protective toward the Action Française. His Holiness was determined to break this disobedient autonomy and place it under hierarchical control in his program of Catholic Action. The primary task to be accomplished was the unification of the episcopate behind his condemnation of the integral nationalists. This would not be easy, for the French hierarchy was divided over the whole issue into three definable segments. First of all, there were those prelates who were committed completely to the condemnation of the Action Française. The most influential of these were the two cardinals Paulin Andrieu of Bordeaux and Louis-Ernest Dubois of Paris. As France's chief prelate, Cardinal Dubois set the tone for those bishops prepared to support the papal offensive by publishing a practical list for Catholics in his religious weekly that would enable them to deal with the Action Française. He warned against the notion and practice of *politique d'abord* and insisted that believers should avoid the newspaper *L'Action Française* at all costs. Finally, he urged all Catholics to "organize themselves beyond all partisan considerations . . . for the defense of the church and its religious liberties." A number of other bishops rallied around the standard of Catholic Action, and in some instances they cautioned that the nationalistic religion of the Action Française was in direct violation of the Christian faith.[11]

Also a significant number of prelates resisted the pope's efforts openly and vehemently. The most striking cases were Msgr. François Marty of Montauban and Cardinal Louis Billot at Rome. In the Montauban religious weekly, Marty softened the papal attack on the Action Française and reserved his harsh words for the French government and Catholic liberals. He accused the Christian Democrats of being motivated by *politique d'abord* and contrasted this behavior with that of the Maurrasians, that "great number of excellent Catholics who above all desire scrupulously to obey the church." The bishop of Montauban insisted that the pope had merely issued a warning rather than a condemnation. Marty continued to laud Maurras as one of the church's most able defenders, and in response to an attack on this assessment he made the following statement: "The Supreme Pontiff has deigned to declare: one is able to join the Action Française league; one is able to be a reader and subscriber to the newspaper *L'Action Française*; and one is able to collaborate with that newspaper." At this point, the Vatican organ *L'Osservatore Romano* intervened to clarify the issue by stating bluntly that "the propositions reported to the bishop of Montauban and published by him never came from the mouth of the Holy Father."[12] Cardinal Louis Billot was only slightly less indiscreet. His protest against the papal anathema was expressed in a letter written privately to a friend in France. He was convinced that "reason, equity, good sense, measure and dignity have been consistently on the side of the accused rather than on the side of the judge and accusers." When Pius XI was apprised of this letter, he held a private meeting with Billot and berated him for over an hour. The upshot of that meeting and of the imprudent epistle was the integral prelate's unprecedented resignation from the cardinalate and his retirement to a Jesuit monastery. Msgr. Penon was more fortunate. His name was listed among the bishops who signed the declaration of the French hierarchy against the Action Française (March 1927), but after his retirement he claimed that an anonymous person had affixed his name without permission. What of the other bishops who had eulogized the Maurrasians so openly in the 1920s? Most of them had died before the papal blow. Cardinal Sevin of Lyon had passed away in 1916, followed by Msgrs. Delassus, de Cabrières, and Dubourg in the early 1920s. Finally, in the spring of 1926 Cardinal Mercier was buried in Belgium. By the time of the Vatican anathema, the monarchist cause was being victimized already by the ravages of aging and chronic mortality. The integrists promoted by Pius X were dying gradually and thus were reducing the extent of episcopal support for the Action Française.[13]

Nevertheless, large numbers of bishops remained cordial toward the beleaguered royalists. As a result of this they vacillated by seeking to combine tacit obedience to the pontiff with sympathy for the Maurrasians. These men constituted the third and largest division of the French hierarchy in this confused affair. Their hope was both to placate the pope and to aid the survival of the Action Française. Some of these prelates claimed that the monarchist league in their own particular dioceses was unquestionably loyal to the church. They hoped to leave the matter at that. Such was the case with Msgr. Germain, the archbishop of Toulouse, who published in his religious weekly a letter of submission by the local Action Française unit. He pointed out that the Toulouse royalists were requesting orthodox theologians from the archdiocese to insure the catholicity of their chapter. Germain's response was enthusiastic: "Having known you for all these years, I have never doubted your obedience and attachment to the directions of the Holy See."[14]

Other prelates confined themselves to external gestures of obedience but coupled such declarations with effusive praise for the Action Française. The royalist bishop of Agen adopted this stance. He began his assessment with a sharp attack on the Third Republic and with a eulogy in praise of the pre–French Revolutionary monarchy. Msgr. Sagot did not deny that the Action Française used "excessive intransigence," "violent language," "*politique d'abord,*" and revolt, all of which he characterized as Sillonist behavior. Nevertheless, he had nothing but praise for Maurras's "notion of order," "attachment to the nationalist tradition," "love of the church" as "an admirable and efficacious bastion of order," and deep sympathies for the papacy. In spite of all this, Sagot felt that his episcopal duty to obey the pope was primary. Reluctantly, he urged monarchical Catholics to break "from a group . . . condemned by the pope" because, he insisted, "it is not necessary to be in vassalage to the Action Française in order to love and defend the royalist view."[15]

Cardinal Alexis-Armand Charost of Rennes was the most striking example of a prelate torn between his own integrist pro-Action Française convictions and external pressure compelling his obedience to the Vatican. Charost had earned the dubious honor of being one of the cardinals who had turned down Pius XI's invitation to inaugurate the campaign against the royalists. As the Vatican's offensive got under way, the archbishop of Rennes sought to salvage the Action Française through a program that could pose as a manifestation of obedience to the pontiff. He called for a retreat designed to teach Catholic orthodoxy to the local royalists. Interestingly enough, the man chosen to lead this effort was the notorious pro-Maurrasian Father Janvier. Charost praised the local integral nationalists and sought to transform them into Catholic Action units. The cardinal heralded the Action Française as "the first vast and ordered counterrevolutionary movement . . . in France" since the ravages of the French Revolution, and he lauded the work accomplished by Charles Maurras in defense of the church. All this led him to conclude: "Therefore we believe it our duty neither to prohibit the league nor the newspaper *L'Action Française.*"[16] Even when the Vatican's condemnation became public, Charost continued to equivocate, yet these vacillations pleased neither the Action Française nor the Vatican. The royalists claimed that the archbishop of Rennes had supported them without reservations at a public dinner when he was conversing there with a Maurrasian named Antoine Schwerer. Their regret was that Charost was unwilling to take up their defense more openly. The archbishop was chagrined by the league's indiscreet exposure of his private talk with Schwerer and said so in no uncertain terms. Also the Holy See was unhappy with Charost. His less than enthusiastic advocacy of the papal condemnation was noted at Rome, as was his continued public esteem for *Le Nouvelliste de Bretagne* and its Maurrasian editor Eugène Delahaye. Indeed, the Breton hierarchy as a whole had rallied to this newspaper's support after the integral nationalists had been anathematized. At this point Father Trochu joined the battle by engineering a campaign to remove Delahaye from his post because of his continued advocacy of the Action Française. *L'Ouest-Eclair*'s democratic priest won his point. The region's bishops were forced by Rome to demand *Le Nouvelliste de Bretagne*'s political neutrality and with it Delahaye's resignation. Charost accepted the fait accompli, and thus the Action Française affair was closed definitively in Brittany.[17]

At no point had Pius XI abandoned his goal to unite the hierarchy behind his offensive against the Maurrasian royalists. His Catholic Action campaign demanded both an end to Gallicanism in its monarchical form and a solid phalanx of episcopal leadership in support of religious defense as he chose to define it. By late winter 1927 he was able to pressure a collective statement of almost the entire French hierarchy in defense of his position against the Action Française. Maurrasian philosophy was called contradictory to Catholic "dogma and morals," and *politique d'abord* was declared inimical to church doctrine. Most of all, the integral royalists were condemned for their "lack of total submission and respect toward the papacy."[18] Inspite of this apparent unanimity, some bishops continued to vacillate. However, by the end of 1928 all resistance had been broken by Rome. By asserting his authority over the French episcopate, Pius XI had crushed integrist Gallicanism, and the Action Française had lost its hierarchical support. With the episcopate in tow, the pope was free to establish control over those three additional segments of the French church so instrumental to his program of Catholic Action: the mainline Catholic press, organized Catholic youth, and the Fédération Nationale Catholique. In each of these, strong sympathizers of the condemned royalists were prepared to resist the papal offensive, but Pius XI was just as determined to crush all signs of opposition.

With respect to the Catholic press, the pontiff had to insure the loyalty of *La Croix,* France's most important religious daily and the semiofficial newspaper of both the hierarchy and the Vatican. However, its position vis-à-vis the papal-royalist controversy was ambivalent at best. For at least a decade *La Croix* had become increasingly impressed with *L'Action Française* and its patriotic fulminations. No wonder, then, that the Assumptionist newspaper was embarrassed by the Vatican's campaign to break the hold that the royalist league exercised over influential Catholics. Throughout the critical period of the controversy from 1926 to 1927, *La Croix* pursued a tortuous policy of silence, hesitant condemnation, and attacks upon the Catholic monarchists' most vocal domestic foes. Both the Assumptionist Father Bertoye and the lay reactionary Jean Guiraud were loath either to criticize a loyal ally or to stand against a declared papal command. As a result, these editors became immobilized and angered both camps. Initially *La Croix* attempted to play down the importance of the issue. The pope's reply to Cardinal Andrieu's letter was printed without editorial comment, and later documents were only excerpted in the newspaper. When Pius XI condemned the royalist league in his consistorial allocution (December 1926), *La Croix* felt pressured to make comments, but even these were vague. The Action Française was not mentioned by name. In the name of charity and calm judgment, the newspaper sought to chastize only the agnosticism of a few royalists in order to salvage the Action Française as a Catholic ally of repute.[19]

However, when the Action Française responded with intransigent disobedience to His Holiness, *La Croix* took a stronger stand against its royalist friends. It deplored the "absolute refusal" to obey the pontiff by both believers and unbelievers among the integral nationalists, and it called upon all dissident Catholic monarchists "to respond to the pope . . . by a filial submission." Nevertheless, this firm stand was followed shortly thereafter by further equivocation. The lay editor Jean Guiraud, a friend of the recalcitrant royalists, made every effort to soften the blow struck against the Action Française. He chose to emphasize the grief experienced by those Catholics caught between their religious loyalty to the pope and their patriotic devotion to the royalist cause. For him, the real villains in the drama were the Christian Democrats of the Parti Démocrate Populaire who were gloating over the tormented Maurrasians caught in the vise of the impossible choice between Catholicism and nationalism. Notwithstanding, the continuing pressure of events forced Guiraud to oppose his royalist allies. The episcopal declaration of March 1927 compelled him to compare the Maurrasian action with the revolt of Luther, but he continued to express the hope that Catholic leaguers could retain their organizational integrity by a definitive break with the agnostic leadership of Charles Maurras. The unrelenting opposition of the Action Française removed the possibility of even this faint hope, yet *La Croix* limped along in its editorial ambivalence for another several months. As late as August 1927, the newspaper was still advocating a strategy of silence among French Catholics in order to calm tempers and to create an aura of Catholic unity in the face of more dangerous anti-Catholic foes.[20]

At the same time, Pius XI could ill afford this hesitancy on the part of the most powerful segment of his French Catholic press. As a result he turned to a tactic employed by one of his predecessors. Leo XIII had shuffled *La Croix*'s administrative machinery in order to enforce a policy change in the newspaper. Pius

XI did the same. The proroyalist Father Bertoye was removed from the daily's directorship, and the Assumptionist Léon Merklen was put in his place. Jean Guiraud was retained as an editor, but his activities were circumscribed severely. His articles were limited largely to broadsides against both the traditional anticlerical left and communism. Polemics against the Action Française and apologies for the papal program of Catholic Action were handled almost exclusively by Merklen. Indeed, it was his efforts which insured that *La Croix* would become the most loyal press organ in France to the papal program.[21]

It must be noted, however, that Merklen's condemnation of the Action Française and his newspaper's support of the Vatican's so-called Second Ralliement were essentially no adoption of modern democratic and social democratic values against the reactionary politics of the royalists. Neither in his polemics against the Maurrasians nor in his defense of Catholic Action can one find the principles of the Christian Democrats. Instead, the newspaper echoed the partly conservative, partly reactionary world view of *Ubi Arcano Dei*. His harsh words against the Action Française were in no sense directed against its authoritarian principles. In fact, he charged that its "non-Christian philosophy of government" was an expression of "the worst kind of liberalism." The Maurrasian propensity "for verbal violence" and demagoguery were called "the two most characteristic traits of vulgar democracy." Merklen, throughout his articles against the Action Française, chose to emphasize Maurras's agnosticism, the royalists' tactics of abusive language, and their rebellion against the papal condemnation; and most interestingly, he accused them of using the democratic principles and tactics they had repudiated so correctly.[22]

Further, as *La Croix*'s apologist for Catholic Action, Merklen defined the papal program of missionary action to the modern world with terminology borrowed from the language of religious defense and ecclesiastical traditionalism. To be sure, he was prepared to allow the legitimacy of moderate republican principles and governments as well as the validity of Christian trade unions and some minimal social reforms, but all of these were built upon traditional Catholic values rooted in the soil of medieval Europe, the Council of Trent, and the Syllabus of Errors. Catholic Action was defined as "a hierarchical apostolate . . . tied strictly to the church's magisterium" and totally dependent "upon episcopal authority." *La Croix* called this program "the strict collaboration of Catholic laymen with the hierarchy for the extension of God's kingdom in the world," but it is equally clear that such lay involvement demanded a complete submission to the Vatican's and the French episcopate's leadership. More concretely, the mission of Catholic Action was to rechristianize the social order and return the world to the medieval scheme of things. The godless anticlerical legislation in France and the rise of the communist menace as a most grave danger to Christian civilization were the direct product of Luther's rebellion and the secular violence of the French Revolution. Merklen's crusade against this modern world and his call for a return to ancien régime society could be accomplished only by "an army of militant laymen educated, specialized and coordinated with each other under the authority and direction of the hierarchy." Such would be the task of Catholic Action.[23]

Thus it would appear that Merklen's success in bringing *La Croix* squarely into the papalist camp, by castigating the Maurrasian rebellion and by heralding the program of Catholic Action, was most significantly a victory of one rightist authoritarian force over another in a battle to win the loyalty of French Catholics. For the Vatican, the triumph of Merklen meant that the Holy See had eliminated a serious competitor among Catholics in the offices of the French church's most important publication. This return of *La Croix* to total support of the papal program earned once again for the Assumptionist daily the status of the quasi-official Catholic newspaper of France, a reputation conferred upon it both by the nation's leading prelates and by Pius XI himself. Soon forgotten by the pontiff was the loyal campaign of Francisque Gay's *La Vie Catholique*. Much to be preferred was a vacillating *La Croix* which had returned to a conservative papalism, a papalism that remained uncomfortable with the autonomy, pluralism, and subliminal Christian Democracy of Gay's weekly.[24]

Although resistance to the Vatican's condemnation of the Maurrasians had been broken within the French hierarchy and among the editors of *La Croix,* Pius XI could not guarantee the success of Catholic Action until he had eliminated all Action Française sympathies from those very mass movements that he hoped to enlist in his lay army. First of all, he had to break the influence that Maurras and his followers held over Catholic youth. In France the integral nationalists had made serious inroads among the bourgeois members of the Association Catholique de la Jeunesse Française. Georges Bidault, a Christian Democrat and vice-president of the organization, had warned that the Action Française was the most serious recruitment competitor of his group, especially in the schools. Fortunately, the more moderate and democratic elements of the ACJF were in control, and they were able to steer their organization into the papal camp. Even former members sent word to the Vatican in praise of the condemnation and Catholic Action.[25]

More important, Pius XI's anathema condemning the Action Française coincided with direct efforts by the church to enter the working class en masse. In fact, a number of priests working in proletarian neighborhoods had sent a letter of gratitude to the pope for his offensive against the Maurrasians. They were convinced that his action had increased the church's repute among the workers. Further, the *Chronique Sociale de France,* the Lyon press voice behind the Semaines Sociales, welcomed the papal condemnation as a profound attack in defense of social Catholicism. Indeed, it was a commitment to Christian mission via social action rather than sterile political combat and divisions. Meanwhile the pontiff had come to adopt an innovative Catholic Action program among working-class youth called the Jeunesse Ouvrière Chrétienne (JOC). Organized by militant priests in Belgium and France, the JOC sought to be an avant-garde mission group in the midst of the proletariat for the express purpose of rechristianizing a level of society that had been lost to the church. In 1925 its founder, the Belgian priest Joseph Cardijn, made a personal visit to Pius XI in order to win a papal endorsement of the program. Cardijn's argument that only a missionary elite of believing workers could win the proletariat for Christ struck a responsive chord within the pontiff. "Not only do I bless your undertaking," the Holy Father stated, "I make it my own." Both the Belgian and French JOC retained some affiliation with larger Catholic youth groups, but essentially the Jocistes were autonomous and under the direct patronage of the papacy. By 1930 the French organization had a monthly newspaper, a woman's unit, and a structure for study and propaganda that would serve it effectively until the defeat of France in 1940.[26] The Jeunesse Ouvrière Chrétienne was one of the most creative forces to emerge in the wake of the Action Française condemnation, but it too would serve the more conservative and counterrevolutionary aspects of Catholic Action. Events of the 1930s would demonstrate this within both the hierarchy and the Jocist leadership. For the moment, however, the JOC was an untried factor in French Catholic life. Only the passage of time would define its nature and activities more accurately.

Such was not the case with the Fédération Nationale Catholique, the second of the two Catholic mass movements which Pius XI hoped to enlist in his Catholic Action program. Its papalism and its Maurrasian sympathies led it to pursue a tortuous path of less than enthusiastic obedience for two years. The federation's monthly *Credo* published Pius XI's positive response to Cardinal Andrieu's letter, and de Castelnau himself attached to this a long statement of his organization's loyalty to the Holy Father and Catholic Action. After this affirmation, the FNC maintained for a year what it felt to be a diplomatic silence on the matter. De Castelnau hoped that his organization's quiescence would placate both the papacy and his Maurrasian friends. In this he was sorely disappointed, for the Vatican was unwilling to tolerate such neutrality. By the end of 1927 the tide had turned against the Action Française, and the FNC was prepared to make peace with the Holy See. Writing in *Credo,* the Jesuit reactionary Yves de la Brière chastized the disobedient royalists and defended the necessity of the pope's condemnation. Yet he equivocated by suggesting that the royalist league had removed the most offensive elements of its philosophy and by pointing out that the authors of the Vatican's anathema had "many ideas and common sympathies with the Catholics of the Action Française."[27]

Such evasion was understandable, given the counterrevolutionary ideology and organizational structure of the federation. Its overt integral nationalism and the high status it enjoyed with the church's hierarchy made it especially susceptible to equivocation. In spite of this, the FNC soon began to benefit from the misfortunes of its Maurrasian friends. Splits were occurring in the Action Française itself. The more devout Catholics among the royalists could not accept their league's disobedience to the pope. Consequently, they were abandoning their memberships in droves and were entering the ranks of the FNC. A compromise was reached between these new recruits and the federation. The former refrained from attacking the church and Vatican, while the latter promised to retain its silence in the issue. In spite of this ambivalence by de Castelnau and his cadres toward the Action Française, the French hierarchy and the pontiff were ready to live with these concessions granted by the FNC to former members of the royalist league. Indeed, these prelates maintained their devotion to and effusive praise of both de Castelnau and his organization. The Fédération Nationale Catholique remained for Pius XI and his bishops the single most important manifestation of Catholic Action in France.[28]

With the federation's acceptance of the Action Française's condemnation, the battle was over. The Maurrasians had been isolated effectively. Their intransigents stood alone, and their conscience-troubled Catholics were able to find an ideological home in the FNC. Pius XI, essentially sympathetic with reactionary ideologies, found de Castelnau's organization ideal for his Catholic Action policies. It was structurally dependent upon his church's hierarchy, more powerful and effective than the Action Française, and ideologically compatible with his own world view. The very reality of the FNC made the Action Française a total liability for the church. Catholic Action demanded the demise of the Maurrasian league so that the Vatican could be assured that its authoritarian program remained under hierarchical control.

As 1927 drew to a close, it was apparent that the Action Française had been defeated seriously. In spite of its profound influence among French Catholics, the pontiff had insured the loyalty of key theologians, the nation's bishops, *La Croix,* the Association Catholique de la Jeunesse Française, and the Fédération Nationale Catholique. Pius XI's campaign of religious defense and missionary expansion was ready to move forward. The war against the Action Française was not over, but the decisive battles had been won by the pope of Catholic Action.

Throughout the relentless papal offensive, the Maurrasians refused to be silent and counterattacked at every turn. After the initial shock of the Andrieu letter, the Action Française spent the next several months developing an apologetic against its manifold foes. From the Andrieu missive to the famous *Non Possumus* broadside against the papal condemnation, the league made every effort to pursue a moderate and respectful line. In the hopes of retaining their Catholic credentials, the integral royalists constructed a reasoned case for their growing disobedience to the papacy. These rationales were published in Charles Maurras's *L'Action Française et le Vatican,* largely a collection of the relevant documents in the controversy; in Maurice Pujo's *Comment Rome est trompée,* a response to the arguments developed in *Pourquoi Rome a parlé;* and in books and articles written by the league's most reputed Catholics.

With few exceptions, the beleaguered royalists responded to their detractors with arguments reminiscent of earlier prewar controversies with the Christian Democrats and their friends. Once again, Maurras indicated that *politique d'abord* was strictly a tactical concern that in no way challenged the primordial character of religion, and once again Action Française militants sought to demonstrate that their philosophical leader's agnosticism was no threat to the Catholic membership of the league. Finally, the royalists used earlier polemics to soften the charges of violence and excessive nationalism which were leveled against them.[29] However, before the war the Action Française had been rescued rather than condemned by the pope. This time the monarchist league was faced with the option of its obedient demise or overt rebellion. Until the official condemnation, it tried to avoid both of these ruinous decisions. It affirmed its loyalty to the papacy and declared that its activities served the Catholic cause by its struggles against both "the enemies of France and religion." As late as November 1926, the Action Française was requesting the church to name theologians for the express purpose of purging errors from the midst of its membership. After the condemnation was published, the Maurrasians turned to reasoned arguments to justify their revolt. One royalist leader made the distinction that was found so unacceptable a decade earlier when Father Jules Lemire had refused to abandon his seat in the Chamber of Deputies, namely the notion that political independence was not incompatible with papal loyalty. Finally, Maurice Pujo and a number of Maurrasian priests turned to arguments of natural law to justify their disobedience. In a small pamphlet these clerics affirmed that *"natural law itself allows the propagation of the newspaper."* Indeed, "natural law requires it."[30]

When it became clear to the royalists that all their efforts were unable to reverse the momentum that Rome had mustered against them, they turned to the path of open revolt. This growing awareness that their cause was hopeless led them to adopt a polemical shrillness that soon created an unbridgeable chasm between the contending parties. The well-known *Non Possumus* letter of December 21, 1926, set the stage for the growing ugliness in the battles of the late 1920s and early 1930s. Although its tone was moderate and respectful, the epistle's content was a clear break with Rome, a blatant refusal to obey the papal wishes. To favor the Vatican's act against them, said the integral nationalists, "would be to commit treason. We will not commit treason." The letter expressed a desire to comply with the pontiff, but because such a submission would be "a sin . . . comparable to parricide" against the nation, "he cannot be obeyed."[31]

The Action Française, unlike the Sillon sixteen years earlier, had chosen the road of rebellion, and for the next eleven years it engaged in sharp polemics with its growing number of Catholic foes, both hierarchical and lay. A new, more hostile tone came into play as the royalist newspaper sought to publicize the idea that the league's condemnation had been the result of a Christian Democratic plot and a pacifistic internationalist conspiracy at the Vatican. Analysis gave way increasingly to virulence and name-calling. The monarchist daily even developed a regular acrimonious column, "Sous la terreur," to deal exclusively with its running feud with the church.

Initially these shrill polemics were directed against the Vatican in the hope that the nationalist spirit of Gallicanism might be resurrected among French Catholics. *L'Osservatore Romano,* the Vatican newspaper, was accused of printing pornography and of fostering policies that aided German interests at the expense of France. Indeed, it was charged with being "politically German above all else *[politique allemande d'abord]."* Also the papal nuncio to Paris Msgr. Maglione and the Vatican's secretary of state Cardinal Gasparri were subjected to scathing attacks. Both were labeled anti-French because of their support of the Locarno peace mood exemplified by the foreign policy of Aristide Briand. Maglione was said to have endorsed the anticlerical Cartel des Gauches, and Gasparri was described as favoring "a German military revival" and the destruction of French patriotism.[32] For the most part, Pius XI himself escaped the harsh attacks that the Maurrasians directed against his underlings, but by the early 1930s he too was subjected to similar broadsides.

The French episcopate, however, was not spared similar barbs. Hostile attacks were directed against those prelates who either had displayed sympathies toward Christian Democratic programs or had campaigned vigorously against the integral nationalists. The bishop of Nice was accused of Sillonism, and the archbishop of Paris Cardinal Dubois was charged with financial scandals. Mostly, however, he was chastized for the constant disciplinary actions that he took against Action Française Catholics and clergy who assisted them. In fact, most Maurrasian critiques in the late 1920s against domestic bishops were prompted by the hierarchy's use of religious sanctions against disobedient royalists. Polemics attacking lay Catholic militants in France were limited in quantity and scope until the 1930s. Most of the league's rage was directed against the Vatican and French episcopate which had been so instrumental in the Action Française's downfall. Nevertheless, the royalist newspaper took the time to castigate its traditional Christian Democratic foes Marc Sangnier and *L'Ouest-Eclair*. However, its most venomous language against the Christian Democrats was reserved for Francisque Gay and his publications. Gay himself was called "an impostor" and "a dog," and his *La Vie Catholique* was viewed as a newspaper of low quality, the Parisian equivalent of *L'Ouest-Eclair*.[33]

By 1930 the reasoned appeals of the Action Française had passed into history. The cold stark logic of Maurras's polemics was giving way slowly to the poisonous pen of Léon Daudet and the vitriolic "Sous la terreur" column. Even limited dialogue came to be replaced by mutual recriminations. Intransigent disobedience by Catholic royalists prompted the church's hierarchy to increase and enforce disciplinary measures against those believers who remained openly sympathetic toward the condemned league. In actions reminiscent of the prewar modernist controversy, the French episcopate began to weed out dissenters. Sacraments were refused to Catholic Maurrasians unless they submitted in writing, and integral nationalists were required to sign an oath of loyalty to the papal campaign against the Action Française if they sought to return to the church's good graces. In addition, bishops were exercising religious sanctions against those priests who continued to give the sacramental services of the church to rebellious leaguers.[34] Although this war continued well into the 1930s, the main battles had been joined, lost, and won by the end of the previous decade. Vatican and French Catholicism had isolated its erstwhile competitor. In three years the hierarchy had destroyed the royalist league's far-reaching influence among French Catholics. Some believers retained their Maurrasian loyalty tenaciously, but as a profound force among Catholics, the Action Française was spent.

In short, why had the integral nationalists been condemned? Why had Pius XI intervened to anathematize an organization that had defended Catholicism so resolutely for over twenty years? Why was a league so beloved by the most powerful sectors of the French church attacked so relentlessly by the Holy See? The Action Française itself believed that a papal policy shift toward Christian Democracy, Briandist internationalism, and social progressivism accounted for the victimization of integral nationalists in France. Outside the polemical interests of the royalists, this opinion has been perpetuated by those historians who speak of the new pontiff's efforts to inaugurate the Second Ralliement in France. Without a doubt the Vatican was coming to embrace a number of positions dear to the hearts of Catholic liberals, and it is also true that an explosion of Catholic republican pluralism had begun in postwar France.[35]

Nevertheless, neither the rise and expansion of Christian Democratic groups in France nor Pius XI's ephemeral use of them is a convincing demonstration that the Second Ralliement embraced by the Vatican was progressive in nature. A careful scrutiny of the relevant papal documents shows no such predilections. Instead, the authoritarian and conservative concerns of the Vatican were at issue. *Ubi Arcano Dei*'s ultraconservative and socially defensive character provides hints that the pope's program and anathema toward the royalists were not inspired by democratic values and hopes. In this respect, there was no difference between the condemnations of the Sillon and the Action Française. In both instances, the papacy intervened to reassert its control over its French constituency and to render impotent a serious competitor. However, there are two significant differences between the two actions. First of all, the Action Française was a more serious threat to the Vatican's control over French Catholics. Sangnier never developed a value system as sophisticated and as total as that promulgated by Maurras. The Sillon, unlike the royalist league, never made serious inroads among the leading princes of the French church. Secondly, the condemnation of the Sillon by Pius X was openly counterrevolutionary and antidemocratic. In contrast, Pius XI's documents against the Action Française were strictly silent on political judgments. Neither the theologians, nor the bishops, nor Merklen of *La Croix,* nor even the pope himself expressed any discomfort with the partisan values of the repudiated royalists, nor did they indicate preferences for the more progressive doctrines of the Christian Democrats. No doubt the Action Française was condemned in part because it did not join the Second Ralliement, but this movement was ultraconservative, authoritarian, and defensive in nature, at least as far as the papacy was concerned. The decade of the 1930s, which witnessed the Ralliement's fruition and collapse, would demonstrate this with clarity, as would the papal absolution given to the Action Française less than a year before the death of the Third Republic. The springtime of Ralliement euphoria would give way to acrimonious divisions among French Catholics. Pius XI would undermine his own Ralliement by supporting counterrevolutionaries against progressives and by setting the stage for the reprieve of the Action Française.[36]

+ 9 +

Shattered Ralliement
and the Reprieve
of the Action Française
(1929–1939)

*B*y *1929 the papalists* in France had achieved a decisive victory. The condemnation of the Action Française and its isolation from the articulate forces of French Catholicism meant that Pius XI had swept aside his most significant foes in the French nation. His program of religious defense and expansion had been secured, and the country's leading Catholics, with few exceptions, stood behind him. He was now free to move forward in these designs without serious competitors. At one level, he planned to continue his policy of enhancing the position of the church within France by using the tactics of official diplomacy to build upon the initial agreements he had worked out with the republic in 1924. At another level, he hoped to restore the French masses to Christianity and thus enable them to fight the church's battles under episcopal control. This shift by the Vatican away from overt reaction and toward concordats and Catholic Action stimulated the further expansion of democratic and progressive groups within the French Church. That the papal Ralliement may have been alien to these new forces scarcely occurred to the *ralliés*. The euphoria produced by the Action Française's condemnation blinded them to the conservative authoritarian and reactionary potential of the pontiff's program. For eight more years Catholic progressive forces continued to expand in France and experienced what could be called the halcyon years of the Second Ralliement. This period witnessed the further growth of the two Christian Democratic political units in France. The Parti Démocrate Populaire fell short of its intended goal to win Catholics to moderate republicanism, but it did lay the groundwork for the mass Mouvement Républicain Populaire which would emerge immediately following World War II. In spite of its modest electoral showing, it was able to challenge the dominance of the Republican Federation in the most heavily Catholic areas of the nation. However, in actual practice it often voted with this rightist coalition in the Chamber of Deputies. Its language was liberal, but its behavior was timid, conservative, and increasingly obsessed with anticommunism. For its part, the Jeune République continued to offer more serious alternatives to French Catholics. Although Marc Sangnier retired from the league in the early 1930s, his visionary internationalism remained stamped upon the organization. Domestically it adopted a radically social democratic program which advocated proletarian liberation from the inhuman capitalist system. Its demands for a graduated income tax, worker control of major industries, democratization of the League of Nations, and international policing bodies to replace national armies made the Jeune République a manifestly left-wing Catholic presence in France throughout the 1930s.[1]

Beyond the specifically Christian Democratic parties, Catholics continued to expand their presence within the French working class. By the mid-1930s both the Confédération Française des Travailleurs Chrétiens and the Jeunesse Ouvrière Chrétienne had consolidated their respective organizations and were thriving. The CFTC continued to view itself as a trade union movement of Christian inspiration with the mission of winning the working class away from the joint errors of economic liberalism and revolutionary Marxism. It offered to the French proletariat a syndicalism that would be "strictly professional" against the politically conscious unions "of socialist and communist inspiration." Capitalism was brutal and competitive, Marxism elevated class hatred to the realm of principle, and fascist corporatism was too authoritarian and statist. Only the social Catholicism of Leo XIII's *Rerum Novarum* could redeem the working class. The CFTC's practice of collaborating with factory owners and managers, its competition with more radical trade union federations, and its class-mixed membership made it continually suspect in the eyes of the nation's proletariat.[2]

Such, however, was not the case with the Jeunesse Ouvrière Chrétienne which reflected a more genuinely proletarian stamp. To be sure, the JOC was openly Catholic in its ideology, and it took seriously the clerical advice rendered by its army of chaplains. Nevertheless, its rank-and-file militants and its lay leadership were conscious members of the working class. Initially, the Jocistes were dominated by the exigencies of internal organization. Local groups were formed on the basis of neighborhood and family. These in turn were amalgamated into larger sections based on population or geographical factors, and finally there was a national headquarters in Paris located in a proletarian neighborhood. Chaplain advisors were present at every level and formed the chief link between JOC militants and the institutional church. Throughout the organizational apparatus and via the discipline that it required, the Jocistes and their priests united to bring Christ to the working class. By the Popular Front the Jeunesse Ouvrière Chrétienne had become the most important proletarian youth group in France. It could boast of over 50,000 adherents, including its feminine counterpart, the Jeunesse Ouvrière Chrétienne Féminine (JOCF), and its monthly *Jeunesse Ouvrière* had a circulation in excess of 270,000. Educational and recruitment campaigns were designed both for the broad purpose of developing a Christian class consciousness among proletarians and for dealing with such specific issues as sexual morality, family life, professional training, unemployment, and the like. Ideologically the JOC was militantly Christian. The model of Jociste virility was the manly worker "Jesus the Carpenter" who affirmed the dignity of every human being, especially the poorest and most humble. As a result of this basic conviction, the Jocistes condemned the inhuman system of capitalism which exalted profit and production above people's lives. However, equally dangerous was Marxism, whose doctrine of class struggle violated Christian charity and demeaned working-class self-respect. The only revolution acceptable to the JOC was one based upon love of the neighbor and class cooperation. These values explain the fraternal collaboration between the Jocistes and the CFTC as well as the hostility between these two Christian groups and the labor organizations inspired by syndicalist or Marxist principles. An element of contradiction thus characterized the interwar Jeunesse Ouvrière Chrétienne. Although it wished to be totally proletarian, its Christian ideology brought it into conflict with the dominant values and organizations of the working class. The chasm was never fully bridged, but in spite of this difficulty, the Jocistes remained the most innovative and influential expression of genuinely Ralliement Catholicism in interwar France.[3]

In addition to those Catholic progressive manifestations which predated the Action Française's condemnation, several newer expressions emerged in the years that followed. One was the Parisian Christian Democratic daily *L'Aube,* which saw the light of day in early 1932. Brought into being by the persistence of Francisque Gay, it could count on the active support of such leading Catholic *ralliés* as Gaston Tessier of the CFTC, the social Catholic industrialists Paul Chanson and Joseph Zamanski, and the former Sillonists Marc Sangnier and Georges Hoog. The mainstays of the paper, however, were Gay himself and his associate the historian Georges Bidault, and they steered the daily along resolutely republican lines in favor of social reform by class collaboration and international peace via the League of Nations. But in spite of Gay's dreams, *L'Aube* barely survived the 1930s. It was always in financial trouble, and its circulation reached only 20,000.[4]

France was also experiencing a theological renaissance during the golden years of the Second Ralliement. Both lay and clerical intellectuals were giving articulate voice to the Catholic pluralism which was dawning after the Great War. *La Vie Catholique* was a manifestation of this. Jacques Maritain turned increasingly to the values of a post–French Revolutionary world, but by the

1930s, even his moderate conservatism was being challenged by the populist personalism of Emmanuel Mounier. Among the clergy the Dominicans produced an innovative spirit which survived the Third Republic into the Fourth. Theologians such as Yves Congar and M.-D. Chenu began their illustrious and controversial careers in the 1930s, but it was largely a series of reviews that reflected most clearly the progressive roles played by certain Dominicans in the Second Ralliement. The beginnings of significant liturgical reform and spiritual renovation appeared in *La Vie Spirituelle*, and a new spirit of critical dialogical theology came to dominate the monthly *La Vie Intellectuelle*. However, the most important publication created by these reformist monks at Juvisy was the weekly newspaper *Sept* which made its appearance in 1934. Whereas the reviews had a somewhat modest readership, the new weekly newspaper had an average circulation of 60,000, and on occasion would even surpass 100,000. Still, it was plagued by constant financial difficulty until its premature death in 1937. The Dominican weekly viewed itself as an arm of Catholic Action without partisan affiliations or preferences. In spite of such apolitical claims, it felt most comfortable with the democratic pluralism expressed by *La Vie Catholique* and *L'Aube*. Need for social reform was stressed, as was a willingness to accept critically a wide range of sociopolitical options as long as they were not extremist.[5] Though viewed as part of the left by traditional Catholics, *Sept* was moderate and reformist in ideology and mood.

Such was not the case with Emmanuel Mounier and the review *Esprit,* which he created in 1932. This sensitive intellectual from Grenoble was the inspiration behind the philosophy of "personalism" and the sociopolitical values which made *Esprit* decidedly radical in character. Mounier and his friends were young middle-class rebels who viewed the Third Republic and its economic liberalism as "the established disorder." Institutional traditional Catholicism was also perceived to be part of this moribund system. Consequently, Mounier called for a profound spiritual revolution which would amalgamate the rightist values of "honor, . . . property, family, fatherland" and "religion" with the leftist mystique of profound renovation. In spite of this seeming centrism, *Esprit* broke with Christian Democratic moderation by condemning capitalism with its pseudodemocratic political manifestations and by repudiating the anti-Marxist crusade as "an organ of capitalist defense." Mounier's alternative to his current society may have been vague, but it was leftist in its vision and reflected democratic and social democratic ingredients.[6]

Thus, by the eve of the Depression in France, most of the progressive forms of emerging Catholic pluralism were in place and were making their presence felt. However, with few exceptions, theirs was a minority voice, a tiny island in the sea of traditional Catholic conservatism. Even a group as large as the JOC was only on the fringe area of church life, a bizarre presence among mainline Catholics. Moreover, most of these expressions were constantly in financial difficulty due to their narrow audiences, and in spite of the earlier balmy mood of Ralliement, they came under the fire of their more conservative foes within the church.[7]

Nevertheless, the Second Ralliement reached its zenith during the high tide of Locarno optimism when the Vatican and French papalists supported the international policies of Aristide Briand and the League of Nations. So strong was this spirit within the church that it went by the unofficial title "Catholic Briandism." Its origins can be traced to the peace proposals of Benedict XV, and it was pursued by his successor well into the 1930s. Pius XI and his entourage endorsed international collaboration, mutual disarmament, and the Wilsonian league. The nuncio carried this message to France, and in one instance Secretary of State Gasparri sent a papal blessing to a Jeune République peace congress.[8] With few exceptions, the articulate sectors of the French church rallied to papal-inspired Briandism. Merklen's *La Croix* stood behind the new policy but chose to emphasize its more defensive and conservative aspects. The renowned Catholic daily insisted that peace required a strong national army, and Franco-German collaboration was justified only upon the basis of a united crusade against Bolshevism. Other Catholic conservatives were equally cautious. Jacques Maritain argued that only the church's internationalism was realizable and that the Briandist form of pan-Europeanism needed to be constructed upon the virtue of nationalism. Even the French episcopal statement of 1931 was only a cautious endorsement of "Catholic Briandism." Class collaboration was urged against Marxism, and pacifism was condemned in the same breath as "exaggerated nationalism."[9]

The more consciously democratic elements of the Second Ralliement were much less cautious. The youth cadres of Catholic Action warned against both communism's repudiation of patriotism and "Maurrasian nationalism," and *L'Aube* supported "Catholic Briandism" without the suspicions found among the Catholic conservatives. Leftist Catholics greeted papal internationalism with joy, but they were committed to its further expansion and to its democratization. *Esprit* gave priority to the entire human community by calling for "a juridic international organism" having authority over national units for the purpose of dispensing justice above and beyond class and sectional lines. Peace would be insured by the abolition of conscription, the end of economic nationalism, and the destruction of colonial imperialism. The more pacifistic Jeune République concentrated on mutual disarmament, the creation of an international police force, and the democratization of the League of Nations. Beyond this program it held multinational peace congresses to encourage and practice the policies of "fraternity between people" that it advocated.[10]

In spite of this apparent solidarity with Vatican Briandism and Locarno optimism, sharp divisions on related issues existed among French Catholics which erupted, on occasion, into open conflict. Most obvious in its resistance to the papal program was the Action Française. By the 1930s its daily newspaper was attacking Pius XI personally for his internationalist views. He was accused of being against patriotism, of having naive views about disarmament, and of endorsing a resurrection of German militarism. In fact, charged Maurras, his reign was "the most German ponficate in history."[11] However, by 1930, *L'Action Française* was no longer perceived by most French people as a Catholic publication.

Even within the recognized expressions of the faith could be found deep hostility toward those Catholics who espoused papal Briandist policies. Unsurprisingly, the chief Catholic foes of this spirit were General de Castelnau and his Fédération Nationale Catholique. The reactionary army officer had lost three sons in the Great War, and in no uncertain terms he repudiated the Locarno mood, Briandism, and the League of Nations. He was convinced that France's trust in such policies undermined its national security and encouraged a resurgent militarism in Germany.[12] Throughout the early 1930s the reactionary general became involved in a number of conflicts with Catholic moderates and radicals who supported Locarno-type programs. He attacked special masses in the name of peace and clashed with Francisque Gay over the same issue. In a series of articles in the right-wing daily *L'Echo de Paris,* de Castelnau called upon the entire nation to support proposed legislation which would increase the duration of required military service for conscripts. The Dominicans of *Sept* responded by warning Catholics against excessive militarism and narrow nationalism. De Castelnau accused these moderates of being defeatists and "foreign agents." Emmanuel Mounier's indiscreet entry into the fray triggered a venomous barrage by the reactionary general, who called the editor of *Esprit* a coward, a transvestite, and a deformed spirit. The continuing controversy over new military legislation and rearmament gave way to recriminations concerning an exposé of the French army brought to light by progressive Dominicans. A Belgian senator Father Rutten claimed that the army had refused to bomb German-occupied Briey during the First World War because of the vested interests of local munitions magnates. *Sept* reprinted immediately the charges of its Belgian confrere, and General de Castelnau rose to the army's defense. He accused both *Sept* and *Esprit* of endorsing a communist revolution which would open the nation's door to foreign invaders. The Juvisy Dominicans ended the controversy by charging de Castelnau with violating Catholic unity.[13]

Throughout all these conflicts *L'Aube, Sept,* and *Esprit* had defended papal Briandism against the resolute attacks of General de Castelnau and his federation while the French hierarchy had remained silent. Only when the reactionary general turned upon the moderate internationalism of the ACJF did the church's ecclesiastical leadership feel compelled to intervene. Even here, where the very unity of Catholic Action was threatened, they hesitated. The controversy opened in 1932 when the *Annales de la A.C.J.F.* attacked the munitions industries of both France and Germany for profiting from xenophobia and "the state of armed peace." De Castelnau called these "stupid and gross charges" by an organization that had been infiltrated by socialist and communist ideas. Francisque Gay and Emmanuel Mounier counterattacked against the FNC leader, but it was the intervention of the church's hierarchy that laid the matter to rest. Pius XI praised the loyal obedience of the ACJF, and Cardinal Achille Liénart, the bishop of Lille, blessed the youth organization publicly, assured the FNC that it was equally esteemed and insisted that both these groups were expected to work together. The general's wrists had been slapped diplomatically by the church's leadership. The unity of Catholic Action had demanded it.[14]

International collaboration among nations was only one facet of the Vatican's Ralliement. Piux XI was also deeply committed to the rechristianization of the working class both in France and beyond. His reputation as a defender of the French proletariat was based upon three incidents: his baptism of the Jeunesse Ouvrière Chrétienne, his vindication of the Confédération Française des Travailleurs Chrétiens, and his encyclical on working-class conditions which was published in 1931. Without hesitation the pontiff had adopted the vision of Joseph Cardijn, and from its birth in 1925 to the end of the Third Republic, the JOC remained under the personal sponsorship of the Holy See. Pius XI had no such direct relations with the French Catholic trade unions. Nevertheless, he proved supportive to the CFTC in the midst of an industrial conflict in northern France. In August, 1924, Eugène Mathon, a representative of Catholic textile employers from the Roubaix-Tourcoing-Lille triangle, appealed to the Holy Father against the CFTC, which was involved in a local strike. The coalition of the area's industrialists, called the Consortium, continued to bombard the Vatican with protests against the Catholic unions. Finally, in June 1928, the Sacred Office made a decision in favor of the CFTC, but it was not published until a year later when feeling at Lille was running high against Bishop Achille Liénart. The newly appointed prelate had supported a campaign to raise money for the strikers' suffering families, and he had called upon the factory owners to negotiate the labor dispute sincerely. The employers were furious with Liénart and accused him of violating his episcopal neutrality. The bishop defended his action on the ground that refusal to assist the poor among the strikers would open the door to their being influenced by communism. At this point the Vatican intervened on Liénart's behalf by publishing the Sacred Congregation's pro-CFTC document and by granting the bishop a cardinal's hat even though he was merely forty-five years of age. The pontiff's reputation as friend of the working class was enhanced further when the encyclical *Quadragesimo Anno* was promulgated in May, 1931, in honor of Leo XIII's *Rerum Novarum*. Like his socially conscious predecessor, Pius XI decried the injustices under which the proletariat lived, and he called for an amelioration of these conditions. He defended the right of property and insisted on peaceful collaboration between workers and owners in each occupation. His unique contribution was his insistence that the state had to regulate the economy in a just manner and arbitrate all labor disputes which could not be resolved by employers and employees operating in the same professional organizations.[15]

Thus, throughout the relatively stable period of the late 1920s and early 1930s, French Catholics responded with a near unanimity to the papal Ralliement. The church's moderates, radicals, and even some conservatives were prepared to support Pius XI's Briandism as well as welcome his initiatives in defense of the working class. Nevertheless, behind this aura of solidarity lurked serious divisions between French Catholics. General de Castelnau's offensives against the French supporters of the Vatican's program were a sign of deeper conflicts to come. With the arrival of the mid-1930s came the end of tolerance for the French Catholic progressives. They would find themselves isolated and attacked by the conservative and reactionary Catholic right. Even the Holy See would turn against them. Such would be the tragic experience waiting for the Second Ralliement in the final years of the

Third Republic. The backdrop for this drama was the Depression and the massive dislocations in Europe that resulted from this economic disaster. Crisis followed crisis all over the Continent. Nazism came to power in Germany, the Soviet Union sought to collaborate with the Western democracies, Spain burst into civil war, fascist Italy continued its bellicosity, and Hitler's chauvinism pushed the nations closer and closer toward armed conflict. In France the Depression created a political polarization throughout the land. Militant right-wing leagues took to the streets in February, 1934, and the left responded by forming an electoral coalition of Communists, Socialists, and Radicals which governed France briefly as the Popular Front. French Catholics reflected the same divisions that these crises had produced in the nation at large. The profound fissures which had remained hidden during the calmer days of Ralliement were now exposed. Crisis in France and Europe revealed the deep chasm between French Catholics as well as the vulnerability of the progressives in the face of conservative and hierarchical opposition.

On the domestic level the events surrounding the street violence of February 6, 1934, brought to the surface the sharp ideological conflicts that divided the nation's Catholics. A government financial scandal had been exploited by the Action Française and other right-wing leagues, and they used the occasion to amass demonstrations in an attempt to march on the Chamber of Deputies.[16] They were met by the police at Place de la Concorde, and in the ensuing clashes fifteen people were killed and another fifteen hundred wounded. The government of Edouard Daladier resigned and was replaced by Gaston Doumergue's rightist National Union. The left responded to these events with a sympathetic general strike on February 12 which marked the first signs of what was to become the Popular Front. French Catholics were polarized sharply into two clearly unequal camps over the bloodletting of February 6 and the events that followed. Christian Democrats and other moderates of both *L'Aube* and *Sept* deplored the violence of the leagues and had deep misgivings about the Doumergue government. Nevertheless, they displayed an equal disdain for the nonviolent strike of the left. Gaston Tessier ordered his CFTC unions to remain aloof from this demonstration, and Georges Bidault insisted that the success of either reactionary or revolutionary bands "would mean the capitulation of the republican state." Meanwhile Catholic radicals were drawn more sympathetically toward the nation's leftists. Although Emmanuel Mounier uttered warnings against both camps, he was most concerned that the immediate right-wing peril be alleviated by a "permanent opposition to capitalist institutions." The Jeune République insisted that massive democratic reform was the only meaningful alternative to both fascism and Marxism, yet it took a first step toward its involvement in the Popular Front by calling upon its membership to join "a broad union of leftists for the defense of the menaced republic."[17] On the other side of the political spectrum, Catholic conservatives and reactionaries sympathized openly with the right-wing leagues. The Republican Federation, which drew heavily from Catholic voters, had supportive, albeit ambivalent, feelings toward the rightist formations, but for General de Castelnau the night of February 6 was a noble attempt to restore a Catholic authoritarian order in place of a Masonic and pro-Marxist state. For *La Croix* the street demonstrators were "defenders of the fatherland" who had resisted a government of "class struggle" and the Masonic lodges. Only a wholehearted support of Doumergue's National Union could redeem the patriotic blood that was shed on the night of February 6. Even the moderate Parti Démocrate Populaire praised the rightist demonstrators and called upon the nation to support the government that followed in their wake.[18]

The French hierarchy was more circumspect, but for the most part, the bishops were partial toward the rightists. To be sure, they reiterated the dangers of both right and left-wing extremism, and they continued to warn Cathlics against participation in the Action Française. In spite of all these caveats, France's leading prelates showed a careful but public solidarity with the activists of February 6. Although clergy and Catholic Action were enjoined again to avoid active politics, exceptions could be noted. Some bishops suggested an alliance between the leagues and Catholic Action, and the entire hierarchy permitted priests to maintain their memberships in the Croix de Feu. However, it was the participation of French cardinals in the memorial masses for those who died in the street fighting of February 6 that demonstrated most clearly the sympathies of these prelates. Achille Liénart eulogized the dead militants as "men who have paid for the fatherland's salvation with their lives." In Paris the new archbishop Cardinal Jean Verdier held a special service for the dead rightists. His sermon contained the following oath: "Let this cruel sacrifice serve the fatherland's redemption! Our children have fallen while demanding a more honest and more beautiful France. Their desire, sealed by their blood, will be granted. We promise it to them!" In cathedrals and churches all over France memorial masses were held in which uniformed contingents of the leagues, with flags unfurled, participated. No corresponding concern was demonstrated for those who died in the antifascist demonstrations of February 12. When a delegation of leftist Catholics suggested a memorial mass for these workers to Cardinal Verdier, France's leading prelate rejected the recommendation.[19] The church's hierarchy had made its choice. Under the pressure of domestic crisis it had opted openly for a rightist stance. The isolation of the Catholic moderates and radicals had begun in earnest. With the arrival of the Popular Front, the Second Ralliement would be in fragments.

Born of serious domestic unrest and a perceived fascist threat, the Rassemblement Populaire united the three major leftist parties into a victorious electoral coalition which would govern France in the name of antifascism, democracy, and social reform. Especially frightening to French moderates and conservatives was the Communist participation in the alliance. In the late spring of 1936 the Popular Front came to power, and the Socialist Léon Blum formed its first government. A wave of strikes and factory occupations followed which pressured the new administration to adopt serious social reforms and progressive legislation regulating labor disputes. Following the increasingly positive Comintern policy toward the Western democracies, the Communists embraced a patriotic moderation designed to make them acceptable to the nation as a whole. One aspect of this stance was a policy called the *main tendue* [the outstretched hand], a deliberate proposal to progressive and working-class Catholics inviting them to collaborate with their Marxist brothers on common goals. By 1937 the leftist spirit of the Popular Front had ground to a halt due to its internal divisions, but in the interim French Catholics had rent asunder any vestiges of unity that may have remained in the Second Ralliement.

The Popular Front was a most serious test of French Catholicism's reputed support for democratic values and advanced social reform. That it failed to rise to the occasion is indicative of both the weakness that plagued Catholic progressivism and the residue of right-wing traditionalism that still dominated the French Church.[20] Only a handful of the more radical Catholics welcomed the Popular Front and sought to assist its efforts. The most striking of these were the believers who called for a direct alliance with the communists. Louis Martin-Chauffier of the review *Vendredi* endorsed this, and Robert Honnert wrote a book in defense of such a coalition. However, the most outspoken partisans of Catholic-communist collaboration were the Christian revolutionaries who produced the monthly review *Terre Nouvelle*. Its front cover, adorned by a red Christian cross with the sickle and hammer emblazoned across it, testified to the review's unabashed commitment to Marxist Christianity. Maurice Laudrain, its Catholic editor, urged Christians to vote Red, supported the strikes and called for an unequivocal endorsement of the *main tendue*. Other segments of the Catholic left were more cautious. The Jeune République was a member group within the Popular Front and advocated a careful acceptance of the *main tendue*. Emmanuel Mounier and *Esprit* welcomed the new government but retained deep suspicions toward the French Communist party.[21] Catholic moderates and traditional Christian Democrats neither supported the Popular Front nor trusted the communists. Particularly notable was the ambivalence of the Confédération Française des Travailleurs Chrétiens and the Jeunesse Ouvrière Chrétienne. Throughout the period, both organizations of working-class Catholics attacked Marxist materialism and class warfare, and both remained aloof from the unity efforts of the other proletarian groups. *Le*

Petit Démocrate and *L'Aube* remained foes of the Popular Front and communism throughout the mid-1930s, and *Sept* shared their misgivings as well. Nevertheless, the Dominican review did not rule out limited forms of collaboration with the left. It was prepared to support serious dialogue about the *main tendue* and accepted the legality of the Blum administration. In an interview with the premier, *Sept* expressed its willingness to collaborate with the Popular Front, not as a manifestation of socialism, but as "the legitimate government of the nation."[22]

No such balance existed among the Catholic traditionals and reactionaries. They were worlds apart from their more radical and moderate brothers, and they employed the language and values of civil war against their foes. The French episcopacy was unanimous in its intransigent rejection of both the Popular Front and all collaboration with Marxists. Catholics were commanded to vote against socialism and communism, and even the reputed progressive cardinals saw the leftist government as the harbinger of bolshevism. *La Croix* was equally hostile. Victory for the Rassemblement Populaire would mean the triumph of "communism, revolution and the . . . destroyers of national grandeur and public morality." Most obstinate of all the Catholic opponents of the new government was General de Castelnau and his Fédération Nationale Catholique. As a rabid anti-Marxist, the reactionary general supported the rightist National Front in the 1936 elections, because only this coalition was capable of defeating "materialistic socialism and Soviet communism." The *main tendue* was rejected utterly. De Castelnau stated bluntly: "We refuse obstinately to collaborate with the enemies of religion, the family, society and the fatherland." So hostile was the FNC to Catholic-Marxist cooperation that one of its militants Gaëtan Bernoville published a widely circulated pamphlet called *La Farce de la main tendue*.[23]

Similar ruptures among French Catholics, in an atmosphere of civil war, spilled over into the arena of foreign policy. Here, as well, can be detected the same ideological fissures. All agreed that a resurgent Nazi Germany was a grave danger to French interests, but the various Catholic factions could not agree upon a unified strategy to resist this menace. The church's leftists continued to uphold democratic internationalism and peace, but they also recognized the need to resist Hitler aggressively. They rejected an alliance with Fascist Italy for ideological reasons and because of Mussolini's invasion of Abyssinia. Democratic England was a suitable friend, but they also came to see that collaboration with the Soviet Union was necessary. Catholic conservatives and reactionaries looked toward Mussolini as a counterweight against the twin dangers of Nazism and bolshevism. European stability demanded a Catholic Latin entente, including France, Italy, and — after 1936 — a Franco-ruled Spain, even if this meant an end to Catholic Briandism and a violation of the League of Nations. Under pressure, these Catholics were more inclined to deal with Hitler than with Stalin. After all, Germany, though inclined to militarist expansion at the expense of France, was a normal patriotic nation that accepted the rules of diplomacy. The Soviet Union, on the other hand, recognized no such principles and was bent on the destruction of civilization. Such an opinion was one chief reason why the French Catholic ultras welcomed the Munich agreement of 1938. Traditional Christian Democrats and moderates vacillated between the two positions. As the international crisis deepened, they were reduced more and more to reflecting upon events that had caught them by surprise. They trusted only Great Britain as a fellow democratic ally and found both Fascist Italy and Communist Russia unworthy partners against racist and totalitarian Germany. Unlike the conservatives, these Catholic moderates opposed Italy in the Abyssinian affair, and unlike the Ralliement's radicals, they were still hesitant to deal with the Soviet Union after the Munich fiasco.[24]

By far the most important foreign policy issue that polarized French Catholics was the civil war in Spain from 1936 to 1939. Both the traditional conservative Catholic majority and tiny groups of Christian leftists took predictable stances. The French bishops, *La Croix,* and the Fédération Nationale Catholique attacked the legal Spanish Republic at every turn and welcomed the Franco rebellion against it. In many instances the revolt of the generals was called a crusade of "Christian civilization against Marxist barbarism." In contrast, Catholic radicals welcomed the democratic republic in Spain, supported its Popular Front government and stood behind its efforts to defeat the Nationalists and their Nazi and Fascist allies.[25] Neither the traditional nor the leftist positions taken were particularly surprising. However, hostility against the Spanish republic, on the part of Catholic moderates, Christian Democrats, and even sober conservatives, gradually evolved into thoughtful neutrality or even mild support. This change was the most striking turn of events in Catholic circles with respect to the Spanish question. During the initial stages of the conflict, well-known Christian Democrats chose to emphasize Spain's anticlerical excesses. Francisque Gay published a small propaganda booklet of religious defense called *Dans les flammes et dans le sang* against the Spanish Popular Front. Nonetheless, both Gay and Georges Bidault insisted that Spain should remain a democracy, supported peaceful arbitration between the contending forces, and scorned the crusade mentality of the Catholic right. *Sept* echoed similar opinions.[26]

Most noteworthy, however, was the defection of some prominent Catholic conservatives to a reasoned neutrality and to a sharp criticism of the Nationalist rebels. The well-known intellectuals Jacques Maritain, Georges Bernanos, and François Mauriac deplored the self-righteous notion that Franco was leading a Christian crusade in Spain against the godless hordes of communism. All three had been former supporters of either the Action Française or the Fédération Nationale Catholique, but what they observed about the Spanish situation appalled them. Maritain affirmed that war was a "profane and secular" matter; to call it sacred was a sacrilege. Mauriac had no sympathy for communism, but he refused to tolerate the notion that the word "crusade" could be used to cover fascist violence or rebellion against a legitimate government. Hitler's bombing of the defenseless shrine town of Guernica in 1937 united these conservative writers with both Catholic moderates and radicals. A protest manifesto called "For the Basque People" was published by *L'Aube* and signed by representatives of all shades of Catholic opinion with the exception of the powerful Catholic right. Joined with the signatures of Francisque Gay, Georges Bidault, Emmanuel Mounier, and Georges Hoog were those of Jacques Maritain and François Mauriac. Even in the midst of crisis, a few thoughtful conservatives had turned toward the Catholic progressives.[27]

Nevertheless, by mid-1937 deep rifts separated French Catholics from each other, and the events in Spain had exacerbated these to the breaking point. Since the outbreak of street violence in Paris on the night of February 6, 1934, the fabric of Second Ralliement unity had begun to unravel. Locarno optimism had served to conceal its superficiality and to hide the deeply rooted hostilities that still polarized the French church. The crises of the middle 1930s exposed these fissures to the public. Events in Spain and the Popular Front put the fragile Ralliement and its reputed dedication to Catholic pluralism on trial. That it failed this test was due, in no small measure, to the fears of the massive Catholic right. Convinced that moderates and radicals within the church were part of a revolutionary wave that threatened both Catholicism and France, the nation's hierarchy, *La Croix,* and the Fédération Nationale Catholique inaugurated a campaign designed to purge the church of such "cryptocommunists."

From 1936 until the outbreak of war, this concerted effort by Catholic ultras succeeded in destroying or isolating their foes within Catholicism. In three short years, the Second Ralliement lay in ruins. The first casualty was the Marxist-Christian *Terre Nouvelle.* Given the crusading anticommunism of French Catholic rightists and given the moderates' inflexible suspicion toward Marxism, it is not surprising that Laudrain's review was soon condemned officially by the church. Both General de Castelnau and *La Croix* despised *Terre Nouvelle* and accused it of flagrant violation of the Christian gospel. *L'Aube*'s Christian Democrats distanced themselves from it publicly, and even the more radical Emmanuel Mounier criticized the Marxist review's attempts to marry Christianity with a particular socioeconomic value system. Such isolation made it a ready victim for the hierarchical assaults that were soon to come. On February 15, 1936, less than a year after its birth, the Vigilance Council of the archdiocese of Paris warned Catholics against the review. Other dioceses soon followed, and in the summer of that year the nation's cardinals and archbishops condemned it by public resolution.[28]

Terre Nouvelle was not the sole victim of rightist Catholic assaults. Other *ralliés*, both radical and moderate, were harassed by right-wing Catholics. The Fédération Nationale Catholique attacked the Jeune République for joining a coalition with Marxists, and General de Castelnau stigmatized all those willing to march to the strains of the *Internationale*. He assailed the review *Esprit* continually, and Mounier felt compelled to defend himself against the charge that he was a "leftist Catholic." Reminiscent of the crossfire over the Briey affair, *Sept* was singled out for special abuse. When the Dominican-inspired weekly interviewed Premier Léon Blum early in 1937, the FNC monthly *Credo* accused it of sympathy for the leftist government, and *La Croix* felt that the interview was tacit acceptance of the condemned *main tendue*.[29] By the height of the Popular Front period, Catholic moderates and radicals were manifestly on the defensive and increasingly isolated. The Catholic polarization of this crisis era worked clearly to the detriment of the church's progressives.

However, it was the entry of the Vatican into the fray that wrecked the Second Ralliement decisively. The signs of the Holy See's rightist preferences were not immediately obvious in the early 1930s, but as crises came to dominate the European scene, Pius XI felt the necessity of identifying himself more openly with fascists and conservatives within France and elsewhere. The growing success of leftists, and especially communists, in western Europe increased his already militant antibolshevism. With a Popular Front government in France and pro-Loyalist Marxists in Spain, the pontiff felt compelled to draft his definitive encyclical *Divini Redemptoris* (March 1937). In it he called upon the world's Catholic church to take up the anticommunist crusade which the French Catholic traditionalists had been advocating for some time. Marxism was the enemy of the family, individual liberties, and authority, as well as the scourge "of Christian civilization." Only a return by modern society to the church and the state's support of ecclesiastical privilege could stem the Bolshevist tide. Central to the encyclical was a categorical rejection of the *main tendue* and the notion of the popular front: "Communism is intrinsically wrong, and no one who would save civilization may collaborate with it in any undertaking whatsoever."[30] *Divini Redemptoris* was Pius XI's marching orders for all Catholics to unite behind hierarchical religious defense and militant anticommunism. Anything less than that, in such critical times, would not be tolerated. This unequivocal condemnation of Catholic-Marxist cooperation had a direct impact on Catholic progressives. The Vatican had banned *Terre Nouvelle* earlier, and Emmanuel Mounier felt isolated by and defensive about his relationship to the encyclical. Francisque Gay continued to uphold his newspaper's orthodoxy; nevertheless, the Vatican intervened twice to warn *L'Aube* to exercize greater caution in what it printed. However, it was the Dominicans of Juvisy who felt the papal blows most heavily. Shortly after *Sept*'s interview with Léon Blum, the Vatican intervened to close down the newspaper. Although monetary matters was the public reason given for the demise, Pius XI had instructed the French Dominican superior to force the weekly's termination. Its sister publication *La Vie Intellectuelle* faced a similar condemnation several months later for suggesting that the church's problems were, in part, her own fault. Under Roman pressure, the author of the offensive article and the Dominican review sent formal retractions to the Holy See. Only a direct appeal by Cardinal Liénart to Rome saved *La Vie Intellectuelle* from extinction.[31] Vatican intervention against the church's moderates and radicals undermined deeply Catholic pluralist and progressive ventures in France. Within a brief decade the euphoria among prorepublican Catholics over the condemnation of the Action Française had given way to despair and isolation. They had been forced into a defensive rearguard action by the massive Catholic right in France. By openly siding with the conservatives and counterrevolutionaries, Pius XI lay to rest the short-lived Ralliement.

Why had the pope of Catholic Briandism made such a choice? Why did the pontiff who had condemned the reactionary Action Française act so hastily against the very forces he had liberated in the 1920s? Why did his defense of the working class allow no room for cooperation with Marxists? Why was he so harsh against

Catholic moderates when he seemed to be the avowed enemy of both leftist and rightist extremes? The most obvious response to these questions is that the pressure of events had forced the pontiff to reassess his previous more moderate judgments. Compromise with or abandonment of earlier tactics seemed necessary in the face of the graver dangers experienced in the mid-1930s. The need for international stability and the destruction of communism came to be judged as more vital than the integrity of constitutional governments and the League of Nations. This shift in polity became apparent in both the Ethiopian crisis and the Spanish Civil War. Mussolini's blatant aggression against the sovereign state of Abyssinia in 1935 put the pope in an obviously embarrassing position. On the one hand, the tiny African nation was a member of the League of Nations, and on the other hand, Italy's strength was vitally necessary to resist potential hostile acts by Germany against corporatist and Catholic Austria. Pius XI sought to maintain the peace via a negotiated settlement which would satisfy some of Fascist Italy's expansionist hunger. In this way moderation would prevail and war would be averted. National sovereignty and the integrity of the Wilsonian league were secondary concerns to the Vatican in the matter.[32] Papal hesitancy and equivocation in this crisis indicated that Catholic Briandism had become an expendable policy, at least outside Europe. The Holy See's response to events in Spain would demonstrate that with respect to Europe.

From the beginning of the Spanish republic, Pius XI had endorsed the reactionary and conservative pro-Catholic elements in Spain who had patterned themselves after the corporatist regime of Engelbert Dollfuss in Austria. Initially, this support was couched behind a circumspect neutrality. However, with the outbreak of civil war, the Holy See began to look with favor more openly upon the rebellious generals. With the passage of time the pope's crusading anticommunism became more obvious. Without mentioning the Nationalists by name, the pontiff praised those in Spain who had undertaken the "perilous task of defending and restoring God's rights and honor as well as religion." By the summer of 1938, when a Franco victory seemed certain, the Vatican established diplomatic relations with the rebels.[33] Once again the Holy See had abandoned Catholic Briandism, and once again the pope turned his back on the League of Nations. The crusade to curb communism and defend occidental civilization with its ecclesiastical privileges was given priority over the sovereign integrity of nation states. Franco and his generals had revolted against a legally constituted nation which was a member state in the League of Nations. This and the intervention on the Nationalist side by Fascist Italy and Nazi Germany were ignored by the Vatican in virtue of the fact that this illegality was in the name of religious defense and crusading anticommunism. The papacy could not even tolerate a mild article in *La Croix* which had suggested that a genuine Christian crusade may not be on either side in the civil war.[34]

In spite of this seeming shift, it would be a distortion of the whole picture to suggest that the spectre of communism in Popular Front France and Loyalist Spain caused Pius XI to abandon his progressive Ralliement. Indeed, there is good reason to believe that the pontiff had always viewed his program with conservative and counterrevolutionary eyes. To be sure, the Christian Democrats and Catholic leftists had viewed his condemnation of the Action Française, his peace with the French republic, his Briandist policies, and his working-class concerns through their own eyes, but such wishful thinking is hardly proof for their convictions. It is a mistake to identify the Catholic pluralism of the 1920s and 1930s with papal intentions unless Pius XI would have endorsed these emerging groups in the name of their democratic values. Such was not the case. Either he tolerated them until they clashed with his anticommunism in the mid-1930s, or he adopted them for purposes of his own. To be sure, the crises of the Popular Front period intensified his counterrevolutionary convictions, yet his entire pontificate had been built consistently upon conservative religious defense and antibolshevism. Those elements of his program that had earned for him a reputation as a progressive pope were, in fact, outgrowths of his more rightist concerns. His peace with the Third Republic was an attempt to safeguard the fortunes of the French church, and his condemnation of the

Action Française was chiefly a victory of one authoritarian competitor over another. The pontiff's Briandism was patterned after the position of *La Croix* rather than the moderate convictions of *L'Aube* or the dreams of the Jeune République. Pius XI advocated international collaboration under the arbitration of the Vatican rather than the League of Nations, which was felt to be inspired by some heretical notions. Cooperation between the League of Nations and the Holy See required the supremacy of the latter over the former. Further, concordats with the separate conservative powers would be used along with the League of Nations to curb the Bolshevik menace and preserve the social order. This explains why Pius XI favored the de Castelnau variety of Catholic Action above all others, even when the FNC vacillated in its loyalty to the papal program.[35] Finally, the pope's identification with the proletariat was based upon the traditional social Catholicism of the preceding century as well as the needs of his anti-Marxist crusade. He and his bishops endorsed the Jeunesse Ouvrière Chrétienne because they saw it as an effective means to bring the workers back under the church's control in order to use them in anticommunist campaigns. The Jocistes were to be an anti-Bolshevik "apostolic army" that would stabilize the social order "by perfect submission to the hierarchy and by obedience to its high and luminous instructions." Similar reasons accounted for the papal vindication of the Confédération Française des Travailleurs Chrétiens in the textile conflicts in the French Nord. His holiness insisted that Catholic industrialists accept the CFTC because it was endorsed by the hierarchy and was dedicated to "social peace" and "social Catholic morality." Further, it repudiated "class struggle and collectivism in principle" and advocated class cooperation in their place. Most important, the pontiff viewed the CFTC as a Christian bulwark against "socialist and communist trade unionism." Like the JOC, the Catholic unions were to be "a dike" against "the religious apostasy provoked among the toiling masses" and against the "impressive progress of socialism and communism." A careful study of *Quadragesimo Anno* reveals a similar counterrevolutionary social Catholicism. Marxism was declared to be a far graver danger than capitalism, and the state was called upon to regulate the economy so that communist and independent trade unions would not take root. Class cooperation would be enforced by the government, and the professional organizations advocated by the pontiff were modeled upon Italian fascist corporatism. *Quadragesimo Anno*'s repudiation of the right to strike was the final indicator that working-class independence was alien to the social doctrine of Pius XI. The pope's dedication to the proletariat was built upon the foundation of charitable paternalism, religious defense, and anticommunism.[36] Counterrevolution, reactionary visions, and pragmatic conservatism had characterized the papal program since *Ubi Arcano Dei.*

However, is this judgment entirely fair? Must not the antileftist militancy of Pius XI be offset by his bold stands against the fascist right? Do not his encyclicals against extremists of the left and right suggest that the pope had earned a well-deserved reputation as the foe of all totalitarianism whatever its color? This was certainly the interpretation of France's Christian Democrats at the time.[37] Pius XI's antifascist fame is based upon two encyclicals and the events surrounding them. *Non abbiamo bisogno* (1931) was a protest against Mussolini's government, and *Mit brennender Sorge* (1937) was directed against Nazi Germany. However, a close examination of both the content and context of the two letters demonstrates that the pontiff's judgments on these two fascist states were compromisng and equivocal. By way of contrast, his *Divini Redemptoris* was a total condemnation of communism and any collaboration with it whatsoever. Further, it was published as a definitive encyclical for the entire church. The other two missives were limited in both scope and audience. Like the papalists who had castigated the excessive nationalism of the Action Française, the Holy See condemned any elements of totalitarian nationalism that might characterize both fascist Italy and Nazi Germany. In both instances Pius XI attacked the state's attempt to eliminate competing Catholic youth groups and suggested that such efforts not only violated the church's rights but also exalted the nation to a divine status. In even stronger language, the pontiff had warned Hitler's Germany against the dangers of racism. Catholic progressives throughout Europe saw these judgments as signs of the Holy Father's commitment against rightist tyranny. However, it must be noted that the papal critiques were not designed to make definitive breaks with either regime. To the contrary, the pope was appealing indirectly to both governments to act moderately and thus honor the concordats they had signed previously with the church. At issue for the Vatican was neither totalitarianism in general nor human liberties. Instead, the Holy See was engaging in an authority struggle over the question of who was to control Catholic youth. In both instances Pius XI was resisting overt governmental attempts to emasculate Catholic Action by the forced integration of all young people into state organizations. In the hope of convincing both the fascist and Nazi regimes to respect the freedom they had promised previously to ecclesiastical institutions, the two encyclicals employed moderate language and praised the contributions that both dictators had made to their respective societies.[38] The significant difference in content between these two papal documents and *Divini Redemptoris* is that in the former potential partners were being described, while in the latter the satanic foes of the church were being condemned.

Even the broader historical context of *Non abbiamo bisogno* and *Mit brennender Sorge* was radically different from that of the anticommunist encyclical. The latter was a document addressed to all Catholics ordering them to participate in an anti-Marxist crusade in order to save civilization. Dialogue was not an issue. The enemy was defined clearly, and Catholics were expected to join up without equivocation. Meanwhile, the former two encyclicals were expressions of wounded outrage that regimes which the Vatican had welcomed earlier were now disappointing the church sorely. Over the years Pius XI had lauded both governments for their law-and-order positions, for their patriotism, and for their antibolshevism. In fact, his concern to regularize diplomatic relations with both states, whether with Fascist Italy by the Lateran Accords (1929) or with Nazi Germany by the concordat of 1933, included a willingness to aid both states in destroying their independent Catholic political parties and their autonomous confessional trade unions. The pontiff had hoped, by such agreements, both to restore control of lay Catholic organizations to the hierarchy and to insure, by the route of diplomacy, an acceptable means whereby the Vatican might negotiate its interests directly with each state in the name of all Catholics within that land. As in the case of the Action Française's condemnation, the issue was one of authority. Who would control Catholic youth? Who would have ultimate authority over Catholic Action? As long as the radical right provided privileges, prestige, and independence for the church, and while it spent its energies against the threatening left, it would receive the Vatican's blessing or, at least, its benign silence. Fascism's and Nazism's violation of civic rights and democratic freedoms, even their disregard of human life, were not at issue. Indeed, the Holy See had contrived with both to destroy Catholic democratic organizations that were not under hierarchical control.[39]

Certainly Pius XI's anticommunism cannot be questioned, but there is serious doubt that his critique of the extreme right could begin to match his intransigent hatred of the Marxist left. His misgivings about such ultrarightist manifestations as Maurras's integral nationalism, Mussolini's fascism, and Hitler's Nazism were sporadic and limited, as was his temporary willingness to let Catholic pluralism flourish in France. However, what remained constant throughout his long reign was his commitment to the restoration of a hierarchically controlled Catholic order in Europe that would aid in the destruction of communism root and branch. Even his brief acceptance of some progressive Catholic forces and his anathema toward certain Catholic reactionaries fit into this broader program, a program pursued singlemindedly from *Ubi Arcano Dei* to his death shortly before the Franco forces entered Madrid in 1939. Conservative authoritarianism and counterrevolution characterized his long reign and gave it consistency. This explains why he adopted the Second Ralliement in the 1920s and why he abandoned it in the 1930s. This accounts for his condemnation of the Action Française in 1926 as well as its reprieve in 1939.

The last decade of the Third Republic marked the nadir of Action Française influence in France in general and among French

Catholics in particular. Censure by the church had marked the beginning of its serious decline, and by the mid-1930s, the Maurrasians found themselves challenged by new more aggressive groups on the ultraright. Leagues like the Croix de Feu, Solidarité Française, and Jeunesses Patriotes were beginning to draw members from constituencies that used to be the exclusive preserve of the integral nationalists. The aging leadership of the organization was locked into place, and the creative potential of younger, more dynamic forces was not welcome. Circulation of the newspaper declined, and even the royalist pretender turned against the league which had served him for almost forty years. To be sure, there were a few optimistic points to be noted by the struggling monarchists. Charles Maurras, their elder statesman, was invited to become a member of the Académie Française, an indication that his organization's philosophy had won a respectable place in the conservative sectors of French society. Finally, the league received a pardon from the Catholic church less than a year before the Republic voted itself out of existence.[40]

The turn of events in Europe, combined with changes both at Rome and in the bureaus of the Action Française, accounts for the Vatican's volte-face toward its royalist foes in France. For their part, the aggrieved Maurrasians softened their anti-Catholic attacks over the years. Sporadic assaults against members of the French hierarchy continued throughout the mid-1930s, and the "Sous la terreur" column would still appear from time to time. The Vatican's ambassador to France, Msgr. Maglione, came under occasional fire in the context of the league's accusation that there was a continued "entente between Aristide and the nuncio against the Action Française." In contrast, its hostility toward moderate and radical Catholics did not slacken. In a spirit of vituperation akin to that of the FNC, the Maurrasians castigated their most vocal Catholic enemies. *Terre Nouvelle* was described as a "frightful outrage against Christ" which deserved richly the anathema the church had bestowed upon it. *Sept* was charged with supporting the Popular Front and the Blum government. However, most of the Maurrasian rancor was directed against the Christian Democrats. Marc Sangnier, Francisque Gay, and Georges Bidault were accused of defending "Red atrocities" in Spain. Indeed, they were "phony Catholics," affirmed the royalist daily. *L'Aube* was condemned for siding with those very procommunists that the hierarchy had anathematized so roundly. Finally, the integral nationalists stood side by side with *L'Osservatore Romano*'s critique of the Catholic intellectuals who had protested the bombing of Guernica.[41]

This odium contrasted sharply with a growing mellowness toward Pius XI. His public discourses received increasing praise from the Maurrasians, and his crusading anticommunism was akin to the league's own policy. Integral nationalist hostility to the Popular Front and the Spanish Loyalist cause knew no bounds. The cry of its daily to "vote against revolution and war" was an appeal to all the French to keep Moscow out of the nation's affairs, and the formation of the Blum government occasioned a new outburst of anti-Semitism from the royalists. Maurice Thorez's *main tendue* was rejected categorically as an act of hypocrisy. *L'Action Française* daily reported the "outrages of Red terror" perpetrated upon the Spanish church, but it spoke of the Franco forces as "combatants of holy war" in the cause of the "Sacred Heart and the crucifix." The Maurrasian perception of the civil war in Spain was clearly one of a religious crusade. A definitive choice had to be made "between two Spains, or to put it better, between two civilizations—that of Russia, which is only a form of barbarism, and that of Christianity, which Spain has honored for centuries and for which she has been an invincible champion."[42]

Quite likely it was this crusade mentality versus communism which was the single leading factor in the success of the campaign to reconcile the Action Française with the papacy. Older hostilities were fading gradually in the face of greater perceived threats. As early as 1929, the royalist sympathizer Cardinal Pacelli, who was not yet papal secretary of state, had asked the Carmelite order of nuns at Lisieux to offer prayers that God might help to settle the tragic Action Française controversy. Six years later, the prior of the order, Mother Agnes, told Pius XI of a young Carmelite nun who had spent all her time in prayer for Charles Maurras until the moment of her death. These incidents served as preludes to the correspondence between Maurras and the pope. While in prison in 1937 for some libelous threats, the aging integral nationalist began brooding over his spiritual life and his relationship to the church. These religious wrestlings led him to draft a letter to Pius XI. In it he promised the pontiff that he would make an annual pilgrimage to Lisieux after his release from jail to express his gratitude both for the Carmelite sister's prayers and for the reigning pope himself. Maurras concluded with a profession of loyalty to the Vatican's anticommunist crusade. Pius XI responded by sending his gratitude and personal benediction to the imprisoned royalist. Encouraged by this reply, the Action Française leader sought to press his case. Once again he praised the Holy See's "glorious crusade against communism" and the pope's "exalted benediction . . . upon the forces of order and peace." Then he made his appeal for a reopening of the case against the condemned monarchists, concluding with the observation that "the enemies of the Action Française are the enemies of the forces for order, the fatherland, the church and the papacy."[43]

Upon his release from prison, Maurras began his yearly pilgrimages to Lisieux. Accompanied by the papal blessing and by Robert de Boisfleury, another Action Française militant, he made his way to the shrine of Saint Thérèse of the Infant Jesus. It was the summer of 1937. Meanwhile negotiations continued in the hope that the papal anathema would be lifted. Georges Goyau, a member of the Académie Française and a conservative Catholic, was able to construct a formula of submission that was agreeable both to Action Française Catholics and the agnostic Maurras. Then Goyau turned to Father Gillet, the Dominican superior who had ordered the termination of *Sept* under Vatican orders, and pleaded with him to intervene with Rome on the royalists' behalf. Gillet agreed to do all that he could in a gesture of religious peace, but his efforts were stalled temporarily by the death of Pius XI early in 1939. The new pope, Pius XII, was eager to effect the reconciliation according to the submission formula designed by Goyau. After some stubborn hesitation on the part of Léon Daudet, the entire leadership of the Action Française signed the document. The royalists promised to reject all erroneous doctrines and comply publicly with "the directives of ecclesiastical authority" in those socioeconomic areas which the hierarchy felt related to divine concerns. Pius XII responded to this document on July 10, 1939, by publicly accepting the Maurrasians' professions of loyalty and by removing their newspaper from the Index. The Action Française had been reprieved.[44]

The restoration of the integral nationalists had gone hand in hand with the collapse of the Second Ralliement. Condemned and isolated French Catholic progressives watched their former enemy's return to favor in the context of their own defeat. Nevertheless, the resurrected royalists never returned to their former prominence within French Catholic circles. A monarchical revival seemed passé in the light of more aggressive rightist forces which were coming to enjoy the favor of pope and traditional French Catholics alike. The moment had passed for the declining Maurrasians and their aging chiefs. Integral nationalists were welcome to join with the church's leadership in its campaign to restore a conservative social order at the expense of leftist democrats and godless communists. Never again could they lead this crusade in the name of Catholicism. Maurrasians and their league were no longer a danger to the hierarchical authority of the church. They were only one ally among many, and a weak and declining one at that. The collapse of the Third Republic did nothing to change this. The emergence of Philippe Pétain and Vichy both cemented and brought to and end the stormy relationship that had existed between the Catholic Church and the Action Française.

+ 10 +

The Final Reckoning

*W*hen the Third Republic crumbled under the force of the Wehrmacht's assaults and gave way to the authoritarian regime of Marshal Pétain, it was a dream come true for both the Action Française and those sectors of the Catholic church that had buried the Second Ralliement. For Charles Maurras, the government of defeat was "a divine surprise" in the sense that he saw in the aged Pétain the beginnings of a national renaissance that would unite the *pays légal* with the *pays réel* in a way that had not been experienced in his lifetime. Certainly, he did not mourn the death of the Republic; neither was he pleased with the German occupation. He sought to resolve this dilemma by endorsing the Vichy government as if it were truly a sovereign entity. To be sure, *L'Action Française* could support wholeheartedly the anti-Bolshevist crusades of the early 1940s, but Maurras became increasingly outraged as more and more of his followers and fellow travelers linked themselves uncritically with Waffen SS programs. Throughout the Vichy period, the integrist newspaper sought to preserve itself as a proud and independent voice, and to some extent was able to do just that. It accepted no subsidies either from the Germans or from Vichy, although it did benefit from the regime's publicity. In the narrowest sense *L'Action Française* was not collaborationist. It stood for Pétain against both Nazi absorption and an allied victory. During the early years, it lauded Vichy legislation against foreigners, Masons and especially the Jews. Further it welcomed the pro-Catholic and corporative solutions proclaimed by the National Revolution. Britain and the Soviet Union remained for France significantly greater dangers than the German occupying forces. Throughout the war years, De Gaulle and the free French were viewed as traitors. At the same time, the more rightist organizations, which argued for direct collaboration with the Germans, were treated critically by Maurras. His loyalty was to the Pétain government, and as such, he lashed out against both the Resistance and the pro-Nazi rightists.

However, in the broadest sense, Maurras and his newspaper were collaborationist. His commitment to Vichy meant an acceptance of military defeat and occupation and a willingness to live in a German-dominated Europe. An authoritarian regime, dedicated to hating the same enemies as the Action Française, was far more tolerable than a republican France. Maurras's myopic *pays réel* was more palatable than a truly free France, if the latter were a democracy granting equal rights to Masons, communists and Jews. The illusion that Vichy was a truly independent alternative between the Resistance and avid French Nazis belied the regime's collaborationist reality. Both the government and Maurras had accepted the Nazi order in Europe, albeit reluctantly. The peace they advocated envisioned a serious place for France in the new scheme of things. Nazi Germany and its extremist French friends were criticized, perhaps feared, but they were still seen as rivals within the same camp. For integral nationalists, both the Allies and the Resistance meant war, chaos, and the spectre of communism. The former were stumbling blocks to the Maurrasian dream; the latter were harbingers of total destruction. In this sense, the Action Française was in the collaborationist camp. That the trial of Charles Maurras after the Liberation was colored by a patriotic spirit of revenge cannot be doubted. Equally clear was the fact that he had used his influence against all those forces that had joined to free French soil from the occupiers.

By the 1940s the Action Française had been reduced largely to one person and his ideology. The organizational apparatus of the league had persisted in its decline, and the ravages of age had continued to decimate the leadership. France's defeat drove the already ill Daudet into retirement. Soon thereafter, in 1942, he died. Occupying Germans in Paris forced a hasty transfer of the league's office to the free zone. By that time, the Action Française had been reduced to its newspaper, which had become almost exclusively the voice of one man. To be sure, some student militant groups of the league survived in a few of the major southern cities, but for most, the Action Française had become Charles Maurras. Under his efforts, and with the assistance of Maurice Pujo, the newspaper continued to appear, first in Limoges, then in Lyon, until that city was liberated. However, in the nation as a whole, his was a declining presence. Age and the vicissitudes of history had forced both Maurras and the Action Française into a marginal position in French political life since the late 1920s. Pétain's regime confirmed that reality.

Nonetheless, Maurrasian ideology thrived in Vichy. France and the Maréchal's government drew heavily upon the values of order, authority, hierarchy, fearful patriotism, anti-Semitism, and anticommunism which the integral nationalist philosopher had developed so effectively in the preceding decades. Only royalism seemed to be absent, but even this conviction proved flexible enough to permit Maurras to applaud the Vichy regime uncritically. Authoritarianism had triumphed over monarchism. Powerful manifestations of this ideology permeated the government's rhetoric and legislation. Indeed, even before the war, integral nationalism was experiencing a resurgence in intellectual circles. The entry of Maurras into the Académie Française acknowledged that. Vichy incorporated this revival into its educational establishment, forcing competitive ideologies underground. The profound intellectual survival of this tradition was in sharp contrast to any direct influence either of the declining Action Française or the aging Charles Maurras upon Vichy France, let alone the Catholic church.[1]

Any relationship between Catholicism and the royalist league in the 1940s was minimal, except for this parallel ideology and the church's attitude toward the government of Philippe Pétain.

In effect, what the Action Française had meant to contending Catholics in 1910 and 1926 was represented by the Vichy regime in the early 1940s. On the one hand, the vast majority of prominent Catholics welcomed and embraced the new government. Led by the episcopate, most of Catholic France greeted the new regime and its aged leader with unbridled enthusiasm. The military disaster was viewed as God's judgment upon the secular and anticlerical republic, and Pétain was the Lord's chosen deliverer who would restore the apostate nation to the church of Christ. Especially welcomed were those laws that returned Catholicism to a prominent place in the nation's educational structure. So supportive was much of the regime's legislation to ecclesiastical concerns that the church was able, for the most part, to ignore Vichy's anti-Semitic laws. Overriding all particular reasons for Catholicism's endorsement of the Pétain government was its ideology and authoritarianism. Overall, Vichy represented order, tradition, authority, hierarchy, social peace, and anticommunism—values that had been advocated by the nation's church hierarchy, *La Croix,* the Fédération Nationale Catholique, and the Vatican during the interwar years. Even some Catholic progressives were attracted to Pétain and his rule. Emmanuel Mounier was impressed initially by the regime's rhetoric promising a national revolution, and the Jeunesse Ouvrière Chrétienne welcomed its class collaborationist principles and the support that its elderly leader gave to Catholic Action youth groups. Few leading Catholics were blatant collaborators, Msgr. Alfred Baudrillart of the Institut Catholique de Paris and Philippe Henriot of the FNC being notable exceptions. Nevertheless, the loyalty of most Catholic elites to Pétain and his government moved far beyond the realm of simple pragmatics.[2]

On the other hand, a minority of Christian Democrats and progressives turned to the uncertain road of resistance. From the beginning of the regime, a number of Catholics from every political persuasion refused to accept defeat and collaboration. Even some members of the Action Française belonged to this handful of early resisters. However, the heart of Catholic opposition to Hitler and his French collaborators were the consciously democratic elements of the shattered Second Ralliement. Activists of the Parti Démocrate Populaire, the Jeune République, *Sept*, *L'Aube*, the Catholic trade unions, and left-wing Jocistes gravitated increasingly to the Resistance. Georges Bidault, Francisque Gay, Marc Sangnier, and later Emmanuel Mounier were the most prominent figures from the 1930s who joined opposition movements against the occupiers as well as Vichy. Democratic Catholics also formed the backbone of the *Témoignage Chrétien* movement, which had been organized by the Jesuit theologian Pierre Chaillet. Even most of the Catholic *maquisards*, priest and lay, had received their baptism of fire in the progressive movements of the interwar period. Nevertheless, it was the collaboration of Vichy with the Nazi-inspired forced labor program that drove large masses of Catholics into direct opposition. This Service du Travail Obligatoire prompted large numbers of Jocistes to turn against the regime and caused a few of the nation's prelates to doubt the Catholic loyalty of the collaborationist government. In spite of this mounting resistance, most of the church's leadership continued to support Vichy while regretting its excesses and sometimes ministering to its victims.[3]

This autonomous, progressive, and lay character of Catholics in the Resistance was vital to the shape that French Catholicism would take in the postwar period. Collaboration on the part of the hierarchy had compromised the bishops' reputation, and traditional conservative Catholicism had been discredited by its pro-Vichy behavior during the war. Consequently, the avant-garde of the nation's church was constituted by those elements of the laity and lower clergy who had been victims of the Second Ralliement's destruction and who were victors in the Resistance. Armed with their antifascist credentials, they formed a powerful force of creativity within French Catholicism that produced manifold alternatives to monolithic ecclesiastical traditionalism. A massive Christian Democratic party, the Mouvement Républicain Populaire, emerged from the fires of Resistance, and *Témoignage Chrétien* became the first leftist newspaper officially recognized as part of the Catholic press. Communist-Catholic cooperation, made necessary by anti-Nazi activity, continued at many levels from the halls of government to the working-class ghettos and factories.[4]

From the more visionary prelates to the lay masses of the Jeunesse Ouvrière Chrétienne and the Action Catholique Ouvrière, a new spirit of mission permeated the French church after the war. Catholicism began to welcome a revolutionary future as much as it had yearned previously for a lost past or a stable present. For some, it was no longer a question of accepting a republican government and democratic political ideas. Instead, they rejected French Revolutionary and liberal values in the name of a more egalitarian society struggling to be born out of a decaying brutal capitalism. Cardinals like Suhard of Paris, Liénart of Lille, and Gerlier of Lyon believed firmly that worker-priests, proletarian Catholic Action, working-class parishes, and a missionary-trained clergy could offer French workers a serious alternative to classical Marxism by way of militant example rather than by a sterile and negative crusade. For their part, these working-class apostolates, endorsed by *Esprit* and the more radical Jeunesse de l'Eglise *équipe*, were convinced that the revolutionary proletariat was the vanguard of an emerging more just humanity. They wanted to be a Christian presence in this process, the "leaven in the lump."[5] The Vatican's attempt to circumscribe this Ralliement resurgence chilled some of its optimism, but it was too strong, too deeply rooted, to be destroyed. This revolutionary élan survived the death of Pius XII and came to be a decisive force in the reigns of his two successors and in the chambers of Vatican II. For the first time in modern history, progressive sectors within Catholicism had penetrated the citadels of the Holy See successfully, and the impetus had come from France.[6]

Forces for substantive religious and societal change have struggled for two centuries against ecclesiastical conservatives within French Catholicism. The impact of the French Revolution and the radical transformation of Europe's socioeconomic order threatened the stability and status of the Catholic church and defined the nature of its subsequent internal struggles. A tiny minority of militant Catholics sought to adapt the church to these new and ominous forces. They felt that democracy and revolution could be christianized. Reactionary and conservative Catholics believed that the church was being confronted with mortal enemies. Consequently, they endorsed an implacable crusade against those within and outside Catholicism who were prepared to make peace with post-French Revolutionary society. At issue was the very survival of the Catholic church, a fact recognized by the contending parties. Since 1789, French Catholics have been in the midst of this conflict. Until the defeat of Louis Napoleon in 1870, a fortress mentality prevailed within Catholicism, and the church progressives were isolated voices crying in the wilderness. After the fall of Vichy, influence and initiative were in the hands of *ralliè* forces, and ecclesiastical reaction was on the defensive. The First Vatican Council defined the victory of the Catholic ultras, and the Second Vatican Council marked the triumph of Catholicism's liberals and radicals. Between these two events were the protracted church conflicts of the Third Republic. Its seventy-year existence formed the backdrop for an intensification of conflict within ecclesiastical institutions. The republic's official anticlericalism stirred these passions even more. From Dreyfus to Pétain, the strife continued and intensified during the decade of the Separation Law and in the turbulent 1930s. Sometimes the "preserve and protect" Catholics won decisive battles only to discover that the "change and expand" Catholics had survived, adapted their tactics and were continuing to grow. The former represented the mentality of Vatican I, and the latter were harbingers of *aggiornamento,* the dialogue spirit of Vatican II. On two occasions the forces for change rose up to challenge the conservative dominance within French Catholicism. Convinced that the Holy See was prepared to adopt their cause, they identified with the two Ralliements that had come from Rome. In both instances they were wrong, and were soon crushed by the more powerful rightists within the church. The papal Ralliements had been largely tactical variations of Vatican I. Until the fortunes of war and resistance struck their decisive blows against the pro-Pétain rightists, French Catholic progressives were a defensive and vulnerable minority. With the fall of Hitler's new order in Europe, the balance of power swung to the *ralliés,* and they began their long march toward Vatican II.

In this context of French crisis and Catholic polarization, the Action Française was born, grew, dominated the nation's political right, and declined. For the last forty years of the Third Republic, its values and membership linked it inexorably with the Catholic church. The study of this relationship and the events which shaped it illuminates one significant facet of the larger struggle within Catholicism between the forces of order and the forces of change. The church's temporary alliance with the Maurrasians was not predicated upon a point-by-point ideological solidarity. It was rather an overall mentality that drew the two groups together. Both Catholic rightists and integral nationalists shared a fortress mentality. They feared change and yearned for a past society which was orderly, hierarchical, authoritarian, and which accorded prominence and privilege to the Catholic church. In the midst of anticlerical crises they possessed a common foe—the republican state, run by Masons and socialists and constructed upon anti-Catholic and revolutionary values. In this context, the Action Française became a powerful ally when the French and Vatican churches felt they had few friends. Only the Christian Democrats remained resolute foes of the Maurrasians, but until the interwar period they were in no position to mount an effective opposition. By the time the church had made its peace with the Third Republic in the early 1920s, the Action Française had outlived its usefulness to Catholicism. Its rigidity, its autonomy from the ecclesiastical hierarchy, and its refusal to adapt to changed Vatican tactics caused Pius XI to condemn it in 1926. In one blow the pontiff crushed one of his serious rivals in France. Only months before the outbreak of World War II was the anathema lifted. By then the Action Française had ceased to be a competitor for anyone, let alone the church.[7]

For its part, Catholicism was a vast organization with a long history of struggles. It had weathered internal and external storms of great magnitude. Its concerns had always been supernational, and its seeming monolithic visage was only a public image covering great diversity. Without this pluralism, internal conflict would never have been serious. The church's temporary alliance with the Action Française was only a marriage of convenience. What was helpful to ecclesiastical interests in the church-state wars of 1905 had become a liability when tactical change was required in 1926. Thirteen years later the Maurrasians could be forgiven and permitted to join the church's anticommunist crusade as one minor ally among several major ones. By then the Action Française was fading into the dust of history, but for forty years it had played a significant role by casting its lot with a certain kind of Catholicism. When the fortunes of Christian Democracy were at their nadir, the league's Catholic reputation was on the rise, but when the church's progressives were in the ascendent, Maurrasian religious credentials were called into question. The royalist organization had been the victor in the counterrevolutionary phases of the French church battles, yet at another time, it had become the victim of Ralliement upsurges within ecclesiastical circles. The stormy relationship between the Catholic church and the Action Française mirrored the French church's conflicts in the last half of the Third Republic. This ambivalent alliance was a barometer of the internal warfare within French Catholicism between the forces of order and the forces of change, between the church of the past and the church of the future.

Notes
Bibliography
Index

Notes

Chapter 1. A Church in Conflict

1. A good summary of the Gallican church during the ancien regime and the French Revolution is McManners, *The French Revolution and the Church*. On the continuing conflict between French Catholicism and post-French Revolutionary society, see Dansette, *Religious History of Modern France*.

2. Details of this sociological picture may be found in Larkin, *Church and State*, pp. 7, 10; Boulard, *Introduction to Religious Sociology*, pp. 28–395; Ariès, *Histoire des populations françaises*, p. 461; and Le Bras, *Etudes de sociologie religieuse* 1:69–84, 207–10.

3. On church-state conflicts in the first decades of the Third Republic, see Dansette, *Religious History of Modern France;* McManners, *Church and State;* and Helmreich. *A Free Church in a Free State?*

4. The most thorough work in English about the Ralliement is Sedgwick, *The Ralliement in French Politics*.

5. These views may be noted in the movement's publication, *L'Association Catholique*. Some examples are H. Danzas, "Les Devoirs de la classe dirigeante," 2, no. 4 (1876), 505–19; P., "Les Classes ouvrières, leurs rapports avec la révolution et le catholicisme," 4, no. 5 (1877), 700-15; E. A., "La Contre-Révolution," 6, no. 3 (1878), 334–50; and La Tour du Pin Chambly, "Le Centenaire de 1789," May 15, 1886, pp. 481–505.

6. Breda, "La Question ouvrière at le gouvernement chrétien," *L'Association Catholique*, Aug. 15, 1882, p. 161.

7. Good studies on social Catholicism in France are Moon, *The Labor Problem;* Elbow, *French Corporative Theory;* Hoog, *Histoire du Catholicisme social en France;* Moody, *Church and Society*. Martin, *Count Albert de Mun*, is a useful biography.

188   +   Notes to Pages 7–16

8. F⁷12880, Dec. 4, 1908, nos. 57–61 (no. 3), Dec. 3, 1906, #27, and Nov. 8, 1911, #1.
9. R. P. Jean Villain, "L'Action Populaire," *Chronique Sociale de France* 60 (Apr. 1952), pp. 215–16. Examples of some of these publications before the Great War were *Revue de l'Action Populaire, Guide Social,* and *Année Sociale Internationale.*
10. "Les Semaines Sociales de France se présentent," *Chronique Sociale de France* 62 (May–June 1964), 223–26. On the activities of these Lyon pioneers, see Ponson, *Les Catholiques lyonnais.*
11. Paul Naudet, quoted in Montuclard, *Conscience religieuse,* p. 75.
12. On the French Christian Democrats of the 1890s and early 1900s, see Byrnes, "The French Christian Democrats in the 1890s"; Irving, *Christian Democracy in France;* and Montuclard, "Aux origines de la démocratie chrétienne."
13. Marc Sangnier, in Hoog, *Histoire du catholicisme,* p. 134.
14. The most thorough study of the Sillon is Caron, *Le Sillon et la démocratie chrétienne.* See also the chapter on Marc Sangnier in Vidler, *A Variety of Catholic Modernists.*

Chapter 2.   *The Birth and Pro-Catholic Values of the Action Française*

1. See D. Johnson, *France and the Dreyfus Affair;* Chapman, *The Dreyfus Case;* and Halasz, *Captain Dreyfus.* 1955. Derfler, ed., *The Dreyfus Affair* is a useful collection of opinions.
2. On the new nationalism in the Third Republic, see Rémond, *The Right Wing in France;* Tannenbaum, *The Action Française;* Halasz, *Captain Dreyfus;* Seager, *The Boulanger Affair;* Byrnes, *Antisemitism;* Soucy, *Fascism in France;* Doty, *From Cultural Rebellion to Counterrevolution;* and Weber, *Nationalist Revival in France.* For biographical information, see Martin, "The Creation of the Action Libérale Populaire," pp. 661–62, and *Count Albert de Mun,* pp. 3–6, 84–89.
3. The history and ideology of the Action Française are ably presented in Weber, *Action Française;* and Tannenbaum, *The Action Française.* See also Nolte, *Three Faces of Fascism;* Osgood, *French Royalism.*
4. See Nolte, *Three Faces of Fascism,* p. 143; Osgood, *French Royalism,* p. 58; and Weber, *Action Française,* pp. 6–13.
5. On the philosophy and ideological development of the Action Française, see Weber, *Action Française,* pp. 6–16; Rémond, *The Right Wing in France,* pp. 233–53; Peter, *Charles Maurras;* Nguyen, "Situation des études Maurrassiennes"; and Wilson, "A View of the Past."
6. Police lists are a good indicator of this growing impact of the Action Française. Files contain citations of large public meetings: B a/1342, Mar. 19, 1910, and Mar. 2, 1909, indicate the growing influence of its militant cadres, especially the Camelots du Roi: F⁷12863, Feb. 3, 1912; F⁷12864, Jan. 17, 1910, p. 5, and Feb. 16, 1909; B a/1342, Sept. 21, 1910, pp. 1–3, and note its aug-

Notes to Pages 16–20 ✦ 189

mentation of significant capital: B a/1341, Nov. 2, 1906, #106. In fact, as early as 1905, one report stated the following: "One cannot say yet what will be the importance of the Ligue d'Action Française nor the extent of its range of action, but one learns that it already has at its disposition important capital" (B a/1341, Feb. 3, 1905, #2).

7. Weber, *Action Française*, pp. 18–55, 182–83, treats the early growth of the Action Française and the important role of Léon Daudet.

8. To be sure, the Action Française had its problems and setbacks during this period as well, as indicated in police files. See F^{7}12862, May 27, 1909, #54; F^{7}12861, Nov. 15, 1907, #16. Yet these Sûreté Générale reports also indicate successes: see F^{7}12862, Aug. 21, 1909, #4; F^{7}12861, Apr. 16, 1907, #5, and Apr. 7, 1910, #7.

9. From the "Action Française: Membership Oath," in *France: Empire and Republic*, ed. Thomson, p. 94.

10. Charles Maurras, "Lectures et discussions," *L'Action Française*, Aug. 1, 1903, p. 273. All translations from the French of these documents is the work of the author.

11. Maurras, *Dictionnaire politique*, 1:237–38. For similar opinions, see "Le Mal et le remède," *L'Action Française*, Oct. 1, 1899, pp. 273–74.

12. Maurras, *L'Action Française et la religion catholique*, p. 47.

13. "La Question politique," *L'Action Française*, July 12, 1914, p. 3.

14. Charles Maurras, "Barbares et Romains," *L'Action Française*, Dec. 15, 1906, p. 712.

15. Léon Daudet, *L'Action Française*, Oct. 27, 1909, p. 1.

16. Auguste Cavalier, "Catholiques et libertins," *L'Action Française*, Feb. 15, 1901, p. 280.

17. Henri Vaugeois, "Notes politiques," *L'Action Française*, Apr. 1, 1901, p. 521.

18. Maurras, *Enquête sur la monarchie*, p. 508.

19. Charles Maurras, "Les Monods peints par eux-mêmes," *L'Action Française*, Oct. 15, 1899, p. 316.

20. Léon de Montesquiou, "Le Fait et l'idée," *L'Action Française*, Oct. 15, 1900, p. 660.

21. Bernard de Vesins, *L'Action Française*, July 19, 1910, p. 1.

22. Maurras, "Le Dilemme de Marc Sangnier," *L'Action Française*, July 1, 1904, p. 71 (italics in original).

23. Maurras, *L'Action Française*, June 5, 1913, p. 1; "La Question politique," *L'Action Française*, July 12, 1914, p. 3.

24. This contrast, even contradiction, can be noted by a comparison of the statue of Joan in the marketplace of Rouen and the sculptor who created it. The statue itself shows a fragile and pious Joan in simple classical beauty. The sculptor was Maxime Réal del Sartre, the leader of the Action Française's violent street gangs.

25. Charles Maurras, "La Difficulté religieuse," *L'Action Française*, Dec. 15,

1900, p. 1020, and "Waldeck-Rousseau anticlérical," *L'Action Française*, Feb. 25, 1911, p. 1.

26. "La Dictature maçonnique," *L'Action Française*, Nov. 15, 1899, pp. 737-38; Henri Vaugeois, "Notes politiques—Pour l'école catholique," *L'Action Française*, Aug. 1, 1902, pp. 174-75.

27. Comte de Bruc, "Droits de l'homme—Devoirs de français," *L'Action Française*, June 1, 1901, pp. 876-77.

28. Robert Launay, "L'Antisémitisme malgré l'église," *L'Action Française*, June 15, 1901, pp. 100-02 (for Launay, the traditional Christian anti-Semitism was not enough; in fact, he charged the church with being too soft on the Jews); ibid., pp. 876-77.

29. Maurras, *Oeuvres capitales* 2:90. Antoine Murat, a jurist in the Parisian Court of Appeals and a militant in the Action Française since the 1930s, argues that the league's anti-Semitism was political and religious rather than racial, pointing out that his wife *had been* "a Jew by origin and religion"; however, by joining the Catholic church she had abandoned her foreign religion (interview, Dec. 1972). Perhaps this was sufficient for Murat and others, but for those Jews caned to the streets and sent to German concentration camps from France with the connivance of the Action Française, such philosophical refinements seem hollow indeed.

30. Maurras, "Les Monods," pp. 316-17, 323.

31. Maurras, *Oeuvres capitales* 2:90.

32. Léon de Montesquiou, "Droit divin ou droits de l'homme," *L'Action Française*, Apr. 1, 1901, p. 564.

33. Maurras, *Oeuvres capitales* 2:52.

34. Maurras, *Dictionnaire politique* 1:239.

35. Léon de Montesquiou, "Notes politiques: Débats de théologiens," *L'Action Française*, Apr. 1, 1904, p. 9.

36. Charles Maurras, "Partie périodique: Positivisme et catholicisme," *L'Action Française*, Oct. 1, 1901, p. 577.

37. Ibid.; Charles Maurras, "Partie périodique: La Difficulté religieuse," *L'Action Française*, Dec. 15, 1900, pp. 1019, 1028-29, 1031.

38. Maurras, "Partie périodique: Positivisme et catholicisme," p. 578.

39. Maurras, "Partie périodique: La Difficulté religieuse," p. 1031.

40. Ibid., p. 1020; "Schisme et ralliement," *L'Action Française*, Oct. 1, 1901, p. 151.

41. Henri Vaugeois, "Notes politiques—Questions de propagande: les terrains," *L'Action Française*, Nov. 1, 1903, p. 187; and "Notes politiques—Nous ignorons les affiches," *L'Action Française*, Aug. 1, 1901, p. 179.

42. J. Bainville, "La France, le génie latin et le génie germanique," *L'Action Française*, July 1, 1900, p. 76.

43. Vaugeois, "Notes politiques—Questions de propagande," p. 187.

44. "M. de Pressensé et les démocrates chrétiens," *L'Action Française*, Mar. 1, 1902, pp. 455-56.

45. Maurras, "Le Dilemme de Marc Sangnier," *L'Action Française,* July 1, 1904, pp. 69–71.
46. Ibid., July 15, 1904, p. 139.
47. Ibid., July 1, 1904, pp. 75–76; Aug. 15, 1904, pp. 260, 272; July 1, 1905, pp. 15, 47, 51; and July 15, 1905, pp. 123–27.
48. Henri Vaugeois, "Notes politiques," *L'Action Française,* Nov. 1, 1903, p. 195.
49. "Lettre ouverte," *L'Action Française,* Sept. 15, 1902, pp. 431–34; "Seconde lettre," *L'Action Française,* Dec. 1, 1902, pp. 855–64.
50. See the following articles in *L'Action Française:* "Schisme et ralliement," Jan. 15, 1902, pp. 135–37; "Une page de Henri des Houx sur la politique de Léon XIII," May 1, 1904, p. 180; "Les Faits," Aug. 1, 1904, p. 229; Charles Maurras, "Partie périodique," Feb. 15, 1901, pp. 341, 343; "La Politique de Léon XIII," July 15, 1903, pp. 105–07.
51. "Quelques adhésions—II. Adhésion d'un prêtre," *L'Action Française,* Feb. 15, 1905, p. 247. This column, "Quelques adhésions," appeared frequently in succeeding issues.

Chapter 3. A Catholic Church Under Fire (1899–1906)

1. Byrnes, *Antisemitism,* p. 143; McManners, *Church and State,* p. 120; Boussel, *L'Affaire Dreyfus,* p. 196.
2. *Civiltà cattolica,* quoted in *The Dreyfus Affair,* ed. Derfler, p. 73.
3. McManners, *Church and State,* p. 122; Montuclard, *Conscience religieuse,* p. 136; Daniel-Rops, *A Fight for God,* p. 117; J. B., *La Croix,* Sept. 10–11, 1899, p. 1. For a thorough study of *La Croix,* see Godfrin and Godfrin, *Une Centrale de press catholique,* 1965.
4. Quoted in Cahm, *Politics and Society,* pp. 93–94.
5. Homo, *L'Ouest-Eclair,* Mar. 23, 1903, p. 1; Emmanuel Desgrées du Loû, *L'Ouest-Eclair,* May 1, 1900, p. 1; Charles Bodin, *L'Ouest-Eclair,* Sept. 26, 1901, p. 1.
6. Byrnes, *Antisemitism* pp. 137–38; Paul Naudet, *Justice Sociale,* July 15, 1893, p. 1; Byrnes, "The French Christian Democrats," pp. 294–97.
7. Byrnes, *Antisemitism,* pp. 221–22, 293.
8. Ibid., pp. 190, 221–22.
9. Larkin, *Church and State,* pp. 80–87, 99; Partin, *Waldeck-Rousseau,* pp. 7–10, 157–66.
10. "Chronique diocésaine," *Semaine Religieuse de Cambrai,* Feb. 23, 1901, p. 126.
11. "Les Faux Dogmes de la Révolution," *Semaine Religieuse de Cambrai,* Oct. 24, 1903, pp. 673–77.
12. See "Nouvelles religieuses," *Semaine Religieuse de Cambrai:* Mar. 31, 1900, pp. 204–05; Nov. 10, 1900, pp. 715–18; Aug. 17, 1901, pp. 524, 526; Apr. 12, 1902, p. 236; July 15, 1905, p. 663; and July 29, 1905, p. 705.

13. Cardinal François Richard, *Les Questions Actuelles*, Aug. 16, 1902, pp. 5–6; "La Loi sur les associations," *Semaine Religieuse de Rennes*, Jan. 26, 1901, pp. 266–68; Cardinal Langénieux, *Les Questions Actuelles*, Apr. 15, 1899, p. 195; Msgr. Luçon *Les Questions Actuelles*, Sept. 7, 1901, p. 105; Cardinal Couillé, *Les Questions Actuelles*, May 22, 1899, p. 332.

14. Cardinal François Richard, *Les Questions Actuelles*, Aug. 16, 1902, p. 7.

15. Albert de Mun (March 15, 1902), in *Les Questions Actuelles*, Mar. 22, 1902, pp. 2–3; Albert de Mun, *Gaulois* (Sept. 21, 1905), in *Les Questions Actuelles*, Oct. 7, 1905, p. 164; Jacques Piou, *Les Questions Actuelles*, Jan. 26, 1901, pp. 192–93, 199, 203; "Avant la bataille," *Action Libérale*, Nov. 20, 1901, p. 15; "M. Piou à Bordeaux," *Action Libérale*, Feb. 12, 1902, p. 3; F⁷12719, Oct. 20, 1905, #776.

16. Cardinal Perraud and Msgr. Isoard, in *Les Questions Actuelles*, May 10, 1902, pp. 261, 260. For hierarchical participation at ALP rallies, see "L'Action Libérale Populaire à Rennes," *Semaine Religieuse de Rennes*, Jan. 21, 1903, p. 284; J. B., *La Croix*, May 14, 1902, p. 1; F⁷12719, Jan. 19, 1907, #433, and Sept. 3, 1907, #489; F⁷12880 (no. 3), May 6, 1909, pp. 7–8; Martin, "The Creation of the Action Liberale Populaire," pp. 665–66, 668–69, 673–75, 681–82, 685; and F⁷12716, June 25, 1903. Certainly Martin is right when he states that both Piou and de Mun sought "to organize their followers and those to both flanks into a grand conservative party . . . a broadly based conservative front of the Right and Center ("The Creation of the Action Liberale Populaire," pp. 661–62). Such an effort would necessitate a nonconfessional party. This was the case de jure, but de facto the ALP became an extension and reflection of ecclesiastical politics. Both de Mun and Piou were caught up in that reality, though they were able to modify it somewhat against their own less flexible right wing (ibid., pp. 677–87).

17. Gayraud, *La Croix*, Feb. 7, 1905, p. 1; Marc Sangnier, *La Croix*, Feb. 5, 1904, p. 1, and Sept. 15, 1904, p. 1.

18. A.P.-B., *La Croix*, Oct. 17, 1902, p. 1; Feron-Vrau, *La Croix*, Dec. 19, 1900, p. 1.

19. Homo, *L'Ouest-Eclair*, Mar. 23, 1903, p. 1; Bodin, *L'Ouest-Eclair*, Sept. 26, 1901, p. 1; Guilloteaux, *L'Ouest-Eclair*, Mar. 11, 1904, p. 1; Trois-Etoiles, *Justice Sociale*, Aug. 10, 1901, p. 1; Gayraud, *Les Questions Actuelles*, Feb. 23, 1901, p. 447; Sangnier, "L'Action morale et sociale du catholicisme," *Le Sillon*, Apr. 10, 1902, pp. 242–43; "Les Ennemis de la république," *Le Sillon*, Aug. 2, 1902, pp. 24–31.

20. Desgrées du Loû, *L'Ouest-Eclair*, Mar. 18, 1900, p. 1; Piou, *L'Ouest-Eclair*, Oct. 11, 1904, p. 1; Bodion, *L'Ouest-Eclair*, Aug. 28, 1902, p. 1; "Avant le congrès national," *Le Sillon*, Jan. 25, 1903, pp. 56–57; H. R., "Une Réunion de l'Action Libérale Populaire," *Le Sillon*, June 25, 1902, p. 479; "L'Action Libérale Populaire à Tourcoing," *Action Libérale*, Sept. 3, 1902, pp. 1–4.

21. Editorial, *Vie Catholique*, Feb. 24, 1899, p. 1; Guilloteaux, *L'Ouest-Eclair*, Nov. 18, 1903, p. 1; Marc Sangnier, "Christianisme et démocratie," *Le*

Sillon, Mar. 25, 1904, pp. 202–05; Joseph Ageorges, "République et catholicisme," *Le Sillon*, Sept. 10, 1900, pp. 166–67. For similar opinions, see the Chamber of Deputies' speeches of Fathers Gayraud and Lemire in *Les Questions Actuelles*, Mar. 8, 1902, p. 337; Feb. 23, 1901, pp. 455–56; and Mar. 2, 1901, pp. 456–60.

22. Bodin, *L'Ouest-Eclair*, Oct. 10, 1903, p. 1; Desgrées du Loû, *L'Ouest-Eclair*, July 2, 1904, p. 1; Gayraud, *Les Questions Actuelles*, Dec. 28, 1901, p. 307; H. Perrières, "La Crise catholique," *Le Sillon*, Aug. 25, 1903, p. 124; Marc Sangnier, "Les Ennemis intérieurs du catholicisme," *Le Sillon*, Nov. 25, 1902, pp. 361–67; Paul Naudet, *Justice sociale*, Mar. 14, 1903, p. 1; Trois-Etoiles, *Justice Sociale*, Aug. 10, 1901, p. 1; and Naudet, *Justice Sociale*, Apr. 30, 1904, p. 1.

23. Naudet, *Justice Sociale*, June 20, 1903, p. 1, and Feb. 3, 1900, p. 1; Pierre Fabre, "La Chronique de l'Echo," *Echo des Cercles D'Etudes*, Oct. 10, 1901, p. 290; L. Meyer, "La Chronique de l'Echo," *Echo des Cercles d'Etudes*, Nov. 25, 1901, p. 331; see the following articles in *Le Sillon*: Marc Sangnier, "Où nous en sommes?" Dec. 10, 1899, pp. 513–25; F. Paul, "Les Cercles d'Etudes," June 10, 1900, pp. 403–06; Jacques Nanteuil, "Les Universitaires populaires at l'emancipation intellectuelle," Feb. 10, 1900, p. 95; Marc Sangnier, "L'Institut populaire de V[e] arrondisement," Feb. 10, 1901, p. 66; L. Antoine, "De l'intervention des syndicats et du gouvernement dans les grèves," Mar. 10, 1901, pp. 134, 139; Sangnier, "L'Obstacle," *Eveil Démocratique*, Dec. 8, 1905, p.1; Sangnier, "L'Avenir des syndicats ouvriers," *Eveil Démocratique*, Aug. 5, 1906, p. 1; Sangnier, "L'Avenir du syndicalisme," *Eveil Démocratique*, Nov. 1, 1908, p. 1.

24. Larkin, *Church and State*, pp. 49, 90–93, 102; Partin, *Waldeck-Rousseau*, pp. 135–37, 167–69.

25. Gayraud, *Les Questions Actuelles*, June 4, 1905, pp. 5–7; de Mun, *La Croix*, May 20, 1904, p. 1.

26. Larkin, "Loubet's Visit," p. 100; Mayeur, ed., *La Séparation*, p. 27. On the church-state conflicts during this period, see Partin, *Waldeck-Rousseau*.

27. Mayeur, ed., *La Séparation*, p. 26. *Nobis nominavit* meant "named by us" (the Holy See). See also Larkin, *Church and State*, pp. 130–36; and Partin, *Waldeck-Rousseau*, pp. 217–55.

28. Merry del Val, letter to the papal nuncio in France, *Les Questions Actuelles*, Jan. 13, 1906, p. 84.

29. Msgrs. le Nordez and Géay, *Les Questions Actuelles*, Oct. 25, 1902, pp. 15–17; and Nov. 1, 1902, p. 46.

30. *Les Questions Actuelles*, Aug. 5, 1904, pp. 290–92; and Aug. 13, 1904, p. 18. See also Partin, *Waldeck-Rousseau*, pp. 226–27; and Albert Monniot's pamphlet *Un Préfet Violet* (1907) printed against Msgr. Géay and the folder against Bishop le Nordez entitled "Incident de la cathédrale" (found, respectively, in F[19]1961 and F[19]1962).

31. See Partin, *Waldeck-Rousseau*; Mayeur, ed., *La Séparation*; and Le-

canuet, *Les Signes avant-coureurs*. The minor role played by Msgr. le Nordez and Msgr. Géay in this drama that affected their personal lives so profoundly can be noted in the following references: For Géay, see "Partie officielle," *Semaine Religieuse de Laval*, Sept. 3, 1904, pp. 739–40; and Sept. 17, 1904, pp. 772–73. For le Nordez, see "Actes officielles et communications de l'évêché," *Semaine Religieuse de Dijon*, July 30, 1904, p. 483; and Sept. 10, 1904, p. 581. The F^{19} files cited in note 30 flesh out the details of this controversy.

32. For examples of this unanimous Catholic protest, see "La Rupture entre Rome et le gouvernement français," *Semaine Religieuse de Rennes*, Aug. 6, 1904, pp. 717–18; Feron-Vrau, *La Croix*, Aug. 2, 1904, p. 1; de Mun, *La Croix*, Aug. 3, 1904, p. 1; "L'Affaire des évêques," *L'Ouest-Eclair*, July 31, 1904, p. 1; Naudet, *Justice Sociale*, Aug. 6, 1904, p. 1; and *Le Sillon*, Aug. 10, 1904, p. 119.

33. See Brugerette, *Le Prêtre français* 2:608; Larkin, *Church and State*, pp. 12–13; Laperrière, *La "Séparation,"* pp. 197–202; Boulard, "La 'Déchristianisation' de Paris"; Doncoeur, *La Crise du Sacerdoce*, pp. 17–108; and le Bras, *Introduction à l'histoire*, p. 124.

34. For a text of the Separation legislation, see Thomson, ed., *France: Empire and Republic*, pp. 246–61

35. Protest letter of the French cardinals, *Les Questions Actuelles*, Apr. 1, 1905, pp. 50–51.

36. "Ce dont nous sommes témoins et ce qui se prépare," *Semaine Religieuse de Cambrai*, June 17, 1905, p. 554.

37. Franc, *La Croix*, June 14, 1905, p. 1; Piou, *L'Ouest-Eclair*, Oct. 11, 1904, p. 1; de Mun, *La Croix*, July 5, 1905, p. 1; Desgrées du Loû, *L'Ouest-Eclair*, Apr. 9, 1905, p. 1; Marc Sangnier, "La Séparation des églises et de l'état," *Le Sillon*, May 25, 1905, p. 380; and Henri Couget, "Vers la séparation," *Le Sillon*, Aug. 25, 1904, p. 137; de Mun, "Le Vote de la Séparation," *Action Libérale Populaire*, Dec. 14, 1905, p. 1.

38. "La question des inventaires," *L'Ouest-Eclair*, Mar. 10, 1906, p. 1.

39. *Semaine Religieuse de Paris* (Aug. 26, 1905), in *Les Questions Actuelles*, Sept. 2, 1905, pp. 269–73; and *Semaine Religieuse de Paris* (Sept. 2, 1905), in *Les Questions Actuelles*, Sept. 9, 1905, pp. 310–12.

40. Letter of the "green cardinals" (i.e., those wearing the regalia of the Académie Française), in Coutrot and Dreyfus, *Les Forces religieuses*, pp. 43–45.

41. Msgr. Fulbert Petit, *Les Questions Actuelles*, Sept. 1, 1906, pp. 66–71; McManners, *Church and State*, p. 163.

42. "La question des inventaires," *L'Ouest-Eclair*, Mar. 10, 1906, p. 1; Desgrées du Lou, *L'Ouest-Eclair*, Mar. 28, 1906, p. 1.

43. Albert de Mun, *Les Questions Actuelles*, Apr. 7, 1906, p. 301; "Nouvelles Religieuses," *Semaine Religieuse de Cambrai*, Feb. 10, 1906, p. 138.

44. *Livre Blanc du Saint-Siège*, in *Les Questions Actuelles*, Jan. 6, 1906, pp. 8–32.

45. Pius X, *Gravissimo Officii* (Aug. 10, 1906), in *Les Questions Actuelles,* Aug. 18, 1906, p. 7.

Chapter 4. Catholic Integrists Purge the Church (1906-1914)

1. Pius X, *Pascendi Dominici Gregis* (Sept. 8, 1907), in *The Papal Encyclicals,* ed. Fremantle, pp. 197, 201. See also pp. 204-06 for *Lamentabili Sane,* which reads like Piux IX's *Syllabus of Errors.* Three studies of the modernist controversy are Reardon, ed., *Roman Catholic Modernism;* Vidler, *A Variety of Catholic Modernists;* and Poulat, *Histoire, dogme et critique.* For Pius X's antimodernist machinery, see the following articles in *Les Questions Actuelles:* Oct. 30, 1909, pp. 67-68; Nov. 30, 1907, p. 199; Aug. 21, 1909, pp. 65, 67-68; Oct. 22, 1910, pp. 7-8, 35; Oct. 22, 1910, pp. 6, 15; and Nov. 12, 1910, p. 94. Harry Paul, in *The Edge of Contingency,* "In Quest of Kerygma," and "Science and the Catholic Institutes," describes the lively intellectual ferment in Catholic academic circles during this period.

2. Barbier, *Histoire du catholicisme,* pp. 187-89; Henri Delassus, "L'Encyclique 'Pascendi' et la démocratie chrétienne," *Semaine Religieuse de Cambrai,* Nov. 16, 1907, p. 1131; Amette, *Les Questions Actuelles,* Mar. 7, 1908, pp. 291-92; see the following articles in *Semaine Religieuse de Rennes:* "Partie Officielle," Aug. 3, 1907, pp. 790-91; "Lettre pastorale de Monseigneur l'Archevêque de Rennes," Sept. 28, 1907, pp. 3-4; "Communications de l'Archevêché," Mar. 26, 1910, pp. 473-74; and "Communication de l'Archevêché," Jan. 14, 1911, pp. 273-74.

3. Msgrs. le Nordez and Géay, *Les Questions Actuelles,* Oct. 25, 1902, pp. 15-17; Msgr. Lacroix, *Les Questions Actuelles,* Nov. 1, 1902, 261; Msgr. Lacroix, *Justice Sociale,* Mar. 11, 1905, p. 1; "La Crise religieuse," *L'Ouest-Eclair,* Jan. 7, 1907, p. 1; "Démission de S.G. Mgr. Lacroix," *La Croix,* Oct. 29, 1907, p. 1; "Nouvelles Religieuses," *Semaine Religieuse de Cambrai,* Nov. 2, 1907, p. 1091; Lovie, *Chambéry,* pp. 226-30.

4. Dansette, *Religious History* 2:250-51; Amette, *Les Questions Actuelles,* Mar. 7, 1908, pp. 291-92; *Semaine Religieuse de Rennes,* Sept. 1, 1906, p. 835; "Chronique Diocesaine," *Semaine Religieuse de Cambrai,* May 21, 1904, p. 327; Pius X, *Semaine Religieuse de Cambrai,* June 29, 1912, p. 605; Ponson, *Les Catholiques Lyonnais,* pp. 230-32.

5. Dansette, *Religious History* 2:251, 310-12; Weber, *Action Française,* pp. 219-20; Daniel-Rops, *A Fight for God,* pp. 230-33. On Msgr. Benigni and the *Sodalitium Pianum,* see Poulat, *Intégrisme,* and *Catholicisme, démocratie et socialisme.* Papal support letters to Benigni are quoted in full in Poulat, *Intégrisme,* pp. 88-89, 93-94, 153-54.

6. Pius X was not entirely singleminded in his pontificate, in spite of his intransigence toward the French government and his suspicion toward liberals and Christian Democrats within the church. With respect to the Italian govern-

ment, he was adopting a more moderate stance than that taken by his predecessor. Perhaps the failure of Leo's Ralliement with France was reflected in this shift. However, these diplomatic nuances did not extend to Christian Democrats within the church. See Helmreich, ed., *A Free Church in a Free State?*

7. "Les Papiers Montagnini," *L'Ouest-Eclair*, Apr. 6, 1907, pp. 1-2, and Apr. 13, 1907, p. 1; Marc Sangnier, *L'Ouest-Eclair*, Apr. 15, 1907, p. 1; "Le Sillon et les papiers Montagnini," *Le Sillon*, Apr. 25, 1907, pp. 311-12. A collection of newspaper articles on this controversy may be consulted in the Archives Nationales file F[19]1983. In the actual Montagnini papers, one can find numerous opinions against France's leading Christian Democrats. Two such examples are statements criticizing sharply Father Jules Lemire and Marc Sangnier (C7377, Jan. 1, 1905).

8. See the following articles in *Le Sillon*: Editorial, "Sages initiatives," Apr. 25, 1904, pp. 292-94; Marc Sangnier, "En marche," Jan. 10, 1902, pp. 22-24; "La Route sure," Jan. 10, 1904, p. 4; "Avant le congrès national," Jan. 25, 1903, pp. 52-55; "Le Troisième Congrès national," Mar. 10, 1904, p. 171; "Le Congrès du Sillon," *Semaine Religieuse de Rennes*, Aug. 20, 1904, pp. 752-53; articles in *Le Sillon:* Pierre Fabre, "Le Sillon à Rome," Oct. 25, 1903, pp. 281-82; Georges Hoog, "Le Sillon à Rome," Apr. 25, 1904, pp. 292-94; "Au séminaire," May 25, 1905, pp. 382-84; *Echo des Cercles d'Études*, in *Le Sillon* Dec. 25, 1900, pp. 316-17; and Marc Sangnier, "Le Sillon et les séminaires," *Le Sillon*, Aug. 10, 1899, p. 119.

9. Barbier, *Les Idées du Sillon;* "Nouvelles Religieuses," *Semaine Religieuse de Cambrai*, July 29, 1905, p. 705; Barbier, *Les Erreurs du Sillon*, pp. 1-3; "Chronique Diocésaine," *Semaine Religieuse de Cambrai*, June 22, 1901, pp. 392-94; Paul Naudet, *Justice Sociale*, Apr. 19, 1902, p. 1; Trois Etoiles, *Justice Sociale*, Apr. 12, 1902, p. 1; Emmanuel Desgrées du Loû, *L'Ouest-Eclair*, Apr. 17, 1902, p. 1; "Nouvelles Religieuses," *Semaine Religieuse de Cambrai*, Apr. 17, 1901, pp. 524, 526, and July 7, 1900, pp. 427-28; Naudet, *Justice Sociale*, Oct. 27, 1900, p. 1, and Sept. 28, 1901, p. 1; Delourme, *Trente-cinq années*, pp. 18, 24-30, 39, 61.

10. McAvoy, *The Americanist Heresy*, pp. 46-48, 61-62, 132, 231-35, 262-68, 275-76; Leo XIII, *Graves de Communi* (1901), in *The Church Speaks*, ed. Gilson, pp. 317, 325-26; Pius X, *Action Populaire Chrétienne*, in *Les Questions Actuelles*, Jan. 9, 1904, pp. 3-4.

11. On the decisive campaign against these republican Catholics, see Arnal, "Why the French Christian Democrats Were Condemned."

12. Dabry, *Vie Catholique*, Nov. 16, 1907, p. 1; "Partie officielle—Communications de l'Archevêché," *Semaine Religieuse du Rennes*, Nov. 23, 1907, pp. 145-46; decree (Feb. 13, 1908), in *Les Questions Actuelles*, Mar. 7, 1908, p. 293.

13. On the pilgrimage and impact of *L'Ouest-Eclair*, see Arnal, "The Nature and Success of Breton Christian Democracy"; Delourme, *Trente-cinq an-*

nées, pp. 61, 121-22; "*L'Univers, Le Monde* et la *Vérité française,*" *Semaine Religieuse de Rennes,* May 25, 1907, p. 631; "Les Réactionnaires contre *L'Ouest-Eclair,*" *L'Ouest-Eclair,* Aug. 9, 1910, p. 1; "Nouvelles du diocèse de Rennes," *Semaine Religieuse de Rennes,* July 17, 1915, p. 710; Bellanger, Godechot et al., *Histoire générale de la presse française* 3:127, 338, 604-05, 610-11; Bosworth, *Catholicism and Crisis,* p. 37; Siegfried, *Tableau politique,* pp. 97-105, 108-09, 126, 146-47, 370-74, 217; Robert Cornilleau, "Emmanuel Desgrées du Loû,"*Petit Démocrate,* Feb. 26, 1933, p. 1-2.

14. H. T., *L'Ouest-Eclair,* Aug. 6, 1910, p. 1; Delourme, *Trente-cinq années,* pp. 120-22, 127-30, 133-37, 140-41; "Les Réactionnaires," *L'Ouest-Eclair,* Aug. 9, 1910, p. 1; "Communications de l'archevêché," *Semaine Religieuse de Rennes,* Aug. 13, 1910, p. 854.

15. Delourme, *Trente-cinq années,* pp. 144-45, 149, 159, 166-70, 174.

16. Abbé Gayraud, *L'Univers* (Mar. 27, 1899), in *Les Questions Actuelles,* Apr. 8, 1899, p. 184; "Un Ami de *l'Univers,*" *L'Univers* (Mar. 19, 1899), in *Les Questions Actuelles,* Apr. 8, 1899, pp. 179-80; *L'Osservatore Romano* (Mar. 25, 1899), in *Les Questions Actuelles,* Apr. 8, 1899, pp. 186-88; Naudet, *Justice Sociale,* Apr. 19, 1902, p. 1; Desgrées du Loû, *L'Ouest-Eclair,* Apr. 17, 1902, p. 1.

17. "Le Cas de l'abbé Lémire," *L'Ouest-Eclair,* Nov. 19, 1907, p. 2; "Chronique diocésaine," *Semaine Religieuse de Cambrai,* Dec. 15, 1906, p. 1217; "Partie officielle," *Semaine Religieuse de Cambrai,* Nov. 23, 1907, pp. 1155-56. On Jules Lemire, see Mayeur, *Un Prêtre démocrate.*

18. Chronique diocésaine," *Semaine Religieuse de Cambrai,* June 18, 1910, pp. 562-64, May 18, 1912, p. 471, and Feb. 1, 1913, pp. 104, 123-32, 137, 146-48.

19. "Partie officielle," *Semaine Religieuse de Cambrai,* Mar. 22, 1913, p. 295; "Chronique diocésaine," *Semaine Religieuse de Cambrai,* Sept. 27, 1913, pp. 944-46; "Petite chronique," *Semaine Religieuse de Rennes,* Nov. 8, 1913, pp. 133-34; "Partie officielle," *Semaine Religieuse de Cambrai,* Jan. 10, 1914, p. 53; "Chronique diocésaine," *Semaine Religieuse de Lille,* Mar. 21, 1914, p. 279, and May 2, 1914, pp. 421-22.

20. See the following articles in *Le Sillon:* Henry du Roure, "Le Journal quotidien de la démocratie," Apr. 10, 1908, p. 252; Léonard Constant, "Vers une action démocratique internationale," Mar. 25, 1908, pp. 201-04; V. Ermoni, "Christianisme et socialisme," Oct. 25, 1908, pp. 296-302; Michel Legendre, "Propriété privée et démocratie," June 10, 1908, pp. 411-13; Georges Renard, "Le Sillon et les élections," Mar. 25, 1906, p. 206; du Roure, "Le Journal quotidien de la démocratie," Apr. 10, 1908, pp. 246-48; "Nos dossiers — L'Élection de Sceaux," Apr. 10, 1909, pp. 247-50, and Apr. 25, 1909, pp. 306-07; see the following articles in *Eveil Démocratique:* Marc Sangnier, "Les Patrons," Oct. 14, 1906, p. 1; Marc Sangnier, "Un Congrès syndical au Sillon," Oct. 21, 1906, p. 1; Marc Sangnier, "Hier et demain," Apr. 7, 1907, p. 1;

François Lespiriat, "En Creusant Le Sillon," Feb. 28, 1909, p. 1; B a/1540, Dec. 17, 1906, #670–#671; Mar. 26, 1907, #703; May, 19, 1908, #846; Nov. 21, 1908, #871–#873.

21. Barbier, *Les Erreurs du Sillon,* pp. 61, 87, 212, 260; "Mgr. l'évêque de Quimper et le Sillon," *Le Sillon,* Aug. 25, 1906, pp. 141–42; "Partie officielle,"*Semaine Religieuse de Rennes,* Mar. 30, 1907, pp. 474–76; Msgr. de Cabrières (May 1907), in *Les Questions Actuelles,* June 25, 1910, p. 138; "Petit chronique — Le Sillon," *Semaine Religieuse de Rennes,* Feb. 6, 1909, p. 335; *Les Questions Actuelles,* June 25, 1910, pp. 126–27; "Le Sillon et l'autorité ecclésiastique," *Le Sillon,* Nov. 26, 1906, pp. 381–82; "Documents," Le Sillon, Apr. 10, 1910, pp. 49–63; Sangnier, "Le Sillon et les évêques," *Eveil Démocratique,* Dec. 12, 1909, p. 1; "Nouvelles lettres épiscopales," *Eveil Démocratique,* Mar. 27, 1910, pp. 1–2; B a/1540, July 17, 1907, #730.

22. "Lettre de notre Saint Père le Pape Pie X à l'épiscopat français sur le Sillon" (Aug. 25, 1910), in *Les Questions Actuelles,* Sept. 3, 1910, pp. 97, 106–07, 110–12. For the position of traditional Catholics regarding the Sillon's condemnation, see Breunig, "The Condemnation of the Sillon."

23. Mayeur, *Un Prêtre démocrate;* p. 394; "Les Papiers Montagnini," *L'Ouest-Eclair,* Apr. 6, 1907, pp. 1–2, and Apr. 13, 1907, p. 1; Barbier, *Le Devoir politique,* pp. 9–10, 135–36, 184, 191, 227–28, 265–67; "Nouvelles Religieuses," *Semaine Religieuse de Cambrai,* Nov. 2, 1907, p. 1056; "Au lendemain des élections," *Semaine Religieuse de Cambrai,* May 21, 1910, pp. 458–59; "Pour l'union des catholiques," *Semaine Religieuse de Rennes,* Mar. 26, 1910, pp. 474, 508; Dansette, *Religious History,* pp. 255–56. *Les Questions Actuelles* has collected most of the relevant primary data in the following issues: June 26, 1909, pp. 130–37, and Mar. 7, 1914, pp. 293, 296, 299. To be sure, the ALP was not abandoned totally by the church's hierarchy, but it is clear that it was under pressure to turn rightward and become more integrist and confessional in its orientation. For this shifting orientation, see L. Laya, "Orientation," *Action Libérale Populaire,* Sept. 15, 1910, pp. 393–94; L. Laya, "Les Deux Doctrines," *Action Libérale Populaire,* May 1, 1912, pp. 129–30; "Les Elections du 26 avril," *Action Libérale Populaire,* Mar. 16, 1914, p. 810; and Martin, "The Creation of the Action Libérale Populaire."

Chapter 5. The Birth of a Friendship (1906–1914)

1. On the league's venture into syndicalist politics, see Mazgaj, *The Action Française and Revolutionary Syndicalism.* These attempts to form links with the syndicalists may be noted in the police files. For example, see B a/1540, Nov. 21, 1908, #871–#873; and B a/1342: Feb. 15, 1910, pp. 1–25.

2. Weber, *Action Française,* pp. 57–61; B a/1540: Mar. 29, 1910, and Sept. 5, 1910; F7 12864 (no. 7), #76, and (no. 4), Jan. 17, 1910, #5.

3. Weber, *Action Française,* p. 65; Tannenbaum, "The Reactionary Mentality," p. 23; Tannenbaum, *The Action Française,* p. 127; see also the follow-

ing articles in *L'Action Française:* "Bulletin de la Ligue," Apr. 1, 1906, pp. 73-74; "Dans un grand séminaire," May 1, 1906, pp. 232-33; "Bulletin de la Ligue," Mar. 15, 1906, p. 459; "Ligue d'Action Française," Aug. 1, 1906, pp. 232-33, and July 15, 1906, pp. 167-69; B a/1342, July 7, 1909; B/1343, Apr. 28, 1911, June 24, 1911, July 6, 1911, Aug. 24, 1912, and Dec. 16, 1912; F⁷12862 (no. 7), Mar. 24, 1911, #38; F⁷12861 (no. 6), Feb. 8, 1909, #60.

4. Weber, *Action Française,* p. 220; "Installation du R. P. Janvier comme chanoine honoraire," *Semaine Religieuse de Rennes,* Aug. 24, 1907, p. 845; "L'Action Française jugée par Dom Besse," *L'Action Française,* Aug. 1, 1907, pp. 236-39; Weber, *Action Française,* pp. 65, 220; "En l'honneur de Jeanne d'Arc," *L'Action Française,* May 24, 1909, p. 1; Marc Sangnier, *La Démocratie,* Mar. 3, 1912, p. 1; B a/1341, Oct. 31, 1906, #92; B a/1342, Apr. 20, 1910; B a/1343, Jan. 28, 1911; F⁷12861 (no. 6), Apr. 16, 1907, #6, and Feb. 3, 1908, #225; F⁷12862 (no. #7), June 1, 1911, #67; F⁷12863 (no. 3), Dec. 4, 1913, #748.

5. Msgr. Touchet, *L'Action Française,* Feb. 11, 1913, p. 1; Charles Turinaz, *L'Action Française,* Mar. 1, 1906, p. 328; Father Penon, in Thomas, *L'Action Française,* p. 72; Msgr. de Cabrières, *L'Action Française,* June 15, 1906, pp. 395-98; "La Souscription des catholiques," *L'Action Française,* Jan. 4, 1909, p. 1; F⁷12863 (no. 7), Mar. 21, 1912, pp. 1-5, and (no. 3), Dec. 3, 1913, #146.

6. "Le Congrès pour la bonne presse," *Semaine Religieuse de Rennes,* Oct. 2, 1909, pp. 27-29; "Les Journaux de M. Feron-Vrau," *L'Ouest-Eclair,* Oct. 1, 1909, p. 1; "Installation du R. P. Janvier," *Semaine Religieuse de Rennes,* 1910, p. 845; "Derrière M. Monniot," *Le'Ouest-Eclair,* Aug. 5, 1910, p. 1; "Communications de l'archevêché," *Semaine Religieuse de Rennes,* Aug. 13, 1910, p. 854.

7. See the following articles in *Semaine Religieuse de Cambrai:* "Une Chaire dite du Syllabus fondée par des laiques," Oct. 20, 1906, p. 1019; "Nouvelles religieuses," Aug. 29, 1911, p. 402; "L'Union des catholiques," Oct. 26, 1907, p. 1057; "Nouvelles religieuses," Oct. 7, 1911, pp. 958-59.

8. "Nouvelles religieuses," *Semaine Religieuse de Cambrai,* Oct. 11, 1913, pp. 997-98.

9. Weber, *Action Française,* pp. 66, 219; Nolte, *Three Faces of Fascism,* p. 103; B a/1343, Jan. 6, 1912; F⁷12863 (no. 7), Mar. 21, 1912.

10. See the following articles in *L'Action Française:* "Le Nationalisme intégral," Mar. 21, 1908, p. 1; Daudet, Oct. 27, 1909, p. 1; De Vésins, July 19, 1910, p. 1; Vaugeois, Dec. 15, 1906, p. 702.

11. See the following articles in *L'Action Française:* Maurras, Sept. 30, 1909, p. 1; "Lettres à un ami," Jan. 5, 1909, p. 1; Dimier, May 3, 1908, p. 2.

12. See the following articles in *L'Action Française:* Mandat-Grancey, July 1, 1904, pp. 34-37; Vaugeois, "Notes politiques—Le Vatican, le Quirinal et la République," June 1, 1904, pp. 346, 352; "L'Eglise et la démocratie," Dec. 15, 1905, p. 416; "Lettre du cardinal Luçon," Sept. 9, 1909, p. 1.

13. See the following articles in *L'Action Française:* "La Question scolaire,"

Dec. 4, 1909, p. 1; "A la Cour de Cassation," Nov. 27, 1909, p. 2; "Les Poursuites contre le cardinal Andrieu," July 10, 1909, p. 1; "Evêque poursuivi," June 14, 1912, p. 2; "Livre d'Or de l'Action Française," Feb. 15, 1906, pp. 233–44; de Vesins, Apr. 1, 1906, p. 11.

14. See the following articles in *L'Action Française:* "Lectures et discussions," Jan. 1, 1904, pp. 83–84; Louis Dimier, "La Position apologétique de M. Loisy," Mar. 15, 1904, pp. 443–49; "Revue de la presse," Oct. 2, 1912, p. 3; de Vesins, Dec. 3, 1912, pp. 1–2; "Le Père Billot," Jan. 19, 1912, p. 1; "Aux amis de la Correspondance de Rome," Aug. 6, 1911, p. 3; "Pour les fêtes," Apr. 12, 1909, p. 1; "En l'honneur de Jeanne d'Arc," May 24, 1909, p. 1; "L'Equivoque du Sillon," Feb. 21, 1909, p. 2, Dimier, Apr. 15, 1907, pp. 81–102; F7 12862 (no. 3), Feb. 8, 1909, #20; B a/1342, Apr. 23, 1910.

15. See the following articles in *L'Action Française:* "Ligue d'Action Francaise," Aug. 1, 1906, p. 228; Aug. 15, 1906, pp. 333–35; Mar. 24, 1908, p. 2; "La Mort du cardinal Lecot," Dec. 21, 1908, p. 1; "Chronique de la ligue," May 1, 1906, pp. 225–26; F7 12862, Mar. 17, 1910, #19.

16. Dimier, "Catholique et républicain," *L'Action Française,* May 1, 1906, pp. 196, 201; "Derrière M. Monniot," *L'Ouest-Eclair,* Aug. 5, 1910, p. 1.

17. See the following articles in *L'Action Française:* "Ralliés contre royalistes," Mar. 1, 1906, pp. 351, 358; "L'Équivoque du Sillon," Feb. 21, 1909, p. 2; Abbé Emmanuel Barbier, "Le Sillon et ses tendances protestantes," Apr. 1, 1907, pp. 41–59; Nel Arlès, "A propos du Sillon," Dec. 1, 1907, pp. 376–84; "Chronique de la ligue," May 1, 1906, p. 225; B a/1342, Feb. 8, 1909.

18. See the following articles in *L'Action Française:* "Le Sillon devant l'épiscopat," Dec. 5, 1909, p. 3; "Condamnation du Sillon," Aug. 30, 1910, p. 1; "La Soumission de Marc Sangnier," Aug. 31, 1910, p. 1; "La Lettre de Marc Sangnier," Sept. 1, 1910, p. 2; Aventino, Sept. 3, 1910, p. 1.

19. See the following articles in *Le Sillon:* Sangnier, "Bulletin 14," Sept. 25, 1901, pp. 179–80; Sangnier, "Une Idole," Mar. 25, 1905, pp. 204–05; Georges Hoog, "Métier de roi, métier de citoyen," Sept. 10, 1905, p. 167; Charles Boucaud, "Catholicisme et démocratie," Aug. 10, 1903, pp. 116–18.

20. Emmanuel Desgrées du Loû, *L'Ouest-Eclair,* Dec. 1, 1903, p. 1, and July 2, 1904, p. 1; Charles Bodin, *L'Ouest-Eclair,* Oct. 10, 1903, p. 1; Fonsegrive, *L'Ouest-Eclair,* Feb. 17, 1908, p. 1; Delourme, *Trente-cinq années,* pp. 166–67, 174; "Derrière M. Monniot," *L'Ouest-Eclair,* Aug. 5, 1910, p. 1.

21. M. S., *La Démocratie,* Dec.3, 1911, p. 1; Leroy-Debasan, "Simples réflexions à propos d'une conversion," *Le Sillon,* June 25, 1908, p. 443; E. D. L., *L'Ouest-Eclair,* Sept. 12, 1908, p. 1; Pierre Aumond, "Armée et patrie," *Le Sillon,* Oct. 10, 1905, p. 255.

22. Fonsegrive, *L'Ouest-Eclair,* Feb. 17, 1908, p. 1; Hoog, "Dangereuses alliances," *Le Sillon,* Apr. 10, 1907, p. 243; Hoog, *La Démocratie,* Mar. 17, 1911, p. 1.

23. Hoog, *La Démocratie,* Mar. 17, 1911, p. 1; Fabre, *La Démocratie,* Oct. 7, 1912, p. 1; Dabry, *Vie Catholique,* Nov. 16, 1907, p. 1; Le Guern,

Notes to Pages 76–84 + 201

L'Ouest-Eclair, Dec. 16, 1910, p. 1; Aumond, "Armée et patrie," *Le Sillon,* Oct. 10, 1905, p. 255.
    24. Paul, *The Second Ralliement,* pp. 23–24. F⁷12863 (no. 7), Mar. 21, 1912, p. 4; J. Vialatoux, "Paganisme et Christianisme," *Chronique du Sud-Est,* Apr. 30, 1908, pp. 110–14.
    25. Paul, *The Second Ralliement,* p. 24; Weber, *Action Francaise,* pp. 65–66. F⁷12863 (no. 1), n.d., pp. 1–5.
    26. Weber, *Action Française,* p. 222; "Nouvelles religieuses," *Semaine Religieuse de Cambrai,* Oct. 7, 1911, pp. 958–59; de la Brière, *L'Action Française,* June 23, 1913, pp. 1–2; F⁷12863 (no. 1), n.d., p. 35; B a/1343, Jan. 16, 1912.
    27. Maurras, *L'Action Française et la religion catholique,* pp. 218–21, 229–30.
    28. Ibid., pp. 43, 50, 131, 139–40, 148–49, 251, 278.
    29. Ibid., pp. 273–74.
    30. Weber, *Action Française,* p. 222; Thomas, *L'Action Française,* p. 83.
    31. Msgr. Charost and Pius X, in Thomas, *L'Action Française,* pp. 83, 81. There is some debate on the exact words used by Pius X in this blessing. Daniel-Rops, *A Fight for God,* p. 298, and Weber, *Action Française,* p. 222, claim that the pope said, "Maurras is a good champion of the Church and the Holy See." Regardless of the specific words, the sense of the pontiff's approval of the royalist's work remains unquestionable.

Chapter 6. *The Apogee of a Friendship (1914–1925)*

    1. Cardinal Luçon, *La Croix,* Mar. 18, 1916, p. 3; Cardinal Dubourg, "Partie officielle," *Semaine Religieuse de Rennes,* Mar. 6, 1915, p. 387.
    2. J. B., *La Croix,* May 15, 1915, p. 1, and Jan. 20, 1915, p. 1; Franc, *La Croix,* Mar. 3, 1916, p. 1; Victor de Bled, "L'Idée de la patrie," *Revue des Deux Mondes,* July 15, 1915, pp. 336–37, 352; Massis, *La Croix,* Mar. 29, 1916, p. 3; Maritain, *La Croix,* Jan. 7, 1915, p. 5, Jan. 20, 1915, p. 6, and May 2–3, 1915, p. 5.
    3. "Son Eminence le cardinal Mercier," *Semaine Religieuse de Rennes,* Feb. 12, 1916, pp. 349–50; "Protestation du cardinal Mercier," *La Croix,* Nov. 15, 1916, p. 2; J. B., *La Croix,* Sept. 22, 1914, p. 1; "Destruction de la cathédrale de Reims," *Semaine Religieuse de Rennes,* Sept. 26, 1914, p. 29; "Voeu de S. Em. le cardinal Luçon," *La Croix,* Apr. 9, 1915, p. 5; "Choses et autres," *La Croix,* June 3, 1916, p. 1; "La France à genoux devant le Sacre-Coeur," *Semaine Religieuse de Rennes,* June 22, 1918, pp. 385–87; "Le Voeu collectif de l'épiscopat pour la fête du Sacre-Coeur," *La Croix,* June 5, 1917, p. 1.
    4. Maurras, *Le Pape,* pp. vi, 59; "A l'Institut d'Action Française," *L'Action Française,* June 20, 1915, p. 1; Dimier, *L'Action Française,* July 19, 1915, p. 1; Maurras, *Le Pape,* p. 232; Dimier, *L'Action Française,* June 7, 1918, pp. 1–2; Msgr. Touchet, *L'Action Française,* Apr. 7, 1919, p. 1.

5. Maurras, *Le Pape*, p. 141; Dimier, *L'Action Française*, Aug. 27, 1917, p. 1, Dec. 2, 1917, p. 1, and June 29, 1915, p. 2; Msgr. Tissier, "La Voix des morts," *Semaine Religieuse de Rennes*, Sept. 22, 1917, p. 814; Guiraud, *La Croix*, Jan. 19, 1918, p. 1; Emmanuel Desgrées du Loû, *L'Ouest-Eclair*, July 1, 1917, p. 1.

6. Franc, *La Croix*, Oct. 11, 1916, p. 1; Guiraud, *La Croix*, July 22, 1919, p. 1; Saint-Léry, *L'Ouest-Eclair*, May 7, 1915, p. 1, and May 10, 1915, p. 1; E. L. B., *L'Ouest-Eclair*, Apr. 2, 1919, p. 1; "Pour l'union des catholiques français et italiens," *L'Action Française*, Dec. 20, 1915, pp. 1–2; Dimier, *L'Action Française*, Nov. 6, 1916, pp. 1–2, and Nov. 28, 1915, p. 2.

7. De Grandmaison, *Impressions de guerre*, and Barrès, *The Faith of France*, are two such books; another is Maurras, *Le Pape*. Alfred Baudrillart, *La France*, pp. 30, 47, 50, 58; Franc, *La Croix*, Dec. 22, 1914, p. 1; "Encore l'*Humanité*," *La Croix*, Jan. 10–11, 1915, pp. 1–2; Franc, *La Croix*, Aug. 11, 1915, p. 1, and Nov. 26, 1915, p. 1; Maurras, *Le Pape*, pp. 91, 99, 115, 141, 152, 173, 178, 180–84, 190, 192. For parallel opinions, see Dimier, *L'Action Française*, Aug. 22, 1916, pp. 1–2; "L'Immunité ecclésiastique," *L'Action Française*, Apr. 9, 1918, pp. 1–2.

8. Franc, *La Croix*, Jan. 26, 1915, p. 1, and May 3, 1917, p. 1; Dimier, *L'Action Française*, Nov. 18, 1915, p. 1; "Une lettre de S. S. Benoît XV, "*L'Action Française*," Oct. 24, 1914, p. 1; "Un Don du pape à la France," *L'Action Française*, May 5, 1915, p. 1; Maurras, *Le Pape*, pp. 5, 11–13, 15, 27, 49.

9. For the salient portions of the papal letter, see Anne Freemantle, ed., *The Papal Encyclicals*, pp. 217–19. *Semaine Religieuse de Rennes*, Nov. 3, 1917, pp. 909–10; Franc, *La Croix*, Aug. 18, 1917, p. 1; Collin, *La Croix*, Aug. 23, 1917, p. 1; Dimier, *L'Action Française*, Aug. 18, 1917, p. 1, and Aug. 19, 1917, p. 2.

10. Marc Sangnier, *La Démocratie*, Aug. 3, 1914, p. 1; Dimier, *L'Action Française*, July 24, 1916, p. 1; "La Patrie et la démocratie," *L'Ouest-Eclair*, Jan. 5, 1915, p. 1; Delourme, *Trente-cinq années*, pp. 179, 182–83, 185–90; "Nouvelles du diocèse de Rennes," *Semaine Religieuse de Rennes*, July 17, 1915, p. 710.

11. F⁷13195, Apr., 1915, pp. 3–4.

12. See the following articles in *L'Action Française:* "Le Cardinal de Cabrières et l'action nationale," Sept. 12, 1917, p. 1; "L'Action Française et la religion catholique," Oct. 11, 1919, p. 2; Dimier, Jan. 16, 1920, p. 2; Maurras, *L'Action Française et le Vatican*, pp. 54–55; "Le Cardinal Sevin," *L'Action Française*, May 14, 1916, p. 2; Thomas, *L'Action Française*, 1965, pp. 130–31.

13. Desgrées du Loû, *L'Ouest-Eclair*, Nov. 8, 1917, p. 1; see the following articles in *La Croix*: "Condamnation du *Bonnet Rouge*," Oct. 14, 1915, p. 1; Guiraud, Nov. 9. 1917, p. 1; Mollet, Oct. 9, 1917, p. 1; "Choses et autres," June 3, 1916, p. 1; Franc, Aug. 26–27, 1917, p. 1.

14. Franc, *La Croix*, July 25, 1917, p. 1.

15. "Lettre pastorale et collective des Monseigneurs," *Semaine Religieuse*

de Rennes, Mar. 1, 1924, pp. 189-900; Msgr. Simon Deploige, *Documentation Catholique*, Apr. 26, 1919, p. 395; Cardinal Dubois, "Lettre," *Semaine Religieuse de Paris*, Apr. 17, 1921, *Documentation Catholique*, June 23, 1923, p. 1592; "La Lettre du pape," *Semaine Religieuse de Lille*, July 15, 1923, p. 352.

16. Franc, *La Croix*, Aug. 6, 1919, p. 1; Capitaine B., *La Croix*, July 1, 1922, p. 1; E. L. B., *L'Ouest-Eclair*, Feb. 15, 1919, p. 1; Desgrées du Loû, *L'Ouest-Eclair*, Jan. 12, 1922, p. 1; R. Le Cholleux, *La Croix*, July 14, 1923, p. 1; "Les Troupes françaises pénétreront ce matin dans la Ruhr," *L'Ouest-Eclair*, Jan. 11, 1923, p. 1; René Pinon, *L'Ouest-Eclair*, Jan. 14, 1923, p. 1.

17. "Lettre de S. Em. le cardinal de Cabrières en vue des élections," *Documentation Catholique*, Sept. 13-20, 1920, pp. 398-99; "Lettre de Mgr. Chapon, évêque de Nice," *Documentation Catholique*, Nov. 1, 1919, p. 556: "Lettre des cardinaux, archevêques et évêques de France aux catholiques français," *Semaine Religieuse de Rennes*, May 31, 1919, pp. 338-44.

18. "Communications de l'archevêché," *Semaine Religieuse de Rennes*, Nov. 1, 1919, pp. 689-90; "Petit catéchisme de l'électeur par S. Em. le cardinal Andrieu archévêque de Bordeaux," *Documentation Catholique*, Oct. 25, 1919, pp. 516-17.

19. Franc, *La Croix*, Sept. 18, 1919, p. 1; "Politique républicaine française," *L'Ouest-Eclair*, Apr. 6, 1919, p. 1.

20. Paul, *The Second Ralliement*, pp. 71, 76-77; Cardinal de Cabrières, *Documentation Catholique*, Oct. 30, 1920, p. 331; Cardinal Andrieu, *Documentation Catholique*, Oct. 23, 1920, p. 300; "Lettre pastorale et collective de Monseigneurs les cardinaux, archevêques et évêques de France," *Semaine Religieuse de Rennes*, Mar. 1, 1924, pp. 191-92; Ministère des Affaires Étrangères, Saint-Siège (1918-1929): vol. 23, "Direction Politique Europe," no. 74, Rome, July 15, 1922; "Direction Politique Europe," no. 53, Rome, June 19, 1923.

21. Guiraud, *La Croix*, July 22, 1919, p. 1; Pinon, *L'Ouest-Eclair*, Apr. 22, 1922, p. 1; Eugène le Breton, *L'Ouest-Eclair*, Dec. 28, 1921, p. 1; "Le Bolchevisme et l'héritage romain," *Revue des Deux Mondes*, Apr. 15, 1927, p. 756. On the origins of French communism, see Wohl, *French Communism in the Making*; and Kriegel, *Aux origines du communisme française*, 1969. The impact of anticommunist policies in the highest circles of government and diplomacy may be noted in Mayer's *Political Origins of the New Diplomacy*.

22. "Lettre des cardinaux, archevêques et évêques de France aux catholiques français," *Semaine Religieuse de Rennes*, May 31, 1919, pp. 343-44; Cardinal Andrieu, *Documentation Catholique*, Oct. 7, 1922, pp. 516-17; "Lettre pastorale de Mgr. Julien, évêque d'Arras" (Feb. 23 and Mar. 2, 1922), in *Documentation Catholique*, Mar. 18, 1922, pp. 647-48; "Lettre de S. G. Mgr. Chollet au clergé de l'archdiocèse de Cambrai," *Documentation Catholique*, Apr. 2-9, 1921, pp. 367-69.

23. Cardinal Dubois, *Documentation Catholique*, May 3-10, 1924, p. 1211; "Lettre," *Documentation Catholique*, May 3-10, 1924, p. 1210; Paul, *Second*

Ralliement, p. 103; Cardinal Andrieu, *Documentation Catholique,* June 14, 1924, p. 1489; Guiraud, *La Croix,* Feb. 23, 1924, p. 1; Eugène le Breton,*L'Ouest-Eclair,* Jan. 24, 1924, p. 1.

24. "La Question de l'ambassade auprès du Vatican," *Documentation Catholique,* Feb. 7, 1925, p. 364; "Le Saint-Siège et la France," *Documentation Catholique,* Apr. 11, 1925, pp. 926–59; "La Vraie raison de la suppression de l'ambassade au Vatican," *Semaine Religieuse de Rennes,* Feb. 14, 1925, pp. 156–57; Cardinal Charost, "Discours," *Semaine Religieuse de Rennes,* Feb. 21, 1925, p. 172; Desgrées du Loû, *L'Ouest-Eclair,* Sept. 28, 1924, p. 1; Sangnier, *Jeune-République,* Feb. 6, 1925, p. 1; d'Anthouard, *Vie Catholique,* Jan. 17, 1925, p. 1.

25. Coutrot and Dreyfus, *Les Forces religieuses,* p. 316; Silverman, "Political Catholicism," Paul, *Second Ralliement,* pp. 116–25; Msgr. Ruch, *Documentation Catholique,* Aug. 2–9, 1924, p. 132.

26. Guiraud, *La Croix,* Feb. 24, 1925, p. 1; Sangnier, *Jeune-République,* Oct. 3, 1924, p. 1; Paul, *Second Ralliement,* pp. 113–15; Dansette, *Religious History of Modern France* 2:349; Daniel-Rops, *A Fight for God,* p. 270; Cardinal Charost, "Lettre pastorale," *Semaine Religieuse de Rennes,* Nov. 2, 1924, pp. 1100–01, 1104; Guiraud, *La Croix,* Nov. 14, 1924, p. 1; Guiraud, *La Croix,* Feb. 14, 1925, p. 1; Général de Castelnau, "Les Leçons de Nancy," *Credo,* May 1926, p. 3; "À travers le pays," *Credo,* Mar.–Apr. 1925), pp. 8–9; "Déclaration de l'assemblée des archevêques et cardinaux de France," *L'Action Française,* Mar. 12, 1925, pp. 1–2; F⁷13223, Dec. 22, 1927, pp. 1–3; F⁷13219, Mar. 1, 1926.

27. See the following articles in *L'Action Française:* "Chronique religieuse," Apr. 3, 1924, p. 2; Jacques Bainville, Jan. 11, 1923, p. 1; Daudet, Jan. 13, 1923, p. 1; "La Société des Nations et la Ruhr," Jan. 22, 1923, p. 1; Daudet, Mar. 6, 1920, p. 1; Pujo, Apr. 6, 1920, p. 1.

28. See the following articles in *L'Action Française:* "Nos relations avec le Vatican," Mar. 12, 1920, pp. 1–2; Maurras, Apr. 6, 1920, p. 1; Daudet, Nov. 26, 1920, pp. 1–2; "Revue de la presse," Oct. 2, 1920, p. 3; Havard de la Montagne, May 19, 1921, pp. 1–2; Daudet, Feb. 22, 1921, p. 1; Gloria, *L'Action Française du dimanche,* Oct. 19, 1924, p. 3; see the following articles in *L'Action Française:* Pujo, July 16, 1921, p. 1, and July 22, 1921, p. 1; "La Résistance alsacienne," July 6, 1924, p. 1; "Contre la pérsecution religieuse," Sept. 27, 1924, pp. 1–2; "Programme de l'Union des Catholiques," Oct. 11, 1924, p. 2; Général de Castelnau, Nov. 8, 1924, p. 2; "Procureur Général à M. Le Garde des Sceaux," in F⁷13196, May 23, 1926, p. 1.

29. See the following articles in *L'Action Française:* "J'ai cru nécessaire," Dec. 27, 1919, p. 1; Daudet, Mar. 6, 1920, p. 1; Pujo, Apr. 12, 1920, p. 1; Havard de la Montagne, Jan. 21, 1922, p. 3; "Chronique religieuse," Apr. 3, 1924, p. 2; "Lettre d'Alsace," Aug. 12, 1924, pp. 1–2; Weber, *Action Française,* p. 142; Desgrées du Loû, *L'Ouest-Eclair,* Nov. 5, 1919, p. 1, and Nov. 18,

1919, p. 1; Delourme, *Trente-cinq années*, pp. 194-96; "Communication de l'archevêché," *Semaine Religieuse de Rennes*, Jan. 10, 1920, pp. 17-18.

30. Weber, *Action Française*, pp. 220, 224, 232.

31. *Semaine Religieuse de Rennes*, Oct. 11, 1919, pp. 644-45; see the following articles in *L'Action Française:* Msgr. Penon, Oct. 11, 1919, p. 2; Cardinal de Cabrières, Aug. 6, 1920, p. 1; "La Mort de Madame Maurras," Nov. 12, 1922, p. 1; "Les Obsèques de Madame Maurras," Nov. 7, 1922, p. 1; Paul, *Second Ralliement*, p. 149; Weber, *Action Française*, p. 224; Daudet, *L'Action Française*, Mar. 1, 1925, p. 1.

32. Weber, *Action Française*, pp. 184-85, 223-24; Rémond, *Les Catholiques, le communisme et les crises*, p. 271; Guiraud, *La Croix*, Jan. 9, 1925, p. 1.

33. Weber, *Action Française*, p. 223; Paul, *Second Ralliement*, p. 149; "À Nantes," *L'Action Française*, Mar. 2, 1925, p. 1; Dansette, *Religious History*, p. 349; "Deuxième assemblée générale de la Fédération Nationale Catholique," *Credo*, Dec., 1925, p. 4; "Hommage de la Fédération Nationale Catholique au Saint-Père," *France Catholique*, June 24, 1933, p. 2; "Affaire rue Hermel," in F⁷13196, June 15, 1925, pp. 10, 12; "Les Funérailles du cardinal Mercier à Bruxelles," *L'Action Française*, Jan. 29, 1926, pp. 1-2; Procureur Général à M. Le Garde des Sceaux, in F⁷13196, May 23, 1926, p. 1; Daage, *France Catholique*, Feb. 17, 1934, p. 3; Georges Viance, "L'Anticléricalisme modèle 1928," *Credo*, Apr. 1928, pp. 27-28; Abbé Luc Lefebvre, interview, Paris, Sept. 23, 1972; "La Fédération Catholique et l'Action française," *L'Ouest-Eclair*, June 26, 1925, p. 2; F⁷13223, Oct. 7, 1927.

34. Weber, *Action Française*, pp. 226-28; Paul, *Second Ralliement*, p. 149; F⁷13195, July 12, 1920.

Chapter 7. The Winds of Change (1914-1925)

1. "La Patrie et la démocratie," *L'Ouest-Eclair*, Jan. 5, 1915, p. 1; Marc Sangnier, *La Démocratie*, Feb. 22, 1920, pp. 1-2.

2. Madiran, *L'Intégrisme*, pp. 30, 57-58; "S. S. Benoît XV et l'ancien Sillon," *Semaine Religieuse de Rennes*, Apr. 28, 1917, p. 522.

3. Basic works about the Second Ralliement are Paul, *The Second Ralliement*, and Rémond, *Les Catholiques, le communisme et les crises*. Both these authors' interpretations of the Second Ralliement contrast sharply with the positions adopted in my study (cf. chapters 7-9). During the earliest phase of Pius XI's reign, it seemed as if the Vatican was prepared to make some sort of accommodation with the Bolshevik government. Four days after the new pope's enthronement, his secretary of state Cardinal Pietro Gasparri said as much at the Genoa Conference. However, nothing came of this gesture, which proved to be only an incidental contrast to the pope's consistent and inflexible anticommunism (Daim, *The Vatican and East Europe*, pp. 55-57; Anderson, *Between Two Wars*, pp. 68-69). Daim summarizes this position well (p. 57): "All

in all, the early contacts between the Vatican and the Soviets were at best an interlude, and Catholicism continued to regard communism and its Russian stronghold as traps laid by Satan."

4. E. D. L., *L'Ouest-Eclair,* Jan. 23, 1923, pp. 1–2; Sangnier, *Jeune-République,* Nov. 3, 1922, p. 1, and Jan. 26, 1923, p. 1; "L'Action Française en 1923," *L'Ouest-Eclair,* Mar. 21, 1924, p. 1.

5. See the following articles in *Jeune-République:* Sangnier, May 11, 1923, p. 1; Maury, Mar. 2, 1923, pp. 1–2; Sangnier, Feb. 22, 1924, p. 1; Rolland, Aug. 14, 1921, p. 1; Sangnier, *La Démocratie,* Dec. 10, 1920, p. 1; articles in *Jeune-République:* Sangnier, Jan. 16, 1921, p. 1, Sept. 4, 1921, p. 1, and Nov. 13, 1921, p. 1; "S. Ex. Mgr. Cerretti: Nonce Apostolique visite la Maison de la Démocratie," Jan. 22, 1922, p. 1; Sangnier, Feb. 22, 1924, p. 1; Rudel, Apr. 25, 1924, p. 1. The minimal quantitative impact of the Jeune-République can be seen by the fact that its weekly publication reached a maximum of 50,000 but had only a subscription list of 10,000. Membership in the league itself was significantly less than that (see Sangnier, *Jeune-République,* Oct. 20, 1922, p. 1; Sangnier, *La Démocratie,* June 23, 1912, pp. 1, 5).

6. Hoog, *Jeune-République,* Feb. 15, 1924, p. 1; Sangnier, *Documentation Catholique,* June 30, 1923, 1614.

7. On this confrontation between the two protagonists, see Arnal, "The Nature and Success of Breton Christian Democracy."

8. Delourme, *Trente-cinq années,* pp. 247, 253–55; articles in *L'Ouest-Eclair:* E. D. L., June 14, 1925, pp. 1–2; Desgrées du Loû, June 19, 1925, p. 1; "Avant l'élection du Maine-et-Loire," June 25, 1925, p. 2; Desgrées du Loû, June 29, 1925, p. 1.

9. "Le Scandale de l'*Ouest-Eclair,*" *L'Action Française,* May 7–8, 1923, p. 1; Daudet, *L'Action Française,* May 15, 1923, p. 1; "*L'Ouest-Eclair* et M. Léon Daudet," *L'Ouest-Eclair,* May 8, 1923, p. 1; Desgrées du Loû, *L'Ouest-Eclair,* May 14, 1923, p. 1; "Les Poursuites contre l'abbé Trochu autorisées par le cardinal Charost," *L'Action Française,* May 26, 1923, p. 1; Delourme, *Trent-cinq années,* pp. 236–37; "Une Lettre du cardinal Charost," *L'Action Française,* May 23, 1923, p. 1; "L'Heure de la justice," *L'Ouest-Eclair,* Apr. 3, 1925, p. 1.

10. On the birth and pilgrimage of the PDP, see Rauch, "From the Sillon"; Einaudi and Goguel, *Christian Democracy in Italy and France;* Fogarty, *Christian Democracy in Western Europe;* and Irving, *Christian Democracy in France.* A primary source is Raymond-Laurent, *Le Parti Démocrate Populaire.*

11. Raymond-Laurent, *Le Parti Démocrate Populaire,* p. 47; *Le Petit Démocrate* (Nov. 27, 1927), in *Documentation Catholique,* Feb. 25, 1928, p. 511; Pagès, *L'Ouest-Eclair,* Nov. 17, 1924, p. 1; Rauch, "From the Sillon," pp. 58–63; Einaudi and Goguel, *Christian Democracy in Italy and France,* p. 114; Paul, *Second Ralliement,* p. 183; see the following articles by Robert Cornilleau in *Le Petit Démocrate:* "Loyalisme républicain," Feb. 20, 1927, p. 1; "Un peuple, une politique, un homme," May 29, 1927, p. 1; "Question de force?" June 5, 1927, p. 1; "Sous l'étoile rouge," Sept. 9, 1934, p. 1.

12. Rémond, *Les Catholiques*, pp. 274, 277; see the following articles in *La Vie Catholique:* Gay, Sept. 20, 1924, p. 1, and Nov. 8, 1924, p. 1; Msgr. Beaupin, Sept. 5, 1925, p. 1; Zamanski, Mar. 20, 1926, p. 1; Lerolle, Apr. 18, 1925, p. 1; Gay, May 8, 1926, p. 1; Lerolle, Feb. 7, 1925, p. 1; "Les Devoirs de l'heure présente" Oct. 4, 1924, p. 1; "Lettre de S. S. Pie XI à la *Vie Catholique* pour le première anniversaire de sa fondation," Oct. 24, 1925, p. 1.

13. For studies of the CFTC, see Lorwin, *The French Labor Movement;* Dolléans and Dehove, *Histoire du travail en France;* Bosworth, *Catholicism and Crisis;* and Deygas, *La C.F.T.C.;* Tessier, *L'Aube,* July 14-15, 1933, p. 1; Zirnheld, *La Vie Catholique,* May 28, 1927, p. 1; Tessier, *La Vie Catholique,* Apr. 21, 1934, p. 1; Flory, *La Vie Catholique,* Aug. 1, 1925, p. 1; *Documentation Catholique,* Dec. 13, 1919, p. 760; "Méthodes de la C.F.T.C.," *Vie Catholique,* Nov. 21, 1931, p. 9.

14. Piux XI, *Ubi Arcano Dei* (Dec. 23, 1922), in *The Papal Encyclicals,* ed. Fremantle, pp. 221-24.

15. Gibier, *La France catholique organisée,* pp. ix, xiii-xv, 216, 218; Pius XI, *Maximam Gravissimamque* (Jan. 18, 1924), in *Documentation Catholique,* Feb. 2, 1924, pp. 263-65; "Modèle de statuts approuvées par le pape pour les associations diocésaines," *Semaine Religieuse de Rennes,* Feb. 16, 1924, pp. 138-42.

16. Général de Castelnau, "Votons!" *Credo,* Mar. 1928, pp. 3, 5, and "Initiatives," *Credo,* Sept. 1925, p. 1; Daage, *France Catholique,* Feb. 17, 1934, p. 3; A. G. Michel "Une Quatrième forme de gouvernement—La République démocratique maçonnique," *Credo* Oct. 1934, pp. 8, 15; Georges Viance, "L'Anticléricalisme modèle 1928," *Credo,* Apr. 1928, pp. 27-28; le Cour Grandmaison, *France Catholique,* Feb. 21, 1938, pp. 1, 3.

17. "La F.N.C. dans le diocèse de Lille," *Credo,* Sept. 25, 1925, p. 10. See also Paul, *Second Ralliement,* p. 114; "Les Conseils du cardinal archevêque de Paris aux catholiques," *Credo,* Jan. 1928, p. 5.

18. "Les Conseils, *Credo,* Jan. 1928, p. 5; "Deuxième assemblée générale de la Fédération Nationale Catholique," *Credo,* Dec. 1925, 4; "Lettre du Souverain Pontife—Son Eminence le cardinal Gasparri à M. le général de Castelnau," *Credo* Dec. 1925, p. 3.

19. Pius XI, *Quando nel principio,* in *Documentation Catholique,* July 21-28, 1923, p. 68; articles in *L'Action Française:* Bainville, Jan. 11, 1923, p. 1; Havard de la Montagne, May 19, 1921, pp. 1-2; Talmeyr, Nov. 16, 1920, p. 1; *L'Action Française du dimanche,* Feb. 17, 1924, p. 3.

20. Shortly before his death and after his conversion to Christianity, Charles Maurras became a champion for the canonization of Pius X and wrote a book to that effect called *Le Bienheureux Pie X, sauveur de la France* (1953). Maurras's acceptance of the Catholic faith was described to me by the priest who catechised him, Canon Alfred Cormier (interview, Tours, Feb. 9, 1973). See also Cormier, *Mes entretiens de prêtre avec Charles Maurras and la vie intérieure de Charles Maurras.* Aventino, *L'Action Française,* Jan. 29, 1922, p. 2;

Havard de la Montagne, *L'Action Française*, Jan. 24, 1922, p. 1; *L'Action Française* (Feb. 4, 1922), in Paul, *Second Ralliement*, p. 150.

Chapter 8. The Church Condemns the Action Française (1925-1929)

1. On the Belgian church campaign against the Action Française, see Weber, *Action Française*, pp. 227-29; Paul, *The Second Ralliement*, pp. 149-50; and Thomas, *L'Action Française*, pp. 333-35.
2. Dansette, "L'Église et l'Action Française," p. 289; Paul, *Second Ralliement*, p. 151; Weber, *Action Française*, p. 230; Cardinal Andrieu, *L'Acquitaine*, Aug. 27, 1926, in Thomas, *Action Française*, pp. 110-12.
3. Maurras, *L'Action Française et le Vatican*, pp. 57, 59, 66; Thomas, *L'Action Française*, pp. 338-40.
4. Weber, *Action Française*, p. 235.
5. "'L'Action Française' contre l'organe officiel du Vatican," *Le Petit Démocrate*, Jan. 9, 1927, p. 25; Robert Cornilleau, "'Nous ne marchons pas!'" *Le Petit Démocrate*, May 22, 1927, p. 1.
6. Pagès, *L'Ouest-Eclair*, Oct. 3, 1926, p. 1; "Une Déclaration des cardinaux, archevêques et évêques de France sur l'Action Française," *L'Ouest-Eclair*, Mar. 9, 1927, p. 1; Sangnier, *Jeune-République*, Jan. 7, 1927, p. 1; Lacroix, *Jeune-République*, Apr. 22, 1927, p. 1.
7. See the following articles in *La Vie Catholique:* Veuillot, Jan. 1, 1927, p. 3; Valensin, Nov. 13, 1926, p. 1; Gay, Jan. 7, 1928, p. 1; Gay, Apr. 16, 1927, p. 5; Gay, *L'Aube*, Feb. 15, 1935, p. 2.
8. See the following articles in *La Vie Catholique:* Vignaux, Oct. 16, 1926, p. 1; May 21, 1927, p. 1; Gay, June 4, 1927, p. 5, Aug. 6, 1927, p. 1, and Aug. 27, 1927, p. 8; "M. Xavier Vallat et l'*Action Française*," Feb. 11, 1928, p. 5; Floriscone, Dec. 8, 1928, p. 1; Weber, *Action Française*, pp. 242, 246.
9. Weber, *Action Française*, pp. 242-43, 245.
10. Paul Doncoeur et al., *Pourquoi Rome a parlé*, pp. 22, 27-29, 59-61, 75, 81-82, 109, 112, 117, 262, 278-79; Maritain, *The Things That Are Not Caesar's*, pp. 30, 37, 47, 55, 69. The title of Maritain's book *Primauté du spirituel*, forms an interesting contrast with the Maurrasian slogan *politique d'abord*. See also Maritain, *Une Opinion sur Charles Maurras*.
11. Cardinal Dubois of Paris, *Documentation Catholique* Jan. 22, 1927, p. 270. See also the following issues of *Documentation Catholique*: Oct. 23, 1926, p. 648; Msgr. Humbrecht of Besançon, Jan. 22, 1917, pp. 299-300; and Msgr. Rivière of Aix, Jan. 22, 1927, pp. 303-05.
12. "Une Communique de Mgr. Marty, évêque de Montauban," *L'Action Française*, Oct. 31, 1926, p. 1; Fernand Passelecq, "Une Remise au point de S. G. Marty, évêque de Montauban," *L'Action Française*, Nov. 9, 1926, p. 1; Msgr. Marty, *Documentation Catholique*, Nov. 27, 1926, p. 991; "Ce que sont exactement les instructions du Pape aux évêques français au sujet de l'Action Française," *L'Ouest-Eclair*, Nov. 18, 1926, p. 1.

13. Thomas *L'Action Française*, p. 344; Weber, *Action Française*, pp. 236, 243, 344; Paul, *Second Ralliement*, pp. 164, 169–70; Daniel-Rops, *A Fight for God*, p. 302. Dansette, *Religious History* 2:402–03; Falconi, *The Popes in the Twentieth Century*, p. 214; *L'Action Française:* articles in "Le Cardinal Sevin," May 14, 1916, p. 2; "Mort de Mgr. Delassus," Oct. 12, 1921, p. 2; "Mort de Cardinal de Cabrières," Dec. 22, 1921, p. 1; "Le Cardinal Mercier est mort," Jan. 24, 1926, p. 1.

14. Msgr. Germain, *Documentation Catholique*, Nov. 27, 1926, p. 978. Three other examples from *Documentation Catholique* are: Msgr. Chassagnon of Autun, Oct. 23, 1926, pp. 664–65; Msgr. Ruch of Strasbourg, Oct. 23, 1926, p. 663; and Cardinal Luçon of Reims, Jan. 29, 1927, p. 261.

15. Msgr. Sagot of Agen, *Documentation Catholique*, Apr. 9, 1927, pp. 912–13, 915, 917–19, 929.

16. Cardinal Charost, "Lettre de son eminence le cardinal archevêque de Rennes à l'occasion du recent avertissement donné par le souverain pontife aux catholiques d'Action Française," *Semaine Religieuse de Rennes*, Nov. 27, 1926, pp. 1138–39, and Dec. 4, 1926, pp. 1162–65.

17. Cardinal Charost, *Semaine Religieuse de Rennes*, Jan. 15, 1927, p. 38; "Lettre du cardinal Charost à la *Croix*," *L'Action Française*, Mar. 13, 1927, p. 1; "Réplique de l'amiral Schwerer à S. E. le cardinal Charost," *L'Action Française*, Mar. 14, 1927, p. 1; "Lettre de son eminence le cardinal Charost archevêque de Rennes au *Nouvelliste*," *Semaine Religieuse de Rennes*, Jan. 29, 1927, pp. 69–70; Delorme, *Trente-cinq années*, pp. 351–52, 357–58, 373; "Lettre collective de NN. SS. les évêques de Bretagne et de Mgr. l'évêque de Laval recommandant aux catholiques de leurs diocèses le *Nouvelliste de Bretagne*," *Semaine Religieuse de Rennes*, Sept. 29, 1928, pp. 434–36, 625–28. Interestingly enough, this was the last victory of *L'Ouest-Eclair* against the integrist Catholic forces in Brittany. In less than two years, the more conservative Emmanuel Desgrées du Loû sought to make peace with Cardinal Charost by supporting archdiocesan and FNC electoral candidates. The more progressive Félix Trochu objected strenuously but to no avail. Charost, Desgrées du Loû, and the papal nuncio Msgr. Maglione united to press for Trochu's resignation from the newspaper early in the summer of 1930. *L'Ouest-Eclair* had abandoned the Second Ralliement definitively. (See Delourme, *Trente-cinq années*, pp. 386–96, 401–02, 407–08, 417, 428; and "Chronique Diocésaine — Communication de l'archevêché," *Semaine Religieuse de Rennes*, July 12, 1930, p. 622).

18. In Maurras, *L'Action Française et le Vatican*, pp. 150, 152–55, 158.

19. Some examples of this initial reticence can be found in the following issues of *La Croix*: Sept. 9, 1926; Sept. 10, 1926; Sept. 26–27, 1926; Oct. 8, 1926; Nov. 13, 1926; and Jan. 9–10, 1927, p. 1. "L'Allocuation consistoriale," Dec. 21, 1926, p. 1; "L'Allocution consistoriale du 20 décembre — La France," Dec. 24, 1926, p. 1; France, Sept. 18, 1926, p. 1; I. F., Sept. 28, 1926, p. 1.

20. See the following articles in *La Croix:* editorial, Dec. 28, 1926, p. 1; Guiraud, Jan. 21, 1927, p. 1, and Feb. 11, 1927, p. 1. For similar articles,

see Guiraud, Feb. 22, 1927, p. 1, and "Une contradiction," May 6, 1927, p. 1; editorial, Aug. 21-22, 1927, p. 1. Guiraud's own ambivalence was enhanced by the massive pro–Action Française correspondence that crossed his desk at *La Croix*. See letters in 362 AP from the following persons: Louis Thery, Oct. 13, 1926; Commandment A. Tuloup, Apr. 1, 1927; Mainfroy Maignial, Apr. 15, 1927; and E. de Beaufour, Mar. 17, 1927.

21. For the details of this papally imposed administrative shift, see Godfrin and Godfrin, *Une Centrale de presse catholique*, 1965.

22. Merklen, *La Croix*, Feb. 23, 1928, p. 1, Oct. 17, 1929, p. 1, and May 10, 1928, p. 1.

23. See Merklen's articles in the following issues of *La Croix:* May 21, 1931, p. 1; May 11, 1939, p. 1; Sept. 5, 1929, p. 1; Jan. 1–2 and 9, 1930, p. 1; Mar. 8, 1929, p. 1; "L'Organisation de l'Action catholique—Union dans la coordination," Jan. 6, 1931, p. 1; Feb. 28, 1929, p. 1; Mar. 19, 1936, p. 1; May 21, 1931; May 11, 1939; June 22, 1939, pp. 1–2; July 16, 1936, p. 1; May 21, 1931; Feb. 25, 1927, p. 2; May 25–26, 1933, pp. 1–2.

24. For a detailed critique of the reputed Ralliement credentials of interwar La Croix, see Arnal, "The Ambivalent *Ralliement* of *La Croix*." For examples of this preferential hierarchical treatment given to *La Croix*, note the front pages of the following issues: Oct. 11, 1929; Nov. 30, 1932; July 31, 1935; May 14, 1937; and Apr. 19, 1939.

25. Weber, *Action Française*, pp. 226–28; Paul, *Second Ralliement*, p. 149; "Adresse de l'A.C.J.F. à S. S. Pie XI" and "Adresse des anciens de l'A.C.J.F. à S. S. Pie XI," *Documentation Catholique*, Oct. 22, 1927, pp. 675, 677–78.

26. *Semaine Religieuse de Paris* (Sept. 10, 1927), in *Documentation Catholique*, Oct. 22, 1927, p. 691; La Rédaction, "Le Pape et l'Action Française," *Chronique Sociale de France*, Nov. 1926, pp. 749–50; Abbé Thellier de Poncheville, "Combat politique ou apostolat social?" *Chronique Sociale de France*, Nov. 1926, pp. 751–60. Joseph Vialatoux, who had written polemics against the Maurrasians before the war, attacked them in "La Doctrine catholique et l'École de Maurras," *Chronique Sociale de France*, Dec. 26, 1926, pp. 833–84. See also Daniel-Rops, *A Fight for God*, pp. 293–94; *La Jeunesse Ouvrière Chrétienne* . . . pp. 1–2; Bosworth, *Catholicism and Crisis*, p. 109; André Villette, former J.O.C. officer and newspaper editor, interview, Paris, June 25, 1980. Useful testimonies of the first years of the JOC are found in Véret, *J'ai vu grandir la J.O.C.;* and Berthe, *JOC je te dois tout*, 1980.

27. Général de Castelnau, "Lettre de Sa Sainteté Pie XI à son Eminence le Cardinal Andrieu Archevêque de Bordeaux," *Credo*, Oct. 1926, p. 4; Yves de la Brière, "Pourquoi Rome a parlé," *Credo*, Dec. 1927, pp. 17–18; F7 13223, Nov. 23, 1927.

28. Police dossiers in F7 13196, Mar. 30, 1927, pp. 1–2, and Mar. 9, 1927, pp. 1–2; "Sur quel terrain l'union des catholiques française doit-elle se faire?" *L'Ouest-Eclair*, Dec. 16, 1926, pp. 1–2; "Le Saint-Siège et la Fédération Nationale Catholique," *Credo*, Feb. 1927, p. 3.

29. Maurras, *Action Française et le Vatican*, pp. 242-43. Antoine Murat, a long-time member of the Action Française, said in an interview (Paris, Dec. 1972), that "*politique d'abord* signified priority of means, not primacy." Pujo, *Comment Rome est trompée*, pp. 72-116, 117-78, 184-85, 191, 291-95, 298. Some royalist fellow travelers even argued that Maurras had never entirely lost his religious faith. Canon Alfred Cormier, the monarchist priest who gave him last rites, was one such example (interview, Tours, Feb. 1973). See also Cormier, *Mes entretiens de prêtre;* De Roux, *Charles Maurras*, 1927, p. 64; M. Vuibert, interview, Paris, Dec. 1972.

30. Maurras, *Action Française et le Vatican*, pp. 76-77, 87. Also see Pujo, *Comment Rome est trompée*, 1929, pp. 88, 272-74; *Après sa mise à l'Index peut-on lire en toute tranquillité de conscience "L'Action Française"*? F⁷13196, p. 2, italics in original.

31. In Coutrot and Dreyfus, *Les Forces religieuses*, p. 102.

32. See the following articles in *L'Action Française:* Daudet, Jan. 3, 1927, p. 1, and Jan. 14, 1927, p. 1; "Revue de la presse," Jan. 5, 1927, p. 3; Daudet, Jan. 6, 1927, p. 1, and Jan. 31, 1927, p. 1; "Sous la terreur," Nov. 13, 1927, p. 1.

33. See the following articles in *L'Action Française:* "Sous la terreur," Nov. 13, 1927, p. 1; Pujo, Aug. 21, 1927, p. 1; Pujo, Dec. 29, 1928, p. 1; "Sous la terreur," Jan.31, 1928, p. 1. F⁷13195, Nov. 14, 1927, pp. 1-2; de Roux, *Charles Maurras*, p. 64; articles in *L'Action Française:* Maurras, Apr. 1, 1928, p. 1; "*L'Ouest-Eclair* condamné par le tribunal ecclésiastique de Rennes," Feb. 3, 1930, p. 2; "Les Palinodies de l'*Ouest-Eclair*," Apr. 16, 1927, p. 2.

34. See the following articles in *Documentation Catholique:* "Ordonnance des cardinaux, archevêques et évêques de France," Apr. 14, 1928, pp. 899-902; "Publication du décret de la Sacrée Pénitencerie Apostolique du 16 nov. 1928," Jan. 19, 1929, pp. 131-32; Cardinal Dubois, Jan. 19, 1929, pp. 133-34; "Sur les confesseurs qui absolvent les adhérents à la faction l'Action Française," Jan. 19, 1929, pp. 132-215.

35. Hilaire Chollet, interview, Paris, Sept.1972; Abbé Luc Léfebvre, interview, Paris, Sept. 1972; Dr. Dijon, interview, Paris, Mar. 1973; and Robert Vuibert, interview, Vincennes, Feb. 1973. For a definitive analysis, see Thomas *L'Action Française*, pp. 333-37. Chief among more recent scholars adopting this opinion are René Rémond, in *Les Catholiques, le communisme et les crises*, and Harry W. Paul, *The Second Ralliement*. See also Rémond, *Les Catholiques dans la France*. Both Weber and Tannenbaum, in their seminal studies, accept a more subdued version of this position as one reason for the league's condemnation.

36. See Weber, *Action Française*, for some elaboration of this position. It is my contention that both Rémond and Paul make unsubstantiated ideological connections between the genuine rise of Catholic democratic pluralism in France and the intentions of Pius XI's peace with the Third Republic, his condemnation of the *Action Française*, and his adoption of Catholic Action.

Chapter 9. Shattered Ralliement and the Reprieve of the Action Française (1929–1939)

1. See Rauch, "From the Sillon" and *Politics and Belief;* Raymond-Laurent, *Le Parti Démocrate Populaire;* Irvine, *French Conservatism in Crisis;* see also the following articles in *Le Petit Démocrate:* Robert Cornilleau, "Chez les Socialistes et les Communistes," July 29, 1934, pp. 1–2; Georges Hourdin, "Ce qui nous sépare," June 21, 1936, pp. 1–2; Cornilleau, "Question de force," June 5, 1927, p. 1; and articles in *Jeune-République:* Hoog, May 19, 1933, p. 1; Sangnier, Nov. 13, 1921, p. 1; "Programme," Mar. 25, 1932, p. 1; "Vers la démocratie économique," Mar. 2, 1923, p. 1; Hoog, July 16, 1926, p. 1; De Richemont, Jan. 27, 1935, p. 1.

2. See the following articles in *Syndicalisme Chrétien:* Tessier, Nov. 1933, p. 875; "Syndicalisme chrétien et corporatisme fasciste," Jan. 1934, pp, 887–89, and Feb. 1934, pp. 895–97. See also Deygas, *La C.F.T.C.,* pp. 57–118.

3. For the birth, expansion, and structure of the early JOC in its Catholic and working-class context, see Dansette, *Destin du catholicisme français,* esp. p. 97; Bron, *Histoire du mouvement ouvrier français,* vol. 2; and Bosworth, *Catholicism and Crisis.* I learned much from my interviews with Roger Cartyrade and André Villette, former JOC leaders, concerning the origins and organization of this apostolate (Paris, July 6, 1979, and June 25, 1980, respectively). See the special commemorative publication of the JOC, *La Jeunesse Ouvrière Chrétienne,* pp. 1–2; and the following articles in *Jeunesse Ouvrière:* "J.O.C. petite guide sociale des familles ouvrières," special issue (Spring 1933), pp. 3–26; "La J.O.C. au Trocadero," Oct. 1930, p. 10; "Le vrai visage de la J.O.C.," Feb. 1933, pp. 1–2; "La J.O.C. au Trocadero," Oct. 1930, p. 1; "Les grèves du textile dans le Nord," Sept. 1930, pp. 1–2; "Le Conflit de Roubaix-Tourcoing," Aug. 1931, p. 1. Even those social Catholic study teams, such as the Jesuit Action Populaire and the lay Semaines Sociales, reflected an ambivalence. They were committed to social justice for the workers, but this concern was often overshadowed by an overriding fear of communism. See "La Conquête des âmes," *Dossiers de l'Action Populaire,* June 10, 1929, pp. 699–706; J. C., "L'Attrait du communisme," *Dossiers de l'Action Populaire,* July 10, 1933, pp. 1393–1414; Marius Gonin, "Une explication du Bolchevisme," *Chronique Sociale de France* 43 (Mar. 1934), 184–207; "Regards sur les classes et au-delà des classes: Semaine Sociale de Bordeaux, 24–30 juillet 1939," *Documentation Catholique,* Aug. 5, 1939, pp. 931–80.

4. On these Ralliement groups old and new, see Hellman, "Vichy Background," and "French 'Left Catholics'"; Rauch, *Politics and Belief;* Dansette, *Destin du catholicisme français;* Remond, *Les Catholiques, le communisme et les crises;* Arnal, "Alternatives to the Third Republic," and "Stillborn Alliance"; Coutrot, "Youth Movements in France." See also Mayeur, *L'Aube: Étude d'un journal d'opinion,* pp. 9–23; Gay and Tessier, *L'Aube,* Jan. 20, 1932, p. 1; Gay, *L'Aube,* Mar. 9, 1932, p. 1.

Notes to Pages 150-153 + 213

5. Dansette, *Destin du catholicisme français*, pp. 121-23, 131. Maritain's pilgrimage from reactionary Catholicism to a moderate conservative theology is described in *The Things That Are Not Caesar's, Freedom in the Modern World*, and especially *Integral Humanism*. Mounier's ideological break with his mentor Maritain can be detected in *Jacques Maritain, Emmanuel Mounier*, ed. Petit, and *Un Théologien en liberté: Jacques Duquesne interroge le Père Chenu*. For a fine study of *Sept*, see Coutrot, *Un Courant de la pensée catholique*, pp. 9, 14-15, 23-28, 52-53, 68-70, 115, 241; Simon, *Sept*, Jan. 17, 1936, p. 4.

6. Mounier, *Oeuvres* 1:139-41, 146, 149, 294-96, 491, 494, 497, 505, 513, 515-16, 519, 523-27, 536, 595, 597, 604, 619-21. On the early opening of *Esprit* and the influence of Emmanuel Mounier, see Hellman, "The Opening to the Left," and "Vichy Background;" Rauch, *Politics and Belief;* Lewis, "Emmanuel Mounier"; Winock, *Histoire politique de la revue "Esprit"*; Amato, *Mounier and Maritain;* Arnal, "Alternatives to the Third Republic."

7. Après le congrès national," *Jeune-République*, Oct. 30, 1922, pp. 1, 3; "Nos finances," *Jeune-République*, Apr. 9, 1939, p. 1; Mayeur, *L'Aube*, pp. 19-22, 173-80; Rémond, *Les Catholiques*, pp. 269, 273-74; headlines in *L'Aube*, Jan. 1-2, 1936, Nov. 14, 1936, and May 9, 1939; "Une campagne d'abonnements," *Esprit*, May, 1936, pp. 145-48; "Appel à nos amis," *Esprit*, Mar. 1, 1935, pp. 875-76; Coutrot, *Un Courant de la pensée catholique*, pp. 25, 52-53, 68-70; Bellanger et al., *Histoire générale de la presse française* 3:555, 596-97.

8. See the following articles in *Documentation Catholique*: Msgr. Cerretti, Jan. 16, 1926, p. 131; Pius XI, "Allocution 'Iam annus,'" Jan. 7, 1928, p. 31; Cardinal Gasparri, Apr. 30, 1927, p. 1115.

9. Merklen, *La Croix*, Feb. 16, 1928, p. 1, and June 30, 1931, p. 1; Guiraud, *La Croix*, Dec. 27, 1929, p. 1; Maritain, *Documentation Catholique*, Jan. 28, 1928, p. 226; "Appel des cardinaux et archevêques de France," *Documentation Catholique*, Oct. 24, 1931, p. 642.

10. René du Ponceau, *Annales de la Jeunesse Catholique*, in *Documentation Catholique*, Feb. 1, 1930, pp. 274-75; Gay, *L'Aube*, Mar. 9, 1932; "M. Aristide Briand est mort," *L'Aube*, Mar. 8, 1932, p. 1; "Les Obsèques nationales d'Aristide Briand," *L'Aube*, Mar. 13-14, 1932, pp. 1, 3; "Notre Patrie," *Esprit*, June 1935, pp. 342-44; Mounier, *Oeuvres* 1:629-30, 632-33; Joseph Folliet, "La Colonisation, son avenir, sa liquidation," *Esprit*, Dec. 1935, pp. 355-65; articles in *Jeune-République*: Sangnier, Jan. 26, 1921, p. 1; "Notre premier congrès démocratique international," Nov. 13, 1921, p. 1; Hoog, July 16, 1926; de Richement, Jan. 27, 1935.

11. See the following articles in *L'Action Française*: Daudet, Dec. 2, 1930, p. 1; Maurras, Oct. 29, 1931, p. 1, and Nov. 14, 1931, p. 1.

12. Général de Castelnau, *Documentation Catholique*, Jan. 8, 1927, pp. 84-86; "La Déclaration du Comité archiépiscopal de l'Action Catholique," *Credo*, Feb. 1933, pp. 3-4. As a manifestation of Catholic Action, the FNC was pressured into proclaiming its loyalty to the Vatican's program, but much as it had

done in the Action Française controversy, the reactionary movement used equivocal language. See "La Fédération Nationale Catholique," *France Catholique*, Feb. 4, 1933, p. 4.

13. Rémond, *Les Catholiques, le communisme et les crises*, pp. 61–66, 82–84, 87–88; Gay, *Vie Catholique*, Apr. 23, 1932, p. 1; De Castelnau, *Documentation Catholique*, Mar. 23, 1935, pp. 721–24, 728; *Sept* (Mar. 1, 1935), in *Documentation Catholique*, Mar. 23, 1935, p. 726; E. M., "La Cité," *Esprit*, Apr. 1935, pp. 133–34; "Conclusions," *Esprit*, Apr. 1936, pp. 89–90; Jacques Bois, "Procès de la conscription," *Esprit*, May 1935, p. 203; De Castelnau, *France Catholique*, July 6, 1935, p. 1; "L'Affaire de Briey," *France Catholique*, July 13, 1935, p. 1. The role of the Wendel industrialists in this scandal is dealt with in Jeanneney, *François de Wendel en République*.

14. Rémond, *Les Catholiques, le communisme et les crises*, pp. 68–69, 72; Gay, *L'Aube*, Dec. 7, 1932, p. 1; E. M., "Notes," *Esprit*, June 1935, p. 424; "S. S. Pie XI félicite l'A.C.J.F. de sa filiale docilité à la sainte hiérarchie," *La Vie Catholique*, Dec. 3, 1932, p. 1; Msgr. Liénart, "Lettre Pastorale," *Semaine Religieuse de Lille*, Dec. 11, 1932, pp. 952–53.

15. Rémond, *Les Catholiques, le communisme et les crises*, pp. 21–23, 26, 39; Dansette, *Religious History* 2:364–65; Pius XI, *Quadragesimo Anno* (May 15, 1931), in *The Papal Encyclicals*, ed. Fremantle, pp. 229–34, and in *Documentation Catholique*, June 6, 1931, pp. 1431, 1436–40.

16. "À bas les voleurs! À bas les assassins! Tous ce soir devant la Chambre," *L'Action Française*, Jan. 9, 1934, p. 1; "Contre les voleurs, contre le régime abject; Tous ce soir devant la Chambre," *L'Action Française*, Feb. 6, 1934, p. 1.

17. *Sept*, in Coutrot, *Un Courant, de la pensée catholique*, p. 102; Gay, *Vie Catholique*, Feb. 17, 1934, p. 1; *Documentation Catholique*, Mar. 17, 1934, p. 699; Prénat, *L'Aube*, Feb. 13, 1934, p. 1; Bidault, *L'Aube*, Mar. 21, 1934, p. 1; Mounier, *Oeuvres* 1:198–99, 363–65, 368, 394; France, *Jeune-République*, July 29, 1934, p. 2; "Aux ligeurs de la Jeune République," *Jeune-République*, Feb. 11, 1934, p. 1.

18. De Castelnau, *France Catholique*, Feb. 17, 1934, p. 1; Loyer, *France Catholique*, Mar. 10, 1934, p. 3; Guiraud, *La Croix*, Feb. 9, 1934, p. 1, and Feb. 14, 1934, p. 1; A. Bastianelli, "Les Leçons de la soirée tragique," *Le Petit Démocrate*, Feb. 18, 1934, p. 1; A. Champetier de Ribes, "Notre devoir,"*Le Petit Démocrate*, Feb. 18, 1934, p. 1.

19. Cardinal Lienart, *Documentation Catholique*, May 5, 1934, p. 1165; "Résolutions de l'Assemblée des cardinaux et archevêques," *Documentation Catholique*, July 4–11, 1936, pp. 13–14; "Chronique diocésaine,"*Semaine Religieuse de Lille*, Feb. 25, 1934, p. 144; Msgr. Bruno de Solages, "L'Union entre les catholiques," *Semaine Religieuse de Rennes*, Apr. 18, 1936, pp. 406, 408; Msgr. du Bois de la Villerabel, *Documentation Catholique*, Apr. 11, 1936, p. 908; Cardinal Verdier, *La Croix*, Feb. 10, 1934, p. 1. For other examples of such episcopal sympathy for the leagues, see *Documentation Catholique*, Mar. 17, 1934, pp. 685–88. Maurice Laudrain, "Après la commémoration reli-

gieuse de l'émeute fasciste du 6 février," *Terre Nouvelle*, 1935, p. 11; Maurice Laudrain, interview, Paris, May 1973.

20. On the relationship of French Catholics to various aspects of the Popular Front, see Christophe, *Les Catholiques et le Front populaire;* Hellman, "French 'Left Catholics,'" and "Vichy Background;" Arnal, "Stillborn Alliance," and "Alternatives to the Third Republic"; J. Murphy, "La Main tendue," and "Maurice Thorez"; and Rice-Maximin, "The Main Tendue."

21. Hellman, "French 'Left Catholics,'" p. 508; Robert Honnert, *Catholicisme et communisme;* see also the following articles in *Terre Nouvelle:* "Manifeste de *Terre Nouvelle*," May 1935, p. 1; Maurice Laudrain, "Pour le regne du Christ, votons rouge!" Apr. 1936, p. 5; André Deléage, "Page d'histoire sociale," July 1936, pp. 7-8; Laudrain, interview, Paris, May 1973. See also Arnal, "The Brief Pilgrimage of *Terre Nouvelle*"; Hoog, *Jeune-Republique*, July 7, 1935, p. 1; Philippe Wolff, "La Jeune République et le communisme," *Esprit*, Oct. 1934, pp. 164-65; André Ulmann, "La Cité," *Esprit*, Sept. 1935, p. 823; Jacques Madaule, "La Mort du rassemblement populaire," *Esprit*, Feb. 1938, pp. 781-82; Rauch, *Politics and Belief,* pp. 172-74; Hellman, "The Opening to the Left," p. 387; Arnal, "Stillborn Alliance," p. D1011, and "Alternatives to the Third Republic," pp. 192-93.

22. See the following articles in *Syndicalisme:* Zirnheld, July 1936, p. 1; "L'Activité de la C.F.T.C. pendant les grèves," July 1936, pp. 1-2; editorial, Apr. 1937, p. 1; "Quelle union?" Jan. 1938, p. 1; articles in *Jeunesse Ouvrière:* Mithot, Jan. 1, 1938, pp. 1-2; "Notre position, les grèves," June 15, 1936, p. 1; Muller, July 1, 1936, p. 1; "Appel aux Electeurs," *Le Petit Démocrate,* Apr. 5, 1936, p. 1; Georges Hourdin, "L'Experience Blum," *Le Petit Démocrate,* July 19, 1936, p. 1; Bidault, *L'Aube,* Mar. 21, 1934, p. 1; Sturzo, *L'Aube,* May 16, 1936, p. 1; Georges Bidault, interview, Paris, Feb. 1973; Sherer, *Sept,* May 1, 1936, p. 7; Jacques Duclos, interview, Paris, May 1973; editorial, *Sept,* May 15, 1936, p. 1; editorial, *Sept,* Feb. 19, 1937, p. 1.

23. Cardinal Maurin, *Documentation Catholique,* Apr. 11, 1936, p. 936; Cardinal Verdier's Christmas message, *La Croix,* Dec. 23, 1937, p. 1; Pierry, *Vie Catholique,* Feb. 15, 1936, p. 3; Cardinal Liénart, "Communiqué," *Semaine Religieuse de Lille,* June 28, 1936, pp. 438-39; "Assemblée des cardinaux et archevêques de France" (Feb. 1937), in *Documentation Catholique,* Dec. 20, 1937, p. 773; Merklen, *La Croix,* Jan. 21, 1937, p. 1; Pierre l'Ermite, *La Croix,* July 14-15, 1935, p. 1; De Castelnau, *France Catholique,* Jan. 18, 1936, p. 1, and Dec. 27, 1937, p. 1; Bernoville, *La Farce de la main tendue,* p. 8.

24. René Vallet, "Le Pacte franco-soviétique et la 'symphonie bourgeoise,'" *Terre Nouvelle,* June 1936, p. 10; Georges Duveau, "De Bilbao à Prague," *Esprit,* July 1937, p. 650; Emmanuel Mounier, "Lendemain d'une trahison," *Esprit* Oct. 1938, pp. 1-15; articles in *Jeune-République:* Masson, Mar. 6, 1938, p. 1; "Après les accords de Munich," Nov. 6, 1938, p. 1; "Le Grand Absent de Locarno," Nov. 13, 1935, p. 1; Viance, *France Catholique,* Nov. 2, 1935,

p. 3; De Castelnau, *France Catholique,* Dec. 14, 1935, p. 1; "Au pays du Négus," *Semaine Religieuse de Rennes,* Oct. 12, 1935, pp. 957–58; "Un Manifeste d'intellectuels pour la défense de l'Occident," *L'Action Française,* Oct. 4, 1935, pp. 1–2; articles in *La Croix:* Caret, Aug. 24, 1935, p. 1, Dec. 14, 1935, p. 1, and Sept. 8, 1934, p. 1; De Harcourt, Oct. 28, 1936, pp. 1–2; Guiraud, Sept. 23, 1938, p. 1; Gabilly, Sept. 30, 1938, p. 1; Irvine, *French Conservatism in Crisis,* pp. 180–96; "Manifeste pour la justice et la paix," *L'Aube,* Oct. 18, 1935, p. 1; Griaule, *Sept,* Jan. 3, 1936, p. 7; Hours, *L'Aube,* Aug. 27, 1935, p. 1; Desmonts, *Jeunesse Ouvrière,* June 15, 1938, p. 2; Zirnheld, *Syndicalisme,* Oct. 1937, p. 1.

25. Cardinal Verdier, *France Catholique,* Sept. 12, 1936, p. 1; Caret, *La Croix,* Jan. 11, 1936, p. 1; Montserrat, *La Croix,* Jan. 9, 1937, p. 1; Bernoville, *France Catholique,* May 9, 1938, pp. 1–2; de Castelnau, *France Catholique,* Dec. 12, 1936, p. 1; J.-M. de Semprun Gurea, "Après les élections en Espagne," *Esprit,* Apr. 1936, pp. 135–36; Jose Berganin, "Espagne victorieuse de soi," *Esprit,* June 1937, p. 500; Lardenois, *Jeune-République,* July 17, 1938, p. 1, and Apr. 24, 1938, p. 1; Serre, *Jeune-République,* Apr. 4, 1937, p. 3; "Des canon, des avions pour l'Espagne," *Terre Nouvelle,* Aug.–Sept. 1936, p. 40.

26. Gay, *Dans les flammes;* Bidault, *L'Aube,* Sept. 1, 1936, p. 1; Bidault, *L'Aube,* Apr. 30–May 1, 1937, p. 1; "La Voix d'un espagnol," *Sept,* Aug. 21, 1936, p. 7; editorial, *Sept,* Sept. 18, 1936, p. 1.

27. Rémond, *Les Catholiques, le communisme et les crises,* pp. 179, 187–88, 193–94; "Pour le peuple basque," *L'Aube,* May 8, 1937, p. 1.

28. "Contre l'alliance impie du marteau et de la faucille avec la croix," *France Catholique,* May 18, 1935, p. 4; Guiraud, *La Croix,* June 18, 1935, p. 1; E. M., "Notes," *Esprit,* June 1935, pp. 423–24; Gay, *L'Aube,* June 9, 1936, p. 1; "Communiqué," *Semaine Religieuse de Paris,* in *France Catholique,* Feb. 29, 1936, p. 1; "Résolutions de l'Assemblée des cardinaux et archevêques de France," *Documentations Catholique,* Nov. 21, 1936, p. 931.

29. Bernoville, *La Farce de la main tendue,* p. 105; Monis, *Jeune-République,* July 21, 1935, p. 3; Rémond, *Les Catholiques,* p. 82; E. M., "Catholicisme et communisme," *Esprit,* Apr. 1936, p. 91; Bernoville, "Toujours la *main tendue," Credo,* March 1937, pp. 12–16; Guiraud, *La Croix,* Apr. 16, 1937, p. 1.

30. Pius XI, *Divini Redemptoris* (March 1937), in *Papal Encyclicals,* ed. Fremantle, pp. 225, 256–57, 260–62.

31. Maurice Laudrain, "Le Vatican mussolinien contre 'Terre Nouvelle,'" *Terre Nouvelle,* Aug.–Sept. 1936, p. 12; Emmanuel Mounier, "Chrétiens et communistes," *Esprit,* May 1937, p. 309; Rémond, *Les Catholiques, le communisme et les crises,* pp. 240, 246, 248; Coutrot, *Un Courant de la pensée catholique,* pp. 289, 301; Henri Guillemin, "Par notre faute," *La Vie Intellectuelle,* Sept. 10, 1937, pp. 327–28, 332–35; 345; "Actes Officielles," *Semaine Religieuse de Lille,* May 9, 1937, p. 367.

32. Pius XI, in E. M., "L'Opinion chrétienne et la guerre d'Ethiopie," *Esprit,* Oct. 1935, p. 136.

33. Sanchez, "The Second Spanish Republic," pp. 67–68; Pius XI, in *Documentation Catholique*, Oct. 3, 1936, pp. 456–58, 460, 464; *Documentation Catholique*, July 20, 1938, pp. 837, 839.
34. "Les Catholiques et la guerre d'Espagne," *L'Osservatore Romano* (Jan. 16–17, 1939), in *France Catholique*, Feb. 6, 1939, pp. 1–2. For further references on the Vatican's anticommunist crusade, see *Documentation Catholique*, June 13, 1936, pp. 1477–84.
35. "Locarno et la note de Benoît XV," *Documentation Catholique*, Mar. 20, 1926, p. 755; Pius IX, "Allocution 'Iam annus,'" p. 31; Pius XI, *Mortalium Animas*, in *Documentation Catholique*, Jan. 3, 1931, pp. 9–10; "Hommage de la Fédération Nationale Catholique au Saint-Père," *France Catholique*, June 24, 1933, p. 1; "Allocution de S. Em. le Cardinal Verdier au pèlerinage annuel de la F.N.C. à Montmartre," *France Catholique*, June 23, 1934, p. 1.
36. Pius XI to Cardinal Verdier, *Documentation Catholique* Sept. 25, 1937, p. 387; Cardinal Pacelli to Cardinal Verdier, *Documentation Catholique*, Feb. 13, 1937, p. 390; "Le Dixième Anniversaire de la J.O.C. à Bruxelles," *Semaine Religieuse de Rennes*, Sept. 7, 1935, p. 842; "La J.O.C. à l'honneur," *Semaine Religieuse de Rennes*, Feb. 27, 1937, p. 181; "Nos Oeuvres," *Semaine Religieuse de Lille*, Mar. 28, 1937, p. 323; Cardinal Liénart, "Allocution," *Semaine Religieuse de Lille*, Jan. 10, 1937, p. 58; "Sacrée Congregation du concile à Sa Grandeur Monseigneur Achille Liénart, évêque de Lille au sujet d'un conflit entre ouvriers et patrons de la region," *Semaine Religieuse de Lille*, Sept. 1, 1929, pp. 441, 446–47; Pius XI, *Quadragesimo Anno*, in *Papal Encyclicals*, ed. Fremantle, pp. 229–30, 233–34; and in *Documentation Catholique*, June 6, 1931, pp. 1431, 1436–40.
37. For one such example, see Robert Cornilleau, "La Condamnation du communisme et du nazisme par le Saint-Siège," *Le Petit Démocrate*, Apr. 4, 1937, p. 1.
38. See the salient sections of these two encyclicals in *Papal Encyclicals*, ed. Fremantle. For *Non abbiamo bisogno*, see pp. 246–49; for *Mit brennender Sorge*, see pp. 250–54.
39. For some Vatican comments favorable to both regimes, see Pius XI, *I Disordini* (Aug. 6, 1922), in *Documentation Catholique*, Aug. 19–26, 1922, pp. 259–60; *L'Osservatore Romano* (Jan. 7–8, 1931), in *Documentation Catholique*, Mar. 21, 1931, p. 760; and "Concordat," *Documentation Catholique*, Oct. 7, 1933, pp. 451–65. On Catholicism in Fascist Italy, see Webster, *The Cross and the Fasces*; on the church in Nazi Germany, see Lewy, *The Catholic Church and Nazi Germany*. On Pius XI's reign in the context of European politics, see Rhodes, *The Vatican in the Age of the Dictators*. See also Conway, *The Nazi Persecution of the Churches*; Helmreich, *The German Churches under Hitler*; Delzell, ed., *The Papacy and Totalitarianism*; Falconi, *The Popes in the Twentieth Century*; and Harrigan, "Nazi Germany."
40. For the last decade of the Action Française in the Third Republic, see Weber, *Action Française*, 1962.

41. See the following articles in *L'Action Française:* "Revue de la presse," May 18, 1936, p. 5; "Sous la terreur," May 22, 1936, p. 1, and Sept. 11, 1936, p. 2; F⁷13199, Apr. 9, 1930; Archives du Ministère des Affaires Etrangères, Saint-Siège (1930–1939): "Direction Politique Europe," no. 334, Rome, Sept. 25, 1932, and no. 320, Rome, Sept. 27, 1937; see the following articles in *L'Action Française:* "Revue de la presse," May 21, 1936, p. 4, July 25, 1936, p. 7, and Aug. 2, 1936, p. 4; "Défense à Dieu d'entrer," Apr. 14, 1937, p. 2; "Voyage d'un démo-chrétien chez les rouges déterreurs de Carmélites," Jan. 8, 1939, p. 3; "Le Mensonge de Guernica," May 16, 1937, p. 1; "Le Juif de l'Aube," July 17, 1937, pp. 1–2; "*L'Osservatore Romano* donne une leçon à MM. F. Mauriac et Maritain," May 10, 1937, p. 1.

42. See the following articles in *L'Action Française:* "La Politique," Sept. 15, 1936, p. 1; "Revue de la presse," July 12, 1937, p. 5; "Votez contre la revolution et la guerre," Apr. 26, 1936, p. 1; Daudet, May 17, 1936, p. 1; "La Révolution juive chante victoire," June 14, 1936, p. 1; "Revue de la presse," Sept. 1, 1936, p. 4; "La Guerre civile en Espagne," Aug. 24, 1936, p. 2; "Les Horreurs de la terreur rouge," Aug. 25, 1936, p. 2; Gaudy, Oct. 28, 1936, p. 1; "Les Massacres espagnols," Feb. 7, 1937, p. 2.

43. Thomas, *L'Action Française,* pp. 355, 364–65, 433–34; Massis, *Maurras et notre temps;* Archives du Ministère des Affaires Etrangères, Saint-Siège (1930–1939): "Direction Politique Europe," no. 68, Rome, Feb. 2, 1939, and no. 190, Rome, May 22, 1939.

44. Thomas, *L'Action Française,* pp. 372–76; Massis, *Maurras et notre temps,* pp. 434–35; Canon Albert Cormier, interview, Tours, Feb. 1973; "Le Saint-Siège a levé l'interdiction de *l'Action Française,*" *L'Action Française,* July 16, 1939, p. 1; Archives du Ministère des Affaires Etrangères, Saint-Siège (1930–1939): "Direction Politique Europe," no. 248, Rome, July 15, 1939.

Chapter 10. The Final Reckoning

1. See Weber, *Action Française,* esp. chs. 25, 26.

2. See Paxton, *Vichy France;* Duquesne, *Les Catholiques français sous l'occupation;* Allen, "Resistance and the Catholic Church in France." It is interesting to note that General de Castelnau broke with his federation over Vichy's collaboration with the Germans. He retired in bitterness and died shortly before the national soil was liberated. Quite likely his loss of three sons in the Great War and deep hatred of the Germans prompted this intransigence.

3. Interviews with André Depierre, worker-priest (Montreuil, June 1979), Robert Pacalet, worker-priest (Lyon, July 1979), and Mme. Renée Bédarida, *Témoignage Chrétien* resister (Guelph, Ontario, Oct. 1977). See Bédarida, *Les Armes de l'Esprit;* Noguères and Degliame-Fouché, *Histoire de la resistance en France;* Duquesne, *Les Catholiques français sous l'occupation;* Kedward, *Resistance in Vichy France;* and Arnal, "Catholic Roots of Collaboration and Resistance."

4. On the various Catholic forces operative within the Fourth Republic, see Bosworth, *Catholicism and Crisis in Modern France.*

5. Interview with M.-D. Chenu, Dominican theologian, Paris, May 15, 1979.

6. On the postwar missionary apostolates in France, see Poulat, *Naissance des prêtres-ouvriers;* Dansette, *Destin du catholicisme français.* A useful sampling of primary material from the postwar Catholic progressives is found in Domenach and de Montvalon, *The Catholic Avant-Garde.*

7. The Action Française did not die with the end of Vichy and the trial of Charles Maurras. It still exists in France and publishes a weekly called *Aspects de la France.* One can see its remnants at Joan of Arc Day parades, on the occasional street corner in the Latin Quarter, at Catholic integrist rallies and in the wall slogan "Vive le roi."

Bibliography

Archival Material

Archives Nationales (AN)

362 AP: Jean Guiraud Papers

F⁷ files
- F⁷12457   *Surveillance des nationalistes* (1899–1907)
- F⁷12716   *La Croix*
- F⁷12719   *Action Libérale*
- F⁷12861   *Royalistes* (1900–1912)
- F⁷12862   *Manifestations Thalmas* (1908–1909) and *Action Française* (1908–1911)
- F⁷12863   *Action Française* (1912–1913)
- F⁷12964   *Camelots du Roi* (1909–1913)
- F⁷12880   *Association Catholique de la Jeunesse Française* (1901–1908) and *Capuchins 30*
- F⁷13195   *Action Française* (1908–1927)
- F⁷13196   *Condamnation de l'Action Française et Activités Diverses* (1926–1927)
- F⁷13199   *Action Française*
- F⁷13219   *Fédération National Catholique*
- F⁷13223   *Fédération National Catholique*

F¹⁹ files
- F¹⁹1961   *Affaire Géay et le Nordez*
- F¹⁹1962   *Affaire Géay et le Nordez*
- F¹⁹1944   *Rapports entre la France et le Saint-Siège* (1891–1906)

F¹⁹1983   *Affaire Montagnini*
F¹⁹1985   *La Séparation au Sénat*
F¹⁹5642   *Action Libérale Populaire et Campagne Politique des Evêques*

C files: Archives de la Chambre des Députés, *Enquête sur les papiers saisis à l'ancienne nonciature*
C7376
C7377
C7378

Archives de la Prefecture de Police (APP)

B a/1540   *Société de Democrates chrétiens dite "Le Sillon"* (1898–1907)
B a/1341   *Ligue d'Action Française* (1905–1907)
B a/1342   *Ligue d'Action Française* (1909–1910)
B a/1343   *Ligue d'Action Française* (1911–1912)

Archives du Ministère des Affaires Etrangères, Saint-Siège (1918–1929, 1930–1939)

Interviews

Auphan, Louis, former AF militant. Paris, Apr. 23, 1973.
Bédarida, Renée, resister for *Témoignage Chrétien*. Guelph, Ontario, Oct. 1977.
Bidault, Georges, Christian Democrat at *L'Aube*. Paris, Mar. 20, 1973.
Cartyrade, Roger, former JOC officer. Paris, July 6, 1979.
Chenu, Père, M.-D., Dominican theologian. Paris, May 16, 1979.
Chollet, Hilaire, former AF militant. Paris, Sept. 6, 1972.
Cormier, Canon Albert, royalist priest. Tours, Feb. 9, 1973.
Depierre, André, worker-priest. Montreuil, June 20, 1979.
Dijon, Doctor, former AF militant. Paris, Mar. 20, 1973.
Duclos, Jacques, Communist leader. Paris, May 7, 1973.
Galmard, Father Robert, AF sympathizer. Paris, Nov. 3, 1972.
Juhel, Pierre, former AF militant. Paris, Oct. 18, 1972.
Laudrain, Maurice, editor of *Terre Nouvelle*, Paris, May 22, 1973.
Lefèvre, Father Luc, theologian sympathizer with AF. Paris, Sept. 23, 1972.
Leger, François, former AF militant. Paris, Nov. 8, 1972.
Murat, Antoine, former AF militant. Paris, Dec. 21, 1972.
Pacalet, Robert, worker-priest. Lyon, July 5, 1979.
Pujo, Pierre, son of Maurice Pujo. Paris, Oct. 18, 1972.
Villain, Père, P., director of Action Populaire. Paris, June 6, 1979.
Villette, André, former J.O.C. officer. Paris, June 25, 1980.
Vuibert, Robert, former AF militant. Vincennes, Feb. 28, 1973.

Periodicals

L'Action Liberale Populaire (newspaper of that party). 1901–1914.
L'Action Française. 1908–1940.
L'Action Française du dimanche. 1923–1925.
Année Sociale Internationale. 1910.
L'Association Catholique. 1876–1907.
L'Aube. 1932–1939.
Les Cercles d'Études Élémentaires. 1911.
Chronique de la Bonne Presse. 1900.
Chronique des Comités du Sud-Est. 1906–1908.
Chronique Sociale de France. 1910–1914, 1919–1939.
Credo: Bulletin Officiel de la Fédération Nationale Catholique. 1925–1939.
La Croix de Paris. 1899–1939.
La Démocratie. 1910–1914, 1919–1921.
La Documentation Catholique. 1919–1939.
Esprit. 1932–1939.
L'Eveil Démocratique. 1905–1910.
La France Catholique. 1933–1939.
Guide Social. 1910.
La Jeune-République. 1919–1939.
Jeunesse Ouvrière. 1930–1939.
La Justice Sociale. 1893, 1899–1908.
L'Ouest-Eclair. 1900–1939.
Les Questions Actuelles. 1899–1914.
Le Petit Démocrate. 1924–1939.
Revue de L'Action Française. 1899–1914.
Revue de L'Action Populaire. 1908–1914, 1920–1940.
Revue des Deux Mondes. 1899–1939.
Semaine Religieuse de Cambrai. 1899–1914.
Semaine Religieuse de Dijon. 1899–1904.
Semaine Religieuse de Laval. 1899–1904.
Semaine Religieuse de Lille. 1914, 1919–1939.
Semaine Religieuse de Rennes. 1899–1939.
Sept: L'Hebdomadaire du Temps Présent. 1936–1937.
Le Sillon. 1899–1910.
Le Syndicalisme. 1936–1939.
Le Syndicalisme Chrétien. 1933–1936.
Terre Nouvelle: Organe des Chrétiens Révolutionnaires. 1935–1939.
La Vie Catholique. 1898–1908.
La Vie Catholique. 1924–1938.

Books and Articles

A.C.J.F.: *Cinquante années d'action.* Paris: Spes, 1936.

A.C.J.F. *(Association Catholique de la Jeunesse Française, 1886–1956): Signification d'une crise: Analyse et documents.* Paris: L'Epi, 1964.

Acomb, Evelyn M. *The French Laic Laws, 1879–1889.* New York: Columbia University Press, 1941.

Actes du Troisième Colloque Maurras; Aix-en-Provence . . . 4, 5, et 6 avril 1972. Aix-en-Provence: Centre Charles Maurras, 1974.

Albert, Phyllis Cohen. *The Modernization of French Jewry: Consistory and Community in the Nineteenth Century.* Hanover, N.H.: Brandeis University Press, 1977.

Alix, Christine. *Le Saint-Siège et les nationalismes en Europe, 1870–1960.* Paris: Sirey, 1962.

Allen, Lewis. "Resistance and the Catholic Church in France," in *Resistance in Europe: 1939–1945*, ed. Stephen Hawes and Ralph White. Baltimore: Penguin Books, 1976.

Alquier, Georges. *Le Président Emil Combes.* Castres: Tarn, 1962.

Amato, Joseph. *Mounier and Maritain.* University, Ala.: University of Alabama Press, 1975.

Amette, Cardinal Léon. *Les Conditions de la paix sociale.* Paris: Maison de la Bonne Presse, 1919.

———. *Pendant la guerre — Lettres pastorales et allocutions.* Paris: Bloud et Gay, 1915.

Anderson, Robin. *Between Two Wars: The Story of Pope Pius XI.* Chicago: Franciscan Herald Press, 1977.

Arnal, Oscar L. "Alternatives to the Third Republic among Catholic Leftists in the 1930's." *Historical Reflections/Réflexions Historiques* 5 (Winter 1978), 177–95.

———. "The Ambivalent *Ralliement* of *La Croix.*" *Journal of Ecclesiastical History* 31 (Jan. 1980), 89–106.

———. "The Brief Pilgrimage of *Terre Nouvelle.*" *Journal of Religious History* 11 (Dec. 1981), 578–94.

———. "Catholic Roots of Collaboration and Resistance in France in the 1930s," *Canadian Journal of History* 17 (Apr. 1982), 87–110.

———. "The Nature and Success of Breton Christian Democracy: The Example of *L'Ouest-Eclair.*" *Catholic Historical Review* 68 (Apr. 1982), 226–48.

———. "Stillborn Alliance: Catholic Divisions in the Face of the *Main Tendue.*" On-demand supplement of the *Journal of Modern History.* Chicago: University of Chicago Press, 1979.

———. "Why the French Christian Democrats Were Condemned." *Church History* 49 (June 1980), 188–202.

Ariès, Philippe. *Histoire des populations francaises et de leurs attitudes devant la vie depuis le XVIIIe siècle.* Paris: Editions Self, 1948.

L'Association Catholique de la Jeunesse Française, 1886–1907: Une prise de conscience du laïcat catholique. Paris: 1968.

Azema, Jean-Pierre. *De Munich à la liberation 1938-1944.* Paris: Editions du Seuil, 1977.
Bainville, Jacques. *La Troisième République.* Paris: Les Grandes Etudes Historiques, 1935.
Ball, Gerard. "Combes et la république des comités!" *Revue d'Histoire Moderne et Contemporaine* 24 (Apr.–June 1977), 260–85.
Barbier, Father Emmanuel. *La Décadence du "Sillon."* Nancy: E. Drioton Librairie, 1907.
———. *Le Devoir politique des Catholiques.* Paris: Joure, 1910.
———. *Les Erreurs du Sillon: Histoire documentaire.* Paris: Librairie P. Lethielleux, 1906.
———. *Histoire du Catholicisme libéral et du catholicisme social en France du Concile du Vatican à l'avènement de S. S. Benoit XV 1870-1914).* 5 vols. Bordeaux: Imprimerie Y. Cardoret, 1924.
———. *Les Idées du Sillon.* 3d ed. Paris: Librairie P. Lethielleux, 1905.
———. *Les Infiltrations maçonniques dans l'église.* Aisne: Association Saint-Remy, 1910.
———. *Le Progrès du libéralisme catholique en France sous le pape Leon XIII.* 2 vols. Paris: P. Lethielleux, 1907.
Barrès, Maurice. *The Faith of France: Studies in Spiritual Differences and Unity.* Trans. Elisabeth Marbury. Boston: Houghton Mifflin, 1918.
———. *Faut-il autoriser les congrégations?* Paris: Plon, 1924.
———. *La Grande Pitié des églises de France.* Paris: Emile Paul, 1914.
Barthelemy-Madaule, Madeleine. *Marc Sangnier (1873-1950).* Paris: Editions du Seuil, 1973.
Baudrillart, Alfred. *The Catholic Church, the Renaissance and Protestantism.* Trans. Mrs. Philip Gibbs. London: Kegan Paul, Trench, Trubner, 1907.
———. *La France, les Catholiques et la guerre: Réponse a quelques objections.* Paris: Bloud et Gay, 1917.
———. *Soyons prêts!* Paris: Flammarion, 1937.
———. *La Vie catholique dans la France contemporaine.* Paris: Bloud et Gay, 1918.
Bedarida, Renée. *Les Armes de l'esprit, "Témoignage Chrétien" (1941-1944).* Paris: Éditions Ouvrières, 1977.
Bellanger, Claude, Jacques Godechot et al. *Histoire générale de la presse française.* Vol. 3: *De 1871 à 1940.* Paris: Presses Universitaires de France, 1972.
Bernanos, Georges. *Nous autres français.* Paris.: Gallimard, 1939.
Bernoville, Gaëtan. *La Farce de la main tendue.* Paris: Éditions Bernard Grasset, 1937.
Berthe, Léon-Noël. *JOC je te dois tout.* Paris: Éditions Ouvrières, 1980.
Bertocci, Philip A. *Jules Simon: Republican Anticlericalism and Cultural Politics in France, 1848-1886.* Columbia: University of Missouri Press, 1978.
Besse, Dom. *Le Catholicisme libéral.* Paris: Société Saint-Augustin, 1911.

Bessières, Albert. *L'Union catholique*. Paris: Gigard, 1924.
Bidault, Georges. *L'A.C.J.F. et les mouvements politiques de jeunesse*. Paris: La Jeunesse Catholique, 1926.
Biton, Louis, *La Démocratie chrétienne dans la politique française*. Angers: H. Siraudeau, 1954.
Bodin, Louis, and Jean Touchard. *Front populaire*. Paris: Armand Colin, 1961.
Bois, Paul, *Paysans de l'ouest*. Paris: Mouton, 1960.
Bosworth, William. *Catholicism and Crisis in Modern France: French Catholic Groups at the Threshold of the Fifth Republic*. Princeton, N.J.: Princeton University Press, 1962.
Boulard, Fernand. "La 'Déchristianisation' de Paris." *Archives de Sociologie des Religions* 31 (Jan.–June 1971), 69–98.
———. Essor ou declin du clergé français. Paris: Editions du Cerf, 1950.
———. *An Introduction to Religious Sociology*. Trans. M. J. Jackson. London: Darton, Longman and Todd, 1960.
Bouscaren, Anthony T. "Origins of French Christian Democracy." *Thought* 21 (Winter 1956–1957), 542–66.
Boussel, Patrice. *L'Affaire Dreyfus et la presse*. Paris: Armand Colin, 1960.
Breunig, Charles. "The Condemnation of the Sillon: An Episode in the History of Christian Democracy in France." *Church History* 26 (Sept. 1957), 227–44.
———. "The *Sillon* of Marc Sangnier: Christian Democracy in France, 1894–1910." Ph.D. diss., Harvard University, 1953.
Briand, Aristide. *La Séparation*. 2 vols. Paris: Bibliothèque Charpentier, 1908–1909.
Brière, Yves de la. *L'Église et l'état durant quatre années d'aprèsguerre, 1920–1924*. Paris: Beauchesne, 1924.
———. *Les Luttes de l'église et les luttes de la patrie*. Paris: Bureau des Études, 1918.
Brodhead, J. Napier. *The Religious Persecution in France, 1900–1906*. London: Kegan Paul, Trench, Trubner, 1907.
Brogan, Denis W. *The Development of Modern France, 1870–1939*. London: Hamish Hamilton, 1967.
Bron, Jean. *Histoire du mouvement ouvrier français*. 3 vols. Paris: Editions Ouvrières, 1968.
Brower, Daniel. *The New Jacobins*. Ithaca, N.Y.: Cornell University Press, 1968.
Brown, Marvin L., Jr. "Catholic Legitimist Militancy in the Early Years of the Third French Republic." *Catholic Historical Review* 60 (July 1974), 233–54.
———. *The Comte de Chambord: The Third Republic's Uncompromising King*. Durham, N.C.: Duke University Press, 1967.
———. *Louis Veuillot: French Ultramontane Catholic Journalist and Layman, 1813–1883*. Durham, N.C.: Catholic University Press, 1977.
Brugerette, J. *Le Prêtre français et la société contemporaine*. Vols. 2–3. Paris: P. Lethielleux, 1935.

Bruhat, Jean. *Histoire du mouvement ouvrier français.* 3 vols. Paris: Editions Ouvrières, 1968.
Brunetière, Ferdinand. *Après une visite.* Paris: Perrin, 1907.
———. *Discours de combat.* Paris: Librairie Académique, 1908.
———. *Les Ennemis de l'âme français.* Paris: Hetzel, 1899.
———. *Sur les chemins de la croyance—L'Utilisation du positivisme.* Paris: Librairie Académique Didier, 1905.
Buell, Raymond L. "France and the Vatican." *Political Science Quarterly* 36 (Mar. 1921), 30-50.
Buisson, Ferdinand, and E. E. Farrington. *French Educational Ideals To-Day.* New York: World Book Co., 1919.
Burton, Katherine. *The Great Mantle: The Life of Giuseppe Melchiore Sarto, Pope Pius X.* New York: Longmans, Green, 1950.
Bush, John W. "Education and Social Status: The Jesuit College in the Early Third Republic." *French Historical Studies* 9 (Spring 1975), 125-40.
Butham, William C. *The Rise of Integral Nationalism in France with Special Reference to the Ideas and Activities of Charles Maurras.* New York: Columbia University Press, 1939.
Byrnes, Robert F. *Antisemitism in Modern France.* New Brunswick, N.J.: Rutgers University Press, 1950.
———. "The French Christian Democrats in the 1890's: Their Appearance and Their Failure." *Catholic Historical Review* 36 (Oct. 1950), 286-306.
Cahm, Eric. *Politics and Society in Contemporary France (1789—1971): A Documentary History.* London: George G. Harrap, 1972.
Callot, Émile-François. *Le Mouvement républicain populaire: Origine, structure, doctrine, programme et action politique.* Paris: M. Rivière, 1978.
Camp, Richard L. *The Papal Ideology of Social Reform: A Study in Historical Development, 1878-1967.* Leiden: E. J. Brill, 1969.
Caperan, Louis. *L'Anticléricalisme et l'affaire Dreyfus, 1897-1899.* Toulouse: Imprimerie regionale, 1948.
———. *Histoire contemporaine de laïcité française.* 3 vols. Paris: M. Rivière, 1957-1961.
———. *L'Invasion laïque de Combes au vote de la séparation.* Paris: Desclée, de Brouwer, 1935.
Caron, Jeanne. *Le Sillon et la démocratie chrétienne, 1894-1910.* Paris: Plon, 1967.
Cassidy, Sally Whelan. "The Catholic Revival." *Catholic World,* May 1950, pp. 138-42.
———. "The Catholic Revival." *Catholic World,* Feb. 1951, pp. 372-75.
Chaigne, Louis. *Paul Claudel: The Man and the Mystic.* Trans. Pierre de Fontnouvelle. Westport, Conn.: Greenwood Press, 1978.
Chaigneau, V.-L. *L'Organisation de l'église catholique en France.* Paris: Editions Spes, 1955.
———. *Les Ouvriers dans la moisson: Institutions et associations catholiques en France.* Paris: Editions Spes, 1955.

Chansou, Joseph. *Sous l'épiscopat du cardinal Saliège, 1929-1956.* Toulouse: J. Chansou, 1978.
Chapman, Guy. *The Dreyfus Case.* London: Hart-Davis, 1955.
Chapon, Msgr. Henri Louis. *Les Églises de France et la loi de 1905.* Paris: Bloud et Gay, 1922.
Charles-Roux, F. *Huit ans au Vatican (1932-1940).* Paris: Flammarion, 1947.
Christophe, Paul. *Les Catholiques et le Front Populaire,* 1936. Reprint. Paris: Desclée, 1979.
"Cinquante années d'apostolat social." *Revue de l'Action Populaire,* June, 1953, pp. 481-98.
Clonmore, Lord. *Pope Pius XI and World Peace.* New York: E. P. Dutton, 1938.
Cobban, Aldred. *A History of Modern France.* 3 vols. Baltimore: Penguin Books, 1965.
Cochin, Denys. *1914-1922 — La Guerre — le bloque, l'union sacrée.* Paris: Plon, 1923.
———. *1923-1924: Entre alliés.* Paris: Plon, 1924.
Cochin, Henry. *Les Deux Guerres — 1870-1871, 1914-1917 — Images et souvenirs.* Paris: Librairie Plon, 1917.
Cochrane, Arthur C. *The Church's Confession Under Hitler.* Philadelphia: Westminster, 1962.
Collins, Ross W. *Catholicism and the Second French Republic, 1848-1852.* New York, Columbia University Press, 1923.
Combes, Émile. *Une campagne laïque, 1902 — 1903.* Paris: Plon, 1924.
———. *Une deuxième campagne laïque, 1902-1903. Vers la separation.* Paris: Bellois, 1905.
———. *Mon Ministère: Mémoires, 1902-1905.* Paris: Plon, 1956.
Constant, Abbé, G. *L'Église de France sous le consulat et l'empire, 1800-1814.* Paris: Lecoffre, 1928.
Conway, John S. *The Nazi Persecution of the Churches, 1933-1945.* New York: Basic Books, 1968.
Cordonnier, Charles. *Le Cardinal Amette.* 2 vols. Paris: Éditions du Mortainais, 1949.
———. *Mgr. Fuzet.* Paris: Beauchesne, 1950.
Cormier, Canon Alfred. *Mes entretiens de prêtre avec Charles Maurras and la vie intérieure de Charles Maurras.* Paris: Nouvelles Editions Latines, 1953.
Cornilleau, Robert. *L'Abbé Naudet.* Paris: Bloud et Gay, 1934.
———. *Du Bloc national au front populaire.* Paris: Éditions Spes, 1939.
———. *Pourquoi les Démocrates populaires ont formé un parti nouveau.* Paris: Le "Petit Democrate," 1929.
———. *Pourquoi pas? Une politique réaliste.* Paris: Valois, 1929.
———. *Le "Ralliement" a-t-il echoué?* Paris: Éditions Spes, 1927.
———. *De Waldeck-Rousseau à Poincaré: Chronique d'une génération.* Paris: Editions Spes, 1926.

Cotta, Michele. *La Collaboration 1940-1944*. Paris: Armand Colin, 1964.
Coutrot, Aline. *Un Courant de la pensée catholique, l'hebdomadaire "Sept" mars, 1934-aout, 1937*. Paris: Editions du Cerf, 1961.
———. "Youth Movements in France in the 1930's." *Journal of Contemporary History* 5 (1970), 23-35.
Coutrot, Aline, and François G. Dreyfus. *Les Forces religieuses dans la société française*. Paris: Armand Colin, 1965.
Cronin, John F. *Catholic Social Principles*. Milwaukee: Bruce, 1950.
Curtis, Michael. *Three Against the Republic: Sorel, Barrès and Maurras*. Princeton, N.J.: Princeton University Press, 1959.
Dabry, Father Pierre. *Les Catholiques républicans: Histoire et souvenirs (1890-1903)*. Paris: Chevalier et Rivière, 1905.
———. *Christianisme et démocratie*. Paris: M. Rivière, 1910.
———. *Mon expérience religieuse*. Paris: Librairie de la France Républicaine, 1912.
Daim, Wilfried. *The Vatican and East Europe*. Trans. Alexander Gode. New York: Frederick Ungar, 1970.
Dal-Gal, Father Hieronymo. *Pius X: The Life, Story of the Beatus*. Trans. Thomas F. Murray. Westminster, Md.: Newman Press, 1954.
Daniel, Yvan, and Gilbert Le Mouel. *Paroisses d'hier, paroisses d'aujourd'hui*. Paris: Grasset, 1957.
Daniel-Rops, H. *A Fight for God, 1870-1939*. Trans. John Warrington. New York: E. P. Dutton, 1965-1966.
Dansette, Adrien. *Destin du catholicisme français (1926-1956)*. Paris: Flammarion, 1957.
———. "L'Église et l'Action Française," *Esprit* 19 (Sept. 1951), 275-99; (Oct. 1951), 446-58.
———. *Religious History of Modern France*. 2 vols. Edinburgh and London: Nelson, 1961.
Darbon, Michel. *Le Conflit entre la droite et la gauche dans le catholicisme français 1830-1953*. Toulouse: Privat, Editeur, 1953.
Daudet, Léon. *Charles Maurras et son temps*. Paris: Flammarion, n.d.
———. *Moloch et Minerve ou l'après-guerre*. Paris: Nouvelle Librairie Nationale, 1924.
Debidour, A. *L'Église catholique et l'état sous la Troisième Republique (1870-1906)*. Paris: Felix Alcan, 1909.
Delahaye, Jules. *La Reprise des relations diplomatiques avec le Vatican*. Paris: Librairie Plon, 1921.
De la Rocque, Lt. Col. François. *Service public*. Paris: Èditions Bernard Grasset, 1934.
Delassus, Father Henri. *L'Américanisme et la conjuration anti-chrétienne*. Lille: Desclée, de Brouwer, 1899.
———. *La Conjuration antichrétienne*. Lille: Desclée, de Brouwer, 1910.

———. *La Démocratie chrétienne.* Paris: Desclée, de Brouwer, 1911.

———. *La Mission posthume, de la bienheureuse Jeanne d'Arc et le règne social de Notre-Seigneur Jésus Christ.* Lille: Desclée, de Brouwer, 1913.

———. *Le Problème de l'heure présente: Antagonisme de deux civilisations.* Lille: Desclée, de Brouwer, 1904.

———. *La Question juive: Notes et documents.* Lille: Desclée, de Brouwer, 1911.

Delay, Paul. *Les Catholiques au service de la France.* 2 vols. Paris: Bloud et Gay, 1916–1917.

Delourme, Paul. *Trente-Cinq années de politique religieuse ou l'histoire de "L'Ouest-Eclair."* Paris: Éditions Fustier, 1936.

Delperrie de Bayac, J. *Histoire de la Milice, 1918–1945.* Paris: Fayard, 1969.

Delumeau, Jean. *Le Diocèse de Rennes.* Paris: Beauchesne, 1979.

Delzell, Charles, ed. *The Papacy and Totalitarianism Between the Two World Wars.* New York: John Wiley, 1974.

De Mun, Albert. *Combats d'hier et d'aujourd'hui.* 6 vols. Paris: P. Lethielleux, 1906–1916.

———. *La Conquête du peuple.* Paris: P. Lethielleux, 1908.

———. *Contre la separation.* 2d ed. Paris: Poussielgue, 1906.

———. *La Guerre de 1914.* Paris: Éditions de l'Echo de Paris, 1914.

———. *L'Heure décisive.* Paris: Paul Frères, 1913.

———. *Lettres addressées à M. Waldeck-Rousseau.* Paris: Plon, 1900.

———. *Ma Vocation sociale.* Paris: P. Lethielleux, 1908.

———. *Pour la patrie.* Paris: Emile-Paul, 1912.

———. *La Question sociale, sa solution corporative.* Reims: n.p., n.d.

———. *The Religious Crisis in France.* San Francisco: Catholic Truth Society, 1902.

Denais, Joseph. *Une Apôtre de la liberté: Jacques Pious.* Paris: Palatine, 1960.

Derfler, Leslie. "Le Cas Millerand: Une nouvelle interpretation." *Revue d'Histoire Moderne et Contemporaine* 10 (Apr.–June 1963), 81–104.

Derfler, Leslie, ed. *The Dreyfus Affair: Tragedy of Errors?* In *Problems in European Civilization.* Boston: D. C. Heath, 1963.

Deroo, André. *L'Épiscopat français, 1930–1954.* Paris: Bonne Press, 1955.

De Roux, Marquis Marie. *Charles Maurras et le nationalisme de l'Action Française.* Paris: Bernard Grasset, 1927.

Derre, Jean René. *Lamennais: Ses amis et le mouvement des idées à l'époque romantique, 1824–1834.* Paris: Klincksieck, 1962.

Dobin, Paul. *L'Apostolat laïque.* Paris: Bloud et Gay, 1931.

Dolléans, Edouard, and Gerard Dehove. *Histoire du travail en France.* Paris: Editions Domat Montchrestien, 1955.

Domenach, J.-M. "Religion and Politics." *Confluence* 3 (Dec. 1954), 390–401.

Domenach, Jean-Marie, and Robert de Montvalon. *The Catholic Avant-Garde: French Catholicism Since World War II.* New York: Holt, Rinehart and Winston, 1967.

Doncoeur, R. P. *La Crise du Sacerdoce.* Paris: Flammarion, 1932.
Doncoeur, P., et al. *Pourquoi Rome a parlé.* Paris: Aux Editions Spes, 1927.
Doty, C. Stewart. *From Cultural Rebellion to Counterrevolution: The Politics of Maurice Barrès.* Athens: Ohio University Press, 1976.
Droulers, Paul. *Politique sociale et christianisme: Le Père Desbuquois et l'Action Populaire (1903-1918).* Paris: Editions Ouvrières, 1969.
Dubief, Fernand. *La Rupture avec le Vatican.* Paris: Edouard Cornely, 1903.
Duployé, Pie. *La Religion de Péguy,* 1965. Reprint. Geneva: Slatkine, 1978.
Duquesne, Jacques. *Les Catholiques français sous l'occupation.* Paris: Bérnard Grasset, 1966.
———. *Les Prêtres.* Paris: B. Grasset, 1965.
Duroselle, Jean-Baptiste, *Les Débuts du catholicisme social en France (1822-1871).* Paris: Presses Universitaires de France, 1951.
Duthoit, Eugène. *Le Catholicisme, lien social.* Paris: Spes, 1929.
———. *L'Économie au service de l'homme.* Paris: Flammarion, 1932.
———. *Le Suffrage de demain.* Paris: Perrin, 1901.
———. *Vers l'organisation professionelle.* Reims: Action Populaire, 1910.
———. *Vers une économie ordonnée.* Lyon: Chronique Sociale de France, 1932.
———. *Vie économique et catholicisme.* Paris: Gabalba, 1924.
Eckhardt, Carl Conrad. *The Papacy and World Affairs: As Reflected in the Secularization of Politics.* Chicago: University of Chicago Press, 1937.
Ehrmann, Henry W. *French Labor: From Popular Front to Liberation.* New York: Oxford University Press, 1947.
Einaudi, Mario, and François Goguel. *Christian Democracy in Italy and France.* Notre Dame, Ind.: University of Notre Dame Press, 1952.
Elbow, Matthew H. *French Corporative Theory, 1789-1848: A Chapter in the History of Ideas.* New York: Columbia University Press, 1953.
Elwitt, Sanford. *The Making of the Third Republic: Class and Politics in France, 1868-1884.* Baton Rouge: Louisiana State University Press, 1975.
Estier, Claude. *La Gauche hebdomadaire, 1914-1962.* Paris: Armand Colin, 1962.
Evans, Joseph W., and Leo R. Ward, ed. *The Social and Political Philosophy of Jacques Maritain: Selected Readings.* London: Geoffrey Bles, 1956.
Fabrègues, J. de. *Le Sillon de Marc Sangnier.* Paris: Perrin, 1964.
Faguet, Emile. *L'Anticléricalisme.* Paris: Société Française d'Imprimerie et de Librairie, n.d.
Falconi, Carlo. *The Popes in the Twentieth Century: From Pius X to John XXIII.* Trans. Muriel Grindrod. Boston: Little, Brown, 1967.
Fauvet, Jacques. *Histoire du Parti communiste français.* 2 vols. Paris: Fayard, 1964-1965.
Ferrata, Cardinal Dominique. *"Memoires,": Ma nonciature en France.* Paris: Spes, 1923.
Flory, Albert. *Albert de Mun.* Paris: Maison de la Bonne Presse, 1941.

Flynn, John T. "Welfare and the Welfare State." *Catholic World* 171 (May 1950), 99–103.

Fogarty, Michael P. *Christian Democracy in Western Europe 1820–1953.* Notre Dame, Ind.: University of Notre Dame Press, 1957.

Folliet, Joseph. "Essai sur l'évolution des idées dans le mouvement catholique social en France." *Chronique Sociale de France* (Apr. 1952), 144–54.

———. *Pacifisme de droite, bellicisme de gauche.* Paris: Éditions du Cerf, 1938.

Fontaine, Nicolas. *Saint-Siège, "Action Française" et "Catholiques intégraux."* Paris: Librairie Universitaire J. Gamber, 1928.

Fraisse, Simone. *Péguy et le Moyen-Âge.* Paris: H. Champion, 1978.

Fremantle, Anne, ed. *The Papal Encyclicals in Their Historical Context.* New York: New American Library, 1956.

Fremont, Father Georges. *Le Conflit entre la république et l'église.* Paris: Librairie Bloud, 1905.

———. *La grande erreur politique des catholiques français.* Paris: Bloud et Gay, 1910.

"French Newspapers of the 1890s Relating to the Dreyfus Case." Microfilm, Harvard University Library.

Friedlander, Saul. *Pius XII and the Third Reich: A Documentation.* Trans. Charles Fullman. New York: Knopf, 1966.

Fumet, Stanislas. *Le Renouveau spirituel en France.* Paris: Desclée, de Brouwer, 1931.

Gabbert, Mark A. "The Limits of French Catholic Liberalisme: Msgr. Sibour and the Question of Ecclesiology." *French Historical Studies* 10 (Fall 1978), 641–63.

Gadille, Jacques. *La Pensée et l'action politique des évêques français au début de la IIIe république (1871–1883).* 2 vols. Paris: Hachette, 1967.

———. "La Politique de défense républicaine a l'égard de l'église de France, 1876–1883." *Bulletin de la Societé d'Histoire Moderne* 1 (1967), 2–9.

Gargan, Edward T., ed. *Leo XIII and the Modern World.* New York: Sheed and Ward, 1961.

Gay, Francisque. *Comment j'ai défendu le pape.* Paris: "Vie Catholique," 1927.

———. *Dans les flammes et dans le sang: Les Crimes contre les églises et les prêtres en Espagne.* Paris: Bloud et Gay, n.d.

———. *Les Démocrats d'inspiration chrétienne à l'épreuve du pouvoir.* Paris: Bloud et Gay, 1950.

———. *La Tchécoslovaqie devant notre conscience et devant l'histoire.* Paris: Éditions de l'Aube, 1939.

Gayraud, Father Hippolyte. *L'Antisémitisme de St. Thomas d'Aguin.* Paris: E. Dentu, 1896.

———. *Un Catholique peut-il être socialiste?* Paris: Bloud, 1904.

———. *Les Démocrates, chrétiens, doctrine et programme.* Paris: V. Lecoffre, 1899.

———. *La République et la paix religieuse*. Paris: Perrin, 1900.
Gibier, Msgr. Charles. *La France catholique organisée*. Paris: Pierre Téqui, 1925.
———. *Le Relèvement national*. Paris: Téqui, 1920.
Gilson, Etienne, ed. *The Church Speaks to the Modern World: The Social Teachings of Leo XIII*. Garden City, N.Y.: Doubleday, 1957.
———. *Pour un ordre catholique*. Paris: Desclée, de Brouwer, 1934.
Giordani, Igino. *Pius X: A Country Priest*. Trans. Thomas J. Tobin. Milwaukee: Bruce, 1954.
Girardet, Raoul, ed. *Le Nationalisme français (1871-1914)*. Paris: Armand Colin, 1966.
Godfrin, Jacqueline, and Philippe Godfrin. *Une centrale de presse catholique: La Maison de la Bonne Presse et ses publications*. Paris: Presses Universitaires de France, 1965.
Godin, Henry, and Yvan Daniel. *France pays de mission?* Paris: Éditions de l'Abeille, 1943.
Goguel, Francois. *La Politique des partis sous le IIIe République*. Paris: Aux Editions du Seuil, 1957.
Goubert, Armand. *Les Associations diocésaines*. Montpellier: Langedoc Medical, 1930.
Goyau, Georges. *Autour du catholicisme social*. 5 vols. Paris: Perrin, 1897–1912.
———. *Le Cardinal Mercier*. Paris: Flammarion, 1930.
———. *Catholicisme et politique*. Paris: Éditions de la Revue des Jeunes, 1923.
———. *Ce que le monde catholique doit à la France*. Paris: Perrin, 1918.
———. *The Church of France during the War*. Paris: Bloud et Gay, 1918.
———. *Dieu chez les soviets*. Paris: Flammarion, 1929.
———. *L'École d'aujourd'hui*. Paris: Perrin, 1899.
———. *L'Effort catholique dans la France d'aujourd'hui*. Paris: Editions de la Revue des Jeunes, 1922.
———. *L'Église libre dans l'Europe libre*. Paris: Desclée, de Brouwer, 1931.
———. *L'Epanouissement social du credo*. Paris: Desclée, de Brouwer, 1931.
———. *La Franc-maçonnerie en France*. Paris: Perrin, 1899.
———. *Le Pape Léon XIII*. Paris: Perrin, 1904.
———. *La Présence de la France au Vatican*. Paris: Spes, 1924.
Graham, Robert A., S.J. *Vatican Diplomacy: A Study of Church and State on the International Plane*. Princeton, N.J.: Princeton University Press, 1959.
Grandmaison, Leonce de. *Impressions de guerre de prêtres soldats*. Paris: Librairie Plon, 1917.
Grandmougin, Jean. *Histoire vivante du Front populaire 1934-1939*. Paris: A Michel, 1966.
Greene, Nathanael. *Crisis and Decline: The French Socialist Party in the Popular Front Era*. Ithaca, N.Y.: Cornell University Press, 1969.
Grenier, J. "To Reach the People: *La Croix* (1883–1890)." Ph.D. diss., Fordham University, 1976.

Griffith, Richard. *The Reactionary Revolution: The Catholic Revival in French Literature, 1870–1914.* London: Constable, 1966.

Grubb, Alan. "The Dilemma of Liberal Catholics and Conservative Politics in the Early Third Republic." *Proceedings of the Western Society for French History* 4 (1977), 368–77.

Guerry, Emile. *L'Église catholique en France sous l'occupation.* Paris: Flammarion, 1947.

Guillemain, Bernard. *Le Diocèse de Bordeaux.* Paris: Beauchesne, 1974.

Guillemin, Henri. *Histoire des catholiques français au dix-neuvième siècle.* Genève: Au Milieu du Monde, 1947.

———. "Par notre faute." *La Vie Intellectuelle* 6, no. 3 (Sept. 10, 1937), 326–62.

Guitton, Georges. *Léon Harmel.* 2 vols. Paris: Spes, 1927.

Gurian, W., and M. Fitzsimons, eds. *The Catholic Church in World Affairs.* South Bend, Ind.: Notre Dame University Press, 1954.

Guy, M. *Vincent de Paul Bailly, fondateur de "La Croix."* Paris: Bonne Presse, 1955.

Halasz, Nicholas. *Captain Dreyfus: The Story of a Mass Hysteria.* New York: Grove Press, 1955.

Hales, E. E. Y. *The Catholic Church in the Modern World.* Garden City, N.Y.: Doubleday, 1960.

———. *Pio Nono: A Study in European Politics and Religion in the Nineteenth Century.* London: Eyre and Spottiswoode, 1954.

Harmel, Léon. *A Key to Labor Problems.* London: Catholic Truth Society, 1896.

———. *Manuel d'une corporation chrétienne.* Tours: Alfred Mame et fils, 1876.

Harrigan, William. "Nazi Germany and the Holy See, 1933–1936." *Catholic Historical Review* 47 (July 1961), 164–98.

———. "Pius XI and Nazi Germany, 1937–1939." *Catholic Historical Review* 51 (Jan. 1966), 457–86.

———. "Pius XII's Efforts to Effect a Detente in German-Vatican Relations, 1939–1940." *Catholic Historical Review* 49 (July 1963), 173–91.

Havard de la Montagne, Robert. *Histoire de l'Action Française.* Paris: Amiot-Dumont, 1950.

———. *Histoire de la Démocratie Chrétienne de Lammenais à Georges Bidault.* Paris: Amiot Dumont, n.d.

Hellman, John. *Emmanuel Mounier and the New Catholic Left, 1930–1950.* (Toronto: University of Toronto Press, 1981).

———. "French 'Left Catholics' and Communists in the 1930's." *Church History* 45 (Dec. 1976), 507–23.

———. "The Opening to the Left in French Catholicism: The Role of the Personalists." *Journal of the History of Ideas* 30 (1973), 381–90.

———. "Vichy Background: Political Alternatives for French Catholics in the

1930's." On-Demand Supplement of *Journal of Modern History*. Chicago: University of Chicago Press, 1977, pp. D1111–D1144.
Helmreich, Ernst, C., ed. *A Free Church in a Free State? The Catholic Church, Italy, Germany, France, 1864–1914*. In *Problems in European Civilization*. Boston: D. C. Heath, 1964.
———. *The German Churches Under Hitler*. Detroit: Wayne State University Press, 1979.
Henriot, Philippe. *Comment mourut la paix*. Paris: Éditions de la France, 1941.
———. *Le 6 février*. Paris: Flammarion, 1934.
Herzog, Wilhelm, *From Dreyfus to Pétain: The Struggle of a Republic*. Trans. Walter Sorell. New York: Creative Age Press, 1947.
Hoffman, Robert L. *More Than a Trial: The Struggle Over Captain Dreyfus*. Glencoe, N.Y.,: Free Press, 1980.
Hoffman, Stanley. "Collaboration in France during World War II." *Journal of Modern History* 40 (1968), 375–95.
Hogarth, Henry. *Henri Brémond: The Life and Work of a Devout Humanist*. London: SPCK, 1950.
Honnert, Robert. *Catholicisme et communisme*. Paris: Éditions Sociales Internationales, 1937.
Hoog, Georges. *Le Drame de L'Espagne: Croisade morale ou guerre sociale?* Paris: La Jeune-République, 1937.
———. *La Guerre des nations*. Bellevue: S. et D., 1917.
———. *Histoire, doctrine, action de la "Jeune République."* Paris: Société cooperative d'édition et de propagande, 1925.
———. *Histoire du catholicisme social en France, 1871–1931*. Paris: Doumat, 1946.
———. *Lettres au neutres sur l'union sacrée*. Paris: Bloud et Gay, 1918.
———. *Vingt années d'histoire politique (1906–1925): La Démocratie et la paix*. Paris: "La Démocratie," 1926.
Hourdin, Georges. *La Presse catholique*. Paris: Arthème Fayard, 1957.
Huckaby, John K. "Roman Catholic Reaction to the Falloux Law." *French Historical Studies* 4 (1965), 203–13.
Hughes, Philip. *Pope Pius the Eleventh*. New York: Sheed and Ward, 1938.
Hunerman, William. *Flame of White: A Life of Saint Pius X*. Trans. M. Ida Adler. Chicago: Franciscan Herald Press, 1959.
Hunter, John C. "The Problem of the French Birth Rate on the Eve of World War I." *French Historical Studies* 2 (Fall 1962), 490–503.
Hyman, Paula. *From Dreyfus to Vichy: The Transformation of French Jewry, 1906–1939*. New York: Columbia University Press, 1979.
"Intégrisme et catholicisme national." *Esprit* 27 (Nov. 1959), 515–43.
Irvine, William D. *French Conservatism in Crisis: The Republican Federation of France in the 1930's*. Baton Rouge: Louisiana State University Press, 1979.

Irving, R. E. M. *Christian Democracy in France.* London: Allen and Unwin, 1973.
Isambert, François. "L'Attitude religieuse des ouvriers français au milieu du XIXe siècle." *Archives de Sociologie des Religions* 6 (July–Dec. 1968), 7–35.
———. *Christianisme et classe ouvrière.* Paris: Casterman, 1960.
Jackson, Gabriel. *The Spanish Republic and the Civil War, 1931–1939.* Princeton, N.J.: Princeton University Press, 1965.
Jacquemet, G., ed. *Catholicisme: Encyclopédie en sept volumes.* Paris: Letouzey et Ane, 1950.
Jarlot, Georges, *Doctrine pontificale et histoire: L'Enseignement social de Leon XIII, Pie X et Benoît XV vu dans son ambiance historique (1878–1922).* Rome: Presses de l'Université Gregorienne, 1964.
Jeanneney, Jean-Noel. *François de Wendel en republique.* 3 vols. Paris: Champion, 1976.
La Jeunesse Ouvrière Chrétienne: 50 ans d'histoire. Paris: Éditions Ouvrières, 1978.
"J.O.C. petit guide social des familles ouvrières." *Jeunesse Ouvrière,* special issue (Spring 1933), 3–26.
Johnson, Douglas. *France and the Dreyfus Affair.* New York: Walker, 1967.
Johnson, Humphrey. *Vatican Diplomacy During the Great War.* Oxford: Blackwell, 1933.
Judet, E. M. G. *Le Vatican et la paix de Léon XIII à Pie XI.* Paris: Despeuch, 1927.
Julien, Claude. "Christian Democracy in France?" *Commonweal,* Oct. 1, 1948, pp. 589–93.
Julien, Msgr. Eugène Louis Ernest. *Les Leçons d'un grand évêque.* Paris: Emmanuel Vitte, 1931.
Kedward, Harry R. *Resistance in Vichy France.* Oxford: Oxford University Press, 1978.
Keller, Emile. *L'Ouvrier libre.* Paris: Lecoffre, 1898.
———. *Les Syllabus de Pie IX et Pie X et les principes de 1789.* 3d ed. Paris: P. Lethielleux, 1909.
Kerlévéo, Father Jean. *L'Église catholique en régime français de séparation.* 3 vols. Tournai: Desclée, de Brouwer, 1956–1962.
Keylor, William R. *Jacques Bainville and the Renaissance of Royalist History in Twentieth-Century France.* Baton Rouge: Louisiana State University Press, 1979.
King, Lawrence T. "The Battle for the Mind of Europe." *Catholic World,* Dec. 1952, pp. 188–94.
Kokel, R. *Vincent de Paul Bailly, un pionnier de la presse catholique.* Paris: Bonne Presse, 1957.
Kriegel, Annie. *Aux origines du communisme français.* Paris: Flammarion, 1969.

Kuehnelt-Leddihn, Erik von. "Reading Dansette." *Catholic World*, Oct. 1952, pp. 6–13.
Labasse, Jean. *Hommes de droite, hommes de gauche*. Paris: Économie et Humanisme, 1947.
Laberthonnière, Lucien. *Positivisme et catholicisme à propos de l'Action Française*. Paris: Bloud, 1911.
Lacoste, E. *Le P. Vincent de Paul Bailly, fondateur de "La Croix" et de la Maison de la Bonne Presse*. Paris: Bonne Presse, 1913.
Lacroix, Jean. *Marxisme, existentialisme, personnalisme: Présence de l'éternité dans le temps*. Paris: Presses Universitaires de France, 1950.
Lahalle, Dominique, and Nicole Lowit-Fratellini. "Opinions religieuses et attitudes syndicales des ouvriers du textile du nord de la France," *Archives de Sociologie des Religions* 13 (Jan.–June 1962), 73–85.
Lamy, Etienne. *Les Catholiques et la salvation présente*. Paris: Discours, 1898.
―――. *Catholiques et socialistes à propos des semaines sociales*. Paris: Bloud et Gay, 1910.
―――. *La Femme de demain*. Paris: Perrin, 1901.
―――. *Témoins de jours passés*. 2 vols. Paris: Calmann-Lévy, 1913.
Langdon, John W. "The Church and the French Concordat, 1891 to 1902." *English Historical Review* 321 (1966), 717–39.
―――. "New Light on the Influence of the Jesuit Schools: The Graduates of the École Sainte-Geneviève, Paris, 1854–1913." *Third Republic/Troisième République* 1 (Spring 1976), 132–51.
Laperrière, Guy. *La "Séparation" à Lyon (1904–1908)*. Lyon: Centre d'Histoire du Catholicisme, 1973.
Larkin, Maurice J.M. *Church and State after the Dreyfus Affair: The Separation Issue in France*. New York: 1974.
―――. "Loubet's Visit to Rome and the Question of Papal Prestige." *Historical Journal* 4 (1961), 97–103.
―――. "The Vatican, French Catholics and the Associations Cultuelles." *Journal of Modern History* 36 (Sept. 1964), 298–317.
Larmour, Peter J. *The French Radical Party in the 1930s*. Stanford, Calif.: Stanford University Press, 1964.
Latourette, Kenneth Scott. *Christianity in a Revolutionary Age*. Vol. 1, *The Nineteenth Century in Europe: Background and the Roman Catholic Phase*. New York: Harper, 1958.
―――. *Christianity in a Revolutionary Age*. Vol. 4, *The Twentieth Century in Europe*. New York: Harper, 1961.
Latreille, André. *De Gaulle, la libération et l'église catholique*. Paris: Editions du Cerf, 1978.
―――. "Les Étapes de l'histoire du catholicisme social." *Chronique Sociale de France* (Apr. 1952), 132–43.
―――. *Napoléon et le Saint-Siège, 1801–1808*. Paris: Alcan, 1935.

Latreille, André, and André Siegfried. *Les Forces religieuses et la vie politique.* Paris: Armand Colin, 1921.

Launay, Michel. "La Crise du Sillon dans l'été 1905." *Revue Historique* 498 (Apr.–June 1971), 393–426.

———. *Le Dossier de Vichy.* Paris: Julliard, 1967.

Laurens, Franklin D. *France and the Italo-Ethiopian Crisis, 1935–1936.* The Hague: Mouton, 1967.

Le Bras, Gabriel. *Etudes de sociologie religieuse.* 2 vols. Paris: Presses Universitaires de France, 1956.

———. *Introduction à l'histoire de la pratique religieuse en France.* 2 vols. Presses Universitaires de France, 1942–45.

Lebret, L.-J. *De l'efficacité politique du chrétien.* Paris: Économie et Humanisme, 1947.

Lecanuet, R. P. *L'Église de France sous la Troisième République.* Vol. 3, *Les Signes avant-coureurs de la séparation.* Paris: Librairie Felix Alcan, 1930.

Le Clère, Marcel. *Le 6 fevrier.* Paris: Hachette, 1967.

Ledre, Charles. *L'Église de France sous la révolution.* Paris: R. Laffont, 1949.

Leflon, Jean. *L'Église de France et la révolution de 1848.* Paris: Bloud et Gay, 1948.

Lemire, Father Jules. *Le Travail de nuit des enfants dans les usines à feu continu.* Paris: F. Alcan, 1911.

Levard, Georges. *Chances et perils du syndicalisme chrétien.* Paris: Arthème Fayard, 1955.

Lewis, David L. "Emmanuel Mounier and the Politics of Moral Revolution: Aspects of Political Crises in French Liberal Catholicism, 1935–1938." *Catholic Historical Review* 56 (July 1970), 266–90.

Lewis, Leicester Crosby. *The Philosophical Principles of French Modernism.* Philadelphia: University of Pennsylvania Press, 1925.

Lewy, Günther. *The Catholic Church and Nazi Germany.* New York: McGraw-Hill, 1965.

Loisy, Alfred. *L'Église et la France.* Paris: Nourry, 1925.

Lorwin, Val R. *The French Labor Movement.* Cambridge, Mass.: Harvard University Press, 1954.

Lovie, Jacques, *Chambery, Tarentaise, Maurrienne.* Paris: Beauchesne, 1979.

Lüthy, Herbert. *France Against Herself.* Trans. Eric Mosbacher. New York: Praeger, 1955.

Machefer, Philippe. "Les Croix de feu, 1927–1936." *L'Information Historique,* Jan.–Feb. 1972, pp. 28–34.

———. "Le Parti social français en 1936–1937." *L'Information Historique,* Mar.–Apr. 1972, pp. 74–80.

McAvoy, Thomas. *The Americanist Heresy in Roman Catholicism, 1895–1900.* Notre Dame, Inc.: University of Notre Dame Press, 1963.

McClelland, J. S., ed. *The French Right: From de Maistre to Maurras.* London: Cape, 1970.

McManners, John. *Church and State in France, 1870-1914.* London: SPCK, 1972.
———. *French Ecclesiastical Society Under the Ancien Regime.* Manchester: University Press, 1960.
———. *The French Revolution and the Church.* New York: Harper, 1969.
Madiran, Jean. *L'Intégrisme: Histoire d'une histoire.* Paris: Nouvelles Éditions Latines, n.d.
Maier, Hans. *Revolution and Church: The Early History of Christian Democracy 1789-1901.* Trans. Emily M. Schossberger. Notre Dame, Ind.: University of Notre Dame Press, 1969.
Maître, Jacques. "Les Sociologies du catholicisme français." *Cahiers Internationaux de Sociologie* 24 (Jan.-June 1958), 104-24.
Mandell, R. D. "Affair and the Fair: Some Observations on the Closing Stages of the Dreyfus Case." *Journal of Modern History* 39 (1967), 253-65.
Manhattan, Avro. *The Vatican in World Politics.* New York: Goer Associates, 1949.
Marion, R.-J. *"La Croix" et le ralliement.* Paris: Presses Universitaires de France, 1957.
Maritain, Jacques. *Antisemitism.* London: Geoffrey Bles; Centenary Press, 1939.
———. *Christianity and Democracy.* Trans. Doris C. Anson. New York: Scribner's, 1947.
———. *France: My Country Through the Disaster.* New York: Longmans, Green, 1941.
———. *Freedom in the Modern World.* Trans. Richard O'Sullivan. New York: Scribner's, 1936.
———. *Integral Humanism: Temporal and Spiritual Problems of a New Christendom.* Trans. Joseph W. Evans, 1936. Reprint. New York: Scribner's, 1968.
———. *Une Opinion sur Charles Maurras et le devoir des catholiques.* Paris: Librairie Plon, 1926.
———. *Religion et culture.* Paris: Desclée, de Brouwer, 1946.
———. *The Things That Are Not Caesar's.* Trans. J. F. Scanlan. New York: Charles Scribner's Sons, 1931.
Marrus, Michael R. *The Politics of Assimilation.* Oxford: Clarendon Press, 1971.
Marteaux, Jacques. *L'Église de France devant la révolution marxiste.* Vol. 1, *Les Catholiques dans l'inquiétude, 1936-1944.* Paris: Table Ronde, n.d.
Martin, Benjamin F., Jr. *Count Albert de Mun, Paladin of the Third Republic.* Chapel Hill: University of North Carolina Press, 1978.
———. "The Creation of the Action Libérale Populaire: An Example of Party Formation in Third Republic France." *French Historical Studies* 9 (1976), 660-89.
———. "A Letter of Albert de Mun on the Papal Condemnation of the Sillon." *Catholic Historical Review* 64 (Jan. 1978), 47-50.
Massis, Henri. *L'Honneur de servir.* Paris: Plon, 1937.

———. *Les Jeunes gens d'aujourd'hui*. Paris: Plon, 1919.
———. *Maurras et notre temps – Entretiens et souvenirs*. Paris: Librairie Plon, 1961.
———. *L'Occident et son destin*. Paris: Bernard Grasset, 1956.
Maugendre, L.-A. *La Renaissance catholique au debut du XXe siècle*. Paris: Beauchesne, 1963–1966.
Maurras, Charles. *L'Action Française et la religion catholique*. Paris: Nouvelle Librairie Nationale, 1913.
———. *L'Action Française et le Vatican: Les pièces d'un procès*. Paris: Ernest Flammarion, 1927.
———. *Au Signe de flore*. Paris: Les Oeuvres Représentatives, 1931.
———. *Le Bienheureux Pie X, sauveur de la France*. Paris: Plon, 1953.
———. *La Démocratie religieuse*. Paris: Nouvelles Editions Latines, 1978 (1921).
———. *Dictionnaire politique et critique*. 2 vols. Paris: À la cité des livres, 1932.
———. *Enquête sur la monarchie*. Paris: Nouvelle Librairie Nationale, 1924.
———. *Oeuvres capitales*. Vol. 2: *Essais politiques*. Paris: Flammarion, 1954.
———. *Le Pape, la guerre et la paix*. Paris: Nouvelle Librairie Nationale, 1917.
Mayer, Arno. *Political Origins of the New Diplomacy*. New Haven, Conn.: Yale University Press, 1959.
Mayeur, Françoise. *L'Aube: Étude d'un journal d'opinion*. Paris: Armand Colin, 1966.
Mayeur, Jean-Marie. "Les Congrès nationaux de la 'Démocratie chrétienne' à Lyon, 1896–1897–1898." *Revue d'Histoire Moderne et Contemporaine* 9 (July–Sept. 1962), 171–206.
———. "Droites et ralliés à la Chambre des Deputés au début de 1894." *Revue d'Histoire Moderne et Contemporaine* 13 (Apr.–June 1966), 117–35.
———. *Un Prêtre démocrate: L'Abbé Lemire (1853–1928)*. Tournai: Casterman, 1968.
Mayeur, Jean-Marie, ed. *La Séparation de l'église et de l'état, 1905*. Reprint. Paris: Imprimerie Firmin-Didot, 1966.
Mazgaj, Paul. *The Action Française and Revolutionary Syndicalism*. Chapel Hill: University of North Carolina Press, 1979.
Mejan, L. V. *La Séparation de l'église et de l'état*. Paris: Presses Universitaires de France, 1959.
Merle, Marcel. *Les Églises chrétiennes et la décolonisation* in *Cahiers de la Fondation Nationale des Sciences Politiques*. Paris: Armand Colin, 1967.
Mermeix. *Le Ralliement et l'Action Française*. Paris: Arthème Fayard, 1927.
Merry del Val, Cardinal. *Memories of Pope Pius X*. Westminster, Md.: Newman Press, 1951.
Meynaud, Jean. *Les Groupes de pression en France* in *Cahiers de la Fondation Nationale des Sciences Politiques*. Paris: Armand Colin, 1958.
Micaud, Charles A. *The French Right and Nazi Germany 1933–1939*. Durham, N.C.: Duke University Press, 1943.

Miguel, Pierre. *L'Affaire Dreyfus*. Paris: Presses Universitaires de France, 1959.
Miller, J. Bleecker. *Leo XIII and Modern Civilization*. New York: Eskdale Press, 1897.
Miller, J. Martin. *The Life of Pope Leo XIII*. Philadelphia: National Publishing Co., 1903.
Molette, Charles. *Albert de Mun, 1872-1890: Exigence doctrinale et préoccupations sociales chez un laïc catholique*. Paris: Beauchesne, 1970.
———. *L'Association catholique de la jeunesse française, 1886-1907*. Paris: Armand Colin, 1968.
Montagnini, Msgr. *Les Fiches pontificales*. Paris: Nourry, 1908.
Montuclard, Maurice. "Aux origines de la démocratie chrétienne." *Archives de Sociologie des Religions* 6 (July-Dec. 1958), 47-89.
———. *Conscience religieuse et démocratie: La Deuxième démocratie chrétienne en France, 1891-1902*. Paris: Editions du Seuil, 1963.
Moody, Joseph N. *The Church as Enemy: Anticlericalism in Nineteenth Century French Literature*. Washington: Corpus, 1968.
———. "The Dechristianization of the French Working Class." *Review of Politics* 20 (Jan. 1958), 46-69.
———. "Dreyfus and After." *Bridge* 2 (1956), 160-87.
———. "French Anticlericalism: Image and Reality." *Catholic Historical Review* 61 (Jan. 1971), 630-48.
Moody, Joseph N., ed. *Church and Society: Catholic Social and Political Thought and Movements, 1789-1950*. New York: Arts, 1953.
Moon, Parker Thomas. *The Labor Problem and the Social Catholic Movement in France*. New York: Macmillan, 1921.
Morienval, Jean. *Sur l'histoire de la presse catholique en France*. Paris: Alsatia, 1936.
Mounier, Emmanuel. *Oeuvres: 1931-1939*. 4 vols. Paris: Éditions du Seuil, 1961.
———. *Le Personalisme*. Paris: Presses Universitaires de France, 1955.
Muret, Charlotte Touzalin. *French Royalist Doctrines since the Revolution*. New York: Columbia University Press, 1933.
Murphy, Francis J. "La Main tendue." *Catholic Historical Review* 60 (July 1974), 255-70.
———. "Maurice Thorez and *La Main Tendue*." Ph.D. diss., Fordham University, 1971.
Naudet, Father Paul. *La Démocratie et les démocrates chrétiens*. Paris: J. Briguet, 1900.
———. *Pour la femme: Etudes féministes*. 4th ed. Paris: Fontemoing, 1904.
———. *Pourquoi les catholiques ont perdu la bataille*. Paris: Fontemoing, 1904.
———. *Premiers principes de sociologie catholique*. Paris: Bloud et Barral, 1899.
Nguyen, Victor. "Situation des études maurrassiennes: Contribution à l'étude

de la presse et des mentalités." *Revue d'Histoire Moderne et Contemporaine* 18 (Oct.–Dec. 1971), 503–38.

Nichols, Peter. *The Politics of the Vatican.* New York: Frederick A. Praeger, 1968.

Noether, Emiliana P. "Political Catholicism in France and Italy." *Yale Review* 44 (1955), 569–83.

Noguerès, Henri, et al. *Histoire de la résistance en France.* Vols. 1–4. Paris: Laffont, 1967–1976.

———. *Munich ou la Drôle de paix (29 septembre 1938).* Paris: Livre de Poche, 1976.

Nolte, Ernst. *Three Faces of Fascism.* Trans. Leila Vennewitz. New York: New American Library, 1965.

Novick, Peter. *The Resistance versus Vichy.* New York: Columbia University Press, 1968.

O'Donnel, J. Dean, Jr. "Cardinal Charles Lavigerie: The Politics of Getting a Red Hat." *Catholic Historical Review* 63 (April 1977), 185–203.

——— *Lavigerie in Tunisia: The Interplay of Imperialist and Missionary.* Athens: University of Georgia Press, 1979.

Osgood, Samuel M. *French Royalism Under the Third and Fourth Republic.* The Hague: Martinus Nijoff, 1960.

———. "The Front Populaire: Views from the Right." *International Review of Social History* (1964), 189–201.

Ott, Barthelemy. *Georges Bidault, l'indomptable.* Paris: Editions du Vivarais, 1978.

Ozouf, Mona. *L'École, l'église et la République, 1871–1914.* Paris: Armand Colin, 1963.

Padburg, John W. *Colleges in Controversy: The Jesuit Schools in France from Revival to Suppression, 1815–1880.* Cambridge, Mass.: Harvard University Press, 1969.

Paraf, Pierre. *La France et l'affaire Dreyfus.* Paris: Droit et Liberté, 1978.

Partin, Malcolm O. *Waldeck-Rousseau, Combes and the Church: The Politics of Anticlericalism, 1899–1905.* Durham, N.C.: Duke University Press, 1969.

Paul, Harry W. *The Edge of Contingency: Catholic Reaction to Scientific Change from Darwin to Duhem.* Gainesville: University of Florida Press, 1979.

———. "In Quest of Kerygma: Catholic Intellectual Life in Nineteenth-Century France." *American Historical Review* 75 (1969), 387–423.

———. "Science and the Catholic Institutes in Nineteenth-Century France." *Societas* 1 (Autumn 1971), 271–85.

———. *The Second Ralliement: The Rapprochement Between Church and State in France in the Twentieth Century.* Washington, D.C.: Catholic University of America Press, 1967.

———. *The Sorcerer's Apprentice: The French Scientist's Image of German Science.* Gainesville: University of Florida Press, 1972.

Paxton, Robert O. *Vichy France: Old Guard and New Order, 1940-1944.* New York: Alfred A. Knopf, 1972.
Perkins, C. Alfred. "French Catholic Opinion and Imperial Expansion, 1880-1886." Ph.D diss., Harvard University, 1964.
Peter, Colette. *Charles Maurras et l'ideologie d'Action Française.* Paris: Seuil, 1972.
Petit, Jacques ed. *Jacques Maritain, Emmanuel Mounier, 1929-1939: Les grandes correspondances,* no. 33. Paris: Seuil, 1973.
Pezet, Ernest. *Chrétiens au service de la Cité, de Léon XIII au Sillon et au M.R.P. (1891-1965).* Paris: Nouvelles Éditions Latines, 1965.
Phillips, C. S. *The Church in France, 1848-1907.* London: Society for Promoting Christian Knowledge, 1936.
Pierce, Roy. *The Politics of Educational Reform in France.* Princeton, N.J.: Princeton University Press, 1969.
Pierre, Jules. *Avec Nietzsche à l'assaut du christianisme.* Limoges: Dumont, 1910.
———. *Reponse à M. Maurras, l'Action Française et ses directeurs paiennes.* Paris: Amat, 1914.
Piou, Jacques. *Le Comte Albert de Mun: Sa vie publique.* Paris: Spes, 1925.
———. *Le Ralliement: Son histoire.* Paris: Spes, 1928.
Ponson, Christian. *Les Catholiques lyonnais et la Chronique sociale.* Lyon: Presses Universitaires de Lyon, 1979.
Potel Julien, *Le Clergé français.* Paris: Centurion, 1967.
Poulat, Emile. *Alfred Loisy: Sa vie, son oeuvre.* Paris: Centre National de la Recherche Scientifique, 1960.
———. *Catholicisme, démocratie et socialisme.* Paris: Casterman, 1977.
———. "Le Catholicisme français et son personnel dirigeant." *Archives de Sociologie des Religions* 19 (Jan.–June 1965), 117–24.
———. "Une Enquête anticlericale de pratique religieuse en Seine-et-Marne 1903." *Archives de la Sociologie des Religions* 6 (July–Dec. 1958), 127–48.
———. *Histoire, dogme et critique dans la crise moderniste.* Paris: Casterman, 1962.
———. *Intégrisme et catholicisme intégral: Un Reseau secret international antimoderniste: La "Sapinière" (1909-1921).* Paris: Casterman, 1969.
———. "'Modernisme' et 'intégrisme' du concept polémique à l'irénisme critique." *Archives de Sociologie des Religions* 27 (Jan.–June 1969), 3–28.
———. *Naissance des prêtres-ouvriers.* Paris: Casterman, 1965.
———. "Pour une nouvelle comprehension de la démocratie chrétienne." *Revue d'Histoire Ecclésiastique* 1 (1975), 5–38.
———. "Religion et politique." *Critique* 123–24 (Aug.–Sept. 1957), 757–70.
———. *Les Semaines religieuses: Approche historique.* Paris: Éditions Sociales, 1957.
Powers, Francis J., ed. *Papal Pronouncements on the Political Order.* Westminster, Md.: Newman Press, 1952.

Prelot, Marcel. "Histoire et doctrine du parti démocrate populaire." *Politique* 19–20 (1962), 307–40.

Prelot, Marcel, and F. Galloudec-Genuys, eds. *Le Libéralisme catholique*. Paris: Armand Colin, 1969.

"Progressisme et intégrisme." *Chronique Sociale* 63 (May 15, 1955), entire issue.

Pujo, Maurice. *Comment Rome est trompée*. Paris Arthème Fayard, 1929.

Rauch, R. William, Jr. "From the Sillon to the Mouvement Républicain Populaire: Doctor Robert Cornilleau and a Generation of Christian Democrats in France, 1910–1940." *Catholic Historical Review* 58 (Apr. 1972), 25–66.

―――. *Politics and Belief in Contemporary France*. The Hague: Nijhoff, 1972.

Raymond-Laurent, Jean. *Les Origines du Mouvement républicain populaire*. Paris: Mail, 1954.

―――. *Le Parti Démocrate Populaire, 1924–1944*. Paris: Petit Démocrate, n.d.

Raymond-Laurent, Jean, and Marcel Prelot. *Manuel politique: Le programme du parti démocrate populaire*. Paris: Éditions Spes, 1928.

Reardon, Bernard M. G., ed. *Roman Catholic Modernism*. Stanford, Calif.: Stanford University Press, 1970.

Rémond, René. "L'ACJF et la Jenuesse Ouvrière." *Vie Intellectuelle* 27 (Mar. 1956), 26–41.

―――. "Les anciens combattants et la politique." *Revue Française de Science Politique* 5 (1955), 267–90.

―――. *Les Catholiques dans la France des années 30*. Paris: Cana, 1979.

―――. *Les Catholiques, le communisme et les crises, 1929–1939*. Paris: Armand Colin, 1960.

―――. "Droit et gauche dans le catholicisme français contemporain." *Revue Française de Science Politique* 8 (1958), 529–44, 803–20.

―――. "Évolution de la notion de laïcité entre 1919 et 1929." *Cahiers d'Histoire* 4 (1959), 71–87.

―――. "L'Évolution du journal 'La Croix' et son role auprès de l'opinion catholique (1919–1939)." *Bulletin de la Société d'Histoire Moderne* 12 (1958), 3–10.

―――. "Explications du six février." *Politique* 1 (1959), 218–30.

―――. *The Right-Wing in France from 1815 to de Gaulle*. Philadelphia: University of Pennsylvania Press, 1966.

Rémond, René, ed. *Forces religieuses et attitudes politiques dans la France Contemporaine*. In *Cahiers de la Fondation Nationale des Sciences Politiques*. Paris: Armand Colin, 1965.

Rémond, René, and Janine Bourdin, eds. *La France et les français en 1938–1939*. Paris: Presses de la Fondation Nationale des Sciences Politiques, 1978.

Reynaud, Jean-Daniel. *Les Syndicats en France*. Paris: Armand Colin, 1966.

Rhodes, Anthony. *The Vatican in the Age of the Dictators*. New York: Holt, Rinehart and Winston, 1973.

Rice-Maximin, Edward. "The Main Tendue: Catholics and Communists during the Popular Front in France." *Contemporary French Civilization*, Winter 1980, pp. 193-210.

Ridley, F. F. *Revolutionary Syndicalism in France: The Direct Action of Its Time*. Cambridge: Cambridge University Press, 1970.

Rollet, Henri. *L'Action sociale des catholiques en France*. Paris: Boivin, 1958.

———. *L'Action sociale des catholiques en France, 1871-1914*. 2 vols. Paris: Boivin, 1947-1958.

———. *Albert de Mun et le parti catholique*. Paris: Boivin, 1949.

———. "Essai sur les travaux législatifs des catholiques sociaux." *Chronique Sociale de France*, Apr. 1952, pp. 155-65.

Rowse, A. L. *All Souls and Appeasement*. London: Macmillan, 1961.

Rudaux, Phillipe. *Les Croix de Feu et le PSF*. Paris: Éditions France-Empire, 1967.

Sabatier, Paul. *Disestablishment in France*. Trans. Robert Dell. London: T. Fisher Unwin, 1906.

Saint-Pierre, Michel de. *Les Nouveaux prêtres*. Paris: Table Ronde, 1964.

Sanchez, José M. "The Second Spanish Republic and the Holy See: 1931-1936." *Catholic Historical Review* 49 (Apr. 1963), 47-68.

Sangnier, Marc. *A l'epreuve de la guerre: Recueil de pages extraites des oeuvres d'avant-guerre de Marc Sangnier et précédées d'une introduction*. Paris: Librairie de "la Démocratie," 1919.

———. *Albert de Mun*. Paris: Alcan, 1932.

———. *L'Armée et la nation*. Paris: "La Démocratie," 1913.

———. *Autrefois*. Paris: Bloud et Gay, 1936.

———. *Conférences aux soldats sur le front*. Paris: Bloud et Gay, 1919.

———. *Le Devoir national*. Paris: "La Démocratie," 1914.

———. *L'Éducation sociale du peuple*. Paris: Au Sillon, 1904.

———. *L'Esprit démocratique*. Paris: Perrin, 1905.

———. *Et maintenant?* Paris: "La Démocratie," 1919.

———. *La Lutte pour la démocratie*. Paris: Perrin, 1908.

———. *Une Méthode d'éducation démocratique*. Paris: Au Sillon, 1906.

———. *Qui a le vrai programme républicain?* Paris: "La Démocratie," 1914.

———. *Les Syndicats et la démocratie*. Paris: Au Sillon, 1906.

Schalk, David. "Professors as Watchdogs: Paul Nizan's Theory of the Intellectual and Politics." *Journal of the History of Ideas* 24 (1973), 79-96.

———. *The Spectrum of Political Engagement: Mounier, Benda, Nizan, Brassilach, Sartre*. Princeton, N.J.: Princeton University Press, 1979.

———. "La Trahison des clercs—1927 and Later." *French Historical Studies* 7 (Fall 1971), 245-63.

Schmitt, Hans A. *Charles Péguy: The Decline of an Idealist*. Baton Rouge: Louisiana State University Press, 1967.

Scholl, S. H. *Cent cinquante ans de mouvement ouvrier chrétien en Europe de l'ouest (1789-1939)*. Louvain-Paris, 1966.

Seager, Frederick H. *The Boulanger Affair.* Ithaca, N.Y.: Cornell University Press, 1969.

Sedgwick, Alexander. *The Ralliement in French Politics, 1890–1898.* Cambridge, Mass.: Harvard University Press, 1965.

———. *The Third French Republic, 1870–1914.* New York: Crowell, 1968.

"Les Semaines Sociales de France se présentent. . . ." *Chronique Sociale de France,* May–June 1954, pp. 223–40.

Serant, Paul. *Les Dissidents de l'Action française.* Paris: Copernie, n.d.

Siegfried, André. *Tableau des partis en France.* Paris: B. Grasset, 1930.

———. *Tableau politique de la France de l'ouest sous la Troisième République.* 2d ed. Paris: Armand Colin, 1964.

Silverman, Dan P. "Political Catholicism and Social Democracy in Alsace-Lorraine, 1781–1914." *Catholic Historical Review* 52 (Apr. 1966), 39–65.

Simon, Pierre-Henri. *Les Catholiques, la politique et l'argent.* Paris: Aubier, 1936.

———. *Discours sur la guerre possible.* Paris: Éditions du Cerf, 1937.

———. *L'Église et la révolution sociale.* Paris: Éditions du Cerf, 1938.

———. *Préparer l'après guerre.* Paris: Bloud et Gay, 1940.

"Le soixantième anniversaire de 'La Chronique Sociale.'" *Chronique Sociale de France* (Feb. 1952), 2–4.

Soltau, Roger H. *French Parties and Politics, 1871–1921.* London: Oxford University Press, 1930.

Sorlin, Pierre. *"La Croix" et les juifs.* Paris: Grasset, 1967.

Soucy, Robert. *Fascism in France: The Case of Maurice Barrès.* Berkeley and Los Angeles: University of California Press, 1973.

———. "French Fascism as Class Conciliation and Moral Regeneration." *Societas* 1 (1971), 287–97.

———. "French Fascist Intellectuals in the 1930's: An Old New Left?" *French Historical Studies* 8 (1974), 445–58.

Souvay, Charles L. "The Catholic Church in Contemporary France (1919–1931)." *Catholic Historical Review* 18 (July 1932), 205–28.

Spencer, Philip. *Politics of Belief in Nineteenth-Century France.* New York: Grove Press, 1953.

St. Aubyn, Frederic C. *Charles Péguy.* Boston: Twayne, 1977.

Stearns, Peter N. *Revolutionary Syndicalism and French Labor: A Cause Without Rebels.* New Brunswick, N.J.: Rutgers University Press, 1971.

Sternhell, Zeev. *La Droite révolutionnaire, 1885–1914: Les origines françaises du fascisme.* Pairs: Editions du Seuil, 1978.

———. *Maurice Barrès et le nationalisme français.* Cahiers de la Fondation Nationale des Sciences Politiques, no. 182. Paris: Armand Colin, 1972.

Suffert, Georges. *Les Catholiques et la gauche.* Paris: F. Maspero, 1960.

Sutter, Jacques. "Analyse organigrammatique de L'église de France." *Archives de Sociologie des Religions* 31 (Jan.–June 1971), 99–149.

Talmy, Robert. *Albert de Mun.* Paris: Bloud et Gay, 1965.

———. *Aux sources du catholicisme social: L'École de la Tour du Pin.* Tournai: Desclée, 1963.
———. *René de la Tour du Pin.* Paris: Bloud et Gay, 1964.
———. *Le Syndicalisme chrétien en France, 1781–1930.* Paris: Bloud et Gay, 1966.
Tannenbaum, Edward R. *The Action Française: Diehard Reactionaries in Twentieth-Century France.* New York: John Wiley, 1962.
———. *The New France.* Chicago: University of Chicago Press, 1974.
———. "The Reactionary Mentality of the Action Française." *Historian* 17 (Autumn 1954), 18–42.
Teeling, William. *The Pope in Politics: The Life and Work of Pius XI.* London: Dickson, 1938.
Tessier, Gaston. *Les Catholiques et la paix.* Paris: Spes, 1927.
———. *Un Progrès social: La Journée de huit heures.* Paris: Spes, 1923.
———. "Souvenirs et portraits." *Chronique Sociale de France,* Apr. 1952, pp. 176–83.
———. *Le Syndicalisme chrétien en 1945.* Paris: Éditions de la C.F.T.C, 1945.
Un Théologien en liberté: Jacques Duquesne interroge le Père Chenu. Paris: Centurion, 1975.
Thibaudet, Albert. *Les Idées de Charles Maurras.* Paris: Flammarion, 1930.
Thierry, Jean-Jacques. *Journal politique d'un cardinal (1914–1965).* Paris: Calmann-Levy, 1967.
Thomas, Lucien. *L'Action Française devant l'église de Pie X à Pie XII.* Paris: Nouvelles Editions Latines, 1965.
Thomson, David, ed. *France, Empire and Republic, 1850–1940: Historical Documents.* New York: Harper and Row, 1968.
Tiersky, Ronald. *French Communism, 1920–1972.* New York: Columbia University Press, 1974.
Tilly, Charles. *The Vendée.* New York: Wiley, 1967.
La Tour du Pin Chambly de la Charce, Charles Humbert René. *Aphorismes de politique.* Paris: Nouvelle Librairie Nationale 1909.
———. *Vers un ordre social: Jalons de route, 1882–1907.* Paris: Nouvelle Librairie Nationale, 1907.
Tournier, Jules. *Le Cardinal Lavigerie et son action politique (1863–1892).* Paris: Perrin, 1913.
Trimouille, Pierre. *Léon Harmel et l'usine chrétienne du Val des Bois (1840–1914).* Lyon: Centre d'Histoire du Catholicisme, 1974.
Truman, Tom. *Catholic Action and Politics.* London: Marlin Press, 1960.
Tucker, William R. *The Fascist Ego: A Political Biography of Robert Brasillach.* Berkeley and Los Angeles: University of California Press, 1976.
Vaussard, Maurice. *Histoire de la démocratie chrétienne.* 2 vols. Paris: Éditions du Seuil, 1956.
Véret, Charles. *J'ai vu grandir la J.O.C.* Paris: Éditions Ouvrières, 1977.
Viance, Georges, *La Fédération nationale catholique.* Paris: Flammarion, 1930.

Vidler, Alec R. *The Modernist Movement in the Roman Church.* Cambridge: Cambridge University Press, 1934.

———. *Prophecy and Papacy: A Study of Lamennais, the Church and the Revolution.* New York: Scribner's, 1954.

———. *A Variety of Catholic Modernists.* Cambridge: Cambridge University Press, 1970.

Vigne, Octave. *Mes souvenirs sur Charles Maurras.* Uzes: H. Peladan, 1978.

Villain, R. P. Jean. "L'Action Populaire." *Chronique Sociale de France,* Apr. 1952, 215–19.

———. *La Charte du travail et l'organisation economique et sociale de la profession.* Paris, Spes, 1942.

———. *L'Enseignement social de l'église.* Paris: Editions Spes, 1954.

———. *Le Mythe du communisme.* Paris: Spes, 1936.

———. *Le Problème de la nationalisation au regard de la pensée sociale chrétienne.* Paris: Spes, 1944.

Villier, Marjorie. *Charles Péguy: A Study in Integrity.* London: Collins, 1965.

Vinatier, Jean. *Le Cardinal Liénart et la Mission de France.* Paris: Centurion, 1978.

Wallace, Lillian Parker. *Leo XIII and the Rise of Socialism.* Durham, N.C.: Duke University Press, 1966.

Ward, James E. "The Algiers Toast: Lavigerie's Work or Leo XIII's?" *Catholic Historical Review* 51 (1965), 173–91.

———. "Cardinal Place and Leo XIII's Ralliement Policy." *Catholic Historical Review* 57 (Jan. 1972), 602–28.

———. "Cardinal Richard versus Cardinal Lavigerie: Episcopal Resistance to the Ralliement." *Catholic Historical Review* 53 (Oct. 1967), 346–71.

———. "Franco-Vatican Relations, 1878–1892." Ph.D. diss., Cornell University, 1962.

———. "The French Cardinals and Leo XIII's Ralliement Policy." *Church History* 33 (Mar. 1964), 60–73.

Weber, Eugen. *Action Française: Royalism and Reaction in Twentieth-Century France.* Stanford, Calif.: Stanford University Press, 1962.

———. *Nationalist Revival in France.* Berkeley and Los Angeles: University of California Press, 1959.

Webster, Richard A. *The Cross and the Fasces.* Stanford, Calif.: Stanford University Press, 1960.

Wilson, Stephen. "A View of the Past: Action Française Historiography and Its Socio-Political Function." *Historical Journal* 19 (1976), 135–61.

Winock, Michel. *Histoire politique de la revue "Esprit" 1930–1950.* Paris: Seuil, 1975.

Wohl, Robert. *French Communism in the Making, 1914–1924.* Stanford, Calif.: Stanford University Press, 1966.

Zirnheld, Jules. *Cinquante années du syndicalisme chrétien.* Paris: Spes, 1937.

Index

Abbés démocrates, 9, 35, 38, 53-54, 59, 75-76. *See also* Trochu
Académie Française, 46, 172, 178
L'Acquitaine, 124
Action Catholique Ouvrière, 181
L'Action Française, 16, 70, 72, 84, 97, 100, 120, 129, 132-33, 173, 176; and the papacy, 87, 96, 121-22, 125, 152; polemics of, 28-29, 53, 70, 85, 152; and Sangnier, 26-27, 73
L'Action Française agricole, 101
L'Action Française du dimanche, 101
Action Libérale Populaire (ALP), 7, 37, 55, 61, 71, 198*n*23; and the Christian Democrats, 39-40, 53-56, 72; and *La Croix,* 36, 38; Sangnier's break with, 59; and the Separation Law, 45, 48
Action Populaire, 7, 8
Alsace-Lorraine, 66, 87, 94, 98, 111
Amette, Léon Adolphe, cardinal of Paris, 50-51, 61, 67
Andrieu, Paulin, archbishop of Bordeaux, 91-93, 126, 133, 138, 140; opposition of, to the Action Française, 129; and Maurras, 88-89; and Pius XI, 124, 128

Anticlericalism, 3-4, 10, 83; and the Bloc National, 91, 99; and the Cartel des Gauches, 82, 94, 95, 96, 98, 99, 112, 142; and the Christian Democrats, 38-40, 62, 75; and the Combes ministry, 41-48, 49, 51; and *La Croix,* 38, 86, 135-36; and the Dreyfus affair, 10, 12, 28, 30, 41; and the Fédération Nationale Catholique, 95-96, 98; and the Ralliement, 6-7; and the Third Republic, 23-24, 97, 99-100, 103; and the Waldeck-Rousseau ministry, 34-36. *See also* Separation Law
Anti-Semitism, 12, 21, 32, 33, 38, 63, 173, 179
Arlès, Nel, 72
Aspects de la France, 219
Assembly of French Cardinals, 118
Association Catholique, 7
Association Catholique de la Jeunesse Française (ACJF), 7, 65, 102-03, 110-11, 137, 153-54; support of Pius XI for, 140, 154
Associations Bill, 34
Associations Catholiques de Chefs de Famille, 95

✢ 249 ✢

Assumptionists, 32, 66, 89; and *La Croix*, 12, 25, 37, 133, 136
L'Aube, 149–50, 156, 160–65, 180; on Briandism, 152–53, 168; and Maurrasians, 172
"Au Milieu des sollicitudes," 6

Bainville, Jacques, 26, 101
Barbier, Emmanuel, 50, 53, 60–61, 72, 77
Baudrillart, Alfred, 86, 179
Belgium, 123, 137
Bellaigue, Camille, papal chamberlain, 80
Benedict XV, 86–87, 105–06, 121
Benigni, Umberto, 52, 71, 105
Bernanons, Georges, 65, 100, 162
Bernoville, Gaëtan, 160
Bertoye, M., 86, 89, 92, 101, 133, 135
Besse, J. M., 65
Bidault, Georges (vice-president of ACJF), 137, 149, 157, 162–63, 172, 180
Billot, Louis, cardinal, 52, 68, 71, 129–30
Bloc National, 81, 90–99, 107–08, 116, 121
Blum, Léon (premier of Popular Front), 164–65, 172–73
Bodin, Charles, 39
Boisfleury, Robert de, 174
Bolshevism, 85, 90–92, 93, 97, 106, 112, 122, 151; and *Ubi Arcano Dei*, 115, 120
Bonaparte, 41
Boulanger, Georges, 12
Boulangism, 13, 16, 21
Briand, Aristide, 47, 92, 104; foreign policy of, 142, 151
Briandism, 117, 144, 151–55, 165–68
Briey affair, 164
Brittany, 6, 39, 53–56, 108, 111; and the Action Française, 67, 132; and Christian Democracy, 56, 74, 88
Brunetière, Ferdinand, 46

Cahiers de la Jeunesse Belge, 103
Calvin, John, 20, 23, 83
Camelots du Roi, 15–16, 64, 66, 70–71, 88, 98, 101–02, 127, 188*n*6; and Sangnier, 73, 98, 108
Cardijn, Joseph (founder of JOC), 137, 154
Cartel des Gauches, 82, 94–99, 112, 142
Catholic Action, 101, 115, 118, 132, 135–39, 146, 150–57, 179, 213*n*12; and Pius XI, 117, 123, 125, 137, 140, 170–71
Catteau, Msgr., 77
Les Cercles d'Etudes Elémentaires, 77
Ceretti, Msgr., 107, 110, 124
Chaillet, Pierre, 180
Chamber of Deputies, 34, 39, 40, 59, 107, 156; and the Christian Democrats, 9, 57, 74
Chapon, Msgr., 72, 77, 91
Charost, Alexis-Armand, cardinal of Lille, 59, 79, 100, 110, 124, 131–32, 209*n*17
Chanson, Paul, 149
Chenu, M.-D., 150
Chesnelong, Jean-Victor, 100
Christian Democracy, 44–48, 77, 88, 111, 117, 184; and the Action Française, 65; and the papacy, 47, 125
Christian Democrats, 5, 9, 28, 35–38, 69, 128–29, 134–35, 149, 156; and the Action Française, 29–30, 67, 68, 71, 72, 73, 89, 99, 123, 142; and the ALP, 39–40; and the Dreyfus affair, 41; and *L'Esprit*, 151; foreign policy of, 161–62; in Lorraine, 66; and Maurras, 76, 78, 80; and the Maurrasians, 98, 125–26, 140–41, 172, 183; and *L'Ouest-Eclair*, 33, 56–57, 74, 108; and the PDP, 110–11; and Pius XI, 49, 127, 144, 163, 169; polemics of, 25–26; and the Popular Front, 159; and the Rallie-

Christian Democrats *(cont.)*
ment, 31, 54, 62; republican centrism of, 35–38, 69, 105–06, 114; and the Union Sacrée, 88
Chronique des Comités du Sud-Est, 8
Chronique Sociale de France, 137
Civiltà Cattolica, 32
Clemenceau, Georges, 11, 84, 90, 104
Cochin, Denys, 46
Combes, Emile, 34, 41–43, 117
Committee for the Defense of Right, 33
Communism, 81, 91, 97, 98, 104, 117, 158–59, 165; and the CFTC, 113; and the FNC, 102, 118; and the PDP, 111; denunciation of, 85, 98, 135–36; and the Popular Front, 156; and *La Vie Catholique,* 112
Comte, Auguste: and the Institut d'Action Française, 15; positivism of, 14, 24–25, 28, 63
Confédération Française des Travailleurs Chrétiens (CFTC), 110–13, 147, 149, 180; and the papacy, 154–55, 168; and the Popular Front, 159
Congar, Yves, 150
Consortium, 154
Correspondance Nationale, 64
Correspondance de Rome, 52–53
Coullié, cardinal of Lyon, 51, 61
Credo, 118, 138, 164
Cri de Flandres, 58
La Croix, 7, 28; and the Action Française, 66, 70, 89, 98, 101, 123, 126–27, 133; and the ALP, 36; and the Assumptionists, 12, 25; and Bertoye, 92; and Briandism, 168; and Catholic Action, 136; circulation of, 32; and *Credo,* 164; and Daudet, 109; enemies of, 38, 55, 86, 93, 94; foreign policy of, 83, 84–85, 91, 151; and Gonin, 8; and Guiraud, 95; and the League of Nations, 90; and de Mun, 42; and the papacy, 34, 71, 87, 133, 134–37, 140, 163;

La Croix (cont.)
167; and the royalists, 134–37, 157; and Sangnier, 59; and the Separation Law, 45, 48
Croix de Feu, 158, 172
"Cultic association," 58, 61, 71, 92, 116; and *La Croix,* 51; and the Maurrasians, 97. *See also* Separation Law

Dabry, Pierre, 9, 39, 53–55
Daladier, Edouard, 156
Daudet, Léon, 12, 16–17, 89, 97, 101, 174, 178–79; in government, 90, 96, 102, 107–08; and *L'Ouest-Eclair,* 109; and the Ruhr invasion, 96–97; and Trochu, 110
de Cabrières, cardinal of Montpellier, 51, 60, 66, 68, 88, 91, 100, 130
de Castelnau, Eduard de Curières (leader of FNC), 95–96, 101, 109, 138–39, 153–57, 160, 164, 168; and the FNC, 98, 117–18, 120–21
Declaration of the Rights of Man, 10, 26, 39, 83, 90. *See also* French Revolution
de Gaulle, Charles, 177, 180
de la Brière, Yves, 77, 138
Delahaye, Eugène, 101, 109, 132
de Laï, Cardinal, 52, 59, 122
Delamaire, bishop of Cambrai, 60
de la Montagne, Robert Havard, 101
Delassus, Henri, 50–51, 53, 58, 61, 67–68, 77, 130; and the Separation Law, 45–47
Delcassé, Théophile, 43
La Démocratie, 73
de Mun, Albert, 8, 13, 31, 33, 37, 42, 55, 61, 113, 192n16; *Oeuvre des cercles d'ouvriers,* 7; and the Separation Law, 46, 48
La Dépêche de Toulouse, 86
Depression, 15, 151, 156
Deroulède, Paul, 12

Desbuquois, Gustave, 7
"Le Dilemme de Marc Sangnier," 26–27
Dimier, Louis, 17, 70, 72, 84, 89; and Benedict XV, 87, 121
Dolfuss, Engelbert, 166
Dominicans, 150, 153
Doumergue, Gaston, 156–57
Dreyfus, Alfred, 10, 11, 20, 25, 182
Dreyfus affair, 3, 4, 10, 12–16, 24, 28, 30–34, 38, 41, 44, 47
Drumont, Edouard, 12, 16, 21, 32, 56, 101
Dubillard, bishop of Quimper, 60, 68
Dubois, Louis-Ernest, archbishop of Paris, 112, 129, 142
Dubourg, August, Cardinal of Rennes, 50–57, 60–61, 65, 87–88, 91, 99–100, 108, 110, 130
du Loû, Emmanuel Desgreés (owner of *L'Ouest-Eclair*), 9, 88, 106, 209*n*17; and the Action Française, 75, 89; and the ALP, 40; and the Bloc National, 99; and the FNC, 109; and *L'Ouest-Eclair*, 32, 39, 55–57, 74; and Trochu, 99
Dupanloup, Félix, bishop of Orleans, 5
Duparc, bishop of Quimper, 109

L'Echo de Paris, 153
Education: and the Action Française, 19, 65, 102, 137, 178; in Alsace-Lorraine, 94–97; and anticlericalism, 6, 31; and the associations bill, 34; Masonic, 20, 22; Protestant, 20–21; in seminaries, 50, 65; state aid for Catholic, 91, 92, 111; and the Vichy regime, 179
Election of 1899, 30
Encyclicals, papal: *Ad Beatissimi*, 105; *Divini Redemptoris*, 164–65, 169, 170; *Graves de Communi*, 54; *Gravissimo Officii*, 47–49, 54, 59, 62, 70; *Lamentabili Sane*, 50; *Maximam Gravissimamque*, 116, 121; *Mit*

Encyclicals, papal (*cont.*)
brennender Sorge, 169–70; *Non abbiamo bisogno*, 169–70; *Pascendi Dominici Gregis*, 50–51, 55, 62; *Quadragesimo Anno*, 155, 168–69; *Rerum Novarum*, 113; *Testem Benevolentiae*, 54; *To the Belligerent Peoples and to Their Leaders*, 87; *Ubi Arcano Dei*, 114–15, 120, 135, 144, 169, 171
L'Esprit, 150–52, 159, 164, 181
L'Eveil Démocratique, 9
L'Express du Midi, 101

Fédération Nationale Catholique (FNC), 95, 98, 101, 109, 179; and the Action Française, 102; and Catholic Action, 118, 138–40; and Franco, 161–63; and the Jeune République, 164; and Pius XI, 133–40, 168; and the Popular Front, 160; principles of, 102, 117–20; and Vallat, 127
Feron-Vrau, Paul, 38, 55
Ferry, Jules, minister of education, 6
France Libre, 33
Freemasons. *See* Masons
French Revolution, 3, 5, 22–23, 31, 33, 35–39, 60, 68, 72, 74, 83, 91, 113, 115, 136, 181; and the Reformation, 83, 102
Fuzet, archbishop of Rouen, 53, 71

Gallicanism, 4, 20, 22, 46, 62, 102, 132–33, 142
Gambetta, Léon, 6
Garrigou-Lagrange, Msgr., 65
Gasparri, Pietro, 105, 116, 122, 142, 151
Le Gaulois, 64
Gay, Francisque, 94, 172–73; and the Action Française, 126, 127, 143; and the anti-Maurrasian campaign, 126–27; and *L'Aube*, 149; and the Bloud and Gay firm, 112, 126–27; and de

Gay, Francisque (*cont.*)
  Castelnau, 153–54; and Pius XI, 136; and the Resistance, 180; on Spain, 162–63
Gayraud, Hippolyte, 9, 26, 39–40, 42, 57; and the Montagnini affair, 53; *La République et la paix religieuse*, 26
Géay, bishop of Laval, 43, 51
Gerlier, cardinal of Lyon, 181
Germain, archbishop of Toulouse, 130–31
Germany: and the Action Française, 96–97, 98; and the Cartel des Gauches, 94; and the church, 160–62, 166, 167, 169–71; as enemy, 22, 38, 81, 83, 84, 90, 92, 104, 122, 142; as Protestant nation, 82, 97
Gibier, bishop of Versailles, 116
Gillet, Msgr., 174
Gonin, Marius, 8
Goyau, Georges, 174
Guillibert, Msgr., 77, 100
Guiraud, Jean (leader of Associations Catholiques de Chefs de Famille), 95, 101, 126, 133–35

Harmel, Léon, 9
Henriot, Philippe, 179
Herriot, Edouard, 82, 94–98, 103, 120
Honnert, Robert, 159
Hoog, Georges, 149, 163
Hugo, Victor, 16
L'Humanité, 85–86

Institut d'Action Française, 15, 66–67
Institut Catholique de Paris, 86, 179
Internationalism, 18, 85, 86, 107, 151
Italy, 42, 161, 166, 169, 171

Janvier, canon at Rennes, 65, 67, 100–01, 118, 131
Jaurès, Jean, 27
Jenouvrier, Senator, 99

Jeune République, 151, 168, 206n5; and the Action Française, 107, 126; and the Bloc National, 105, 107; and the FNC, 164; and the PDP, 110–11; policies of, 98, 114, 152; and the Popular Front, 159; and the Resistance, 180
Jeunesse de l'Eglise, 181
Jeunesse Ouvrière Chrétienne (JOC), 137–38, 147, 151, 179, 181; policies of, 148–49; and the JOCF, 138, 148; and Pius XI, 154, 168; and the Popular Front, 159. *See also* Jocistes
Jeunesse Ouvrière Chrétienne Féminine, 138, 148
Jeunesses Patriotes, 172
Jews: as enemies, 4, 16, 18, 20–24, 32–35, 38–39, 63, 69–70, 78, 93; as Bolsheviks, 85; Daudet on, 97; Dreyfus as, 10, 11, 32; and *France Libre*, 33; and the Separation Law, 45; and the Vichy regime, 177. *See also* Anti-Semitism
Joan of Arc, 20, 66, 70–72, 83–84, 189n24, 219n7; and the Camelots du Roi, 16; and Dame Liberty, 36
Jocistes, 138, 149, 180
Le Journal de Rennes, 55
Julien, Eugéne Louis Ernest, bishop of Arras, 93
La Justice Sociale, 33, 54

Keller, Colonel Emile (leader of Union Catholique), 61, 117

Laberthonnière, Lucien, 76
Labouré, Cardinal, 54
Lacroix, Lucien-Léon, bishop of Tarentaise, 51
Lammenais, Msgr., 5
Laudrain, Maurice (editor of *Terre Nouvelle*), 159, 163
League of Nations: denounced by the Action Française, 97; and *L'Aube*,

League of Nations (*cont.*) 149; and the Bloc National, 90; and the Cartel des Gauches, 94; and the Jeune République, 98, 152; and the PDP, 111; and Pius XI, 114–15, 151, 166, 168; and *La Vie Catholique*, 112
Lecot, Cardinal, 71
Le Floch, Msgr., 68
Lemire, Jules, 9, 33, 57–59; and the Maurrasians, 141; and the Montagnini affair, 53; and the Separation Law, 45–46
Lemmonier, bishop of Bayeux, 60
le Nordez, bishop of Dijon, 43, 51
Leo XIII, 6, 8, 13, 41, 91; and the Action Française, 121; and *La Croix*, 38, 134; encyclicals of, 54, 113; and Pius X, 52, 155; policies of, 30–31, 33, 106, 117; and the Ralliement, 6, 13, 28–29, 62; and Sangnier, 53
Leroy, Henri-Joseph, 7–8
La Libre Belgique, 124
La Libre Parole, 7, 32
Liénart, Achille, cardinal of Lille, 154, 165, 181; and the Lille strike, 155, 158
Ligue Antisémite, 12
Ligue Catholique d'Anjou, 102, 109
Ligue de la Patrie Française, 12
Ligue des Patriotes, 12
Lille strike, 154–55
Locarno Treaty, 90, 97, 142, 163; and the Second Ralliement, 151
Loisy, Alfred, 50, 71
Lorin, Henri, 8
Loubet, Emile, 36, 42, 47
Luçon, Cardinal, 82, 124
Luther, Martin, 22, 82–84, 97, 134, 136

Maglione, Msgr. (papal nuncio to Paris), 142, 172, 209*n*17
Main tendue, 159–60, 164, 173
Malvy, Louis-Jean, 84, 85

Maritain, Jacques, 65, 84, 100, 151; and *La Croix*, 83; and Mounier, 149–50; *Primauté du spirituel*, 128; and the Spanish Civil War, 162–63
Martin-Chauffier, Louis, 159
Marty, François, bishop of Montauban, 51, 66, 100, 129
Marxism: and *L'Action Française*, 85; and Briandism, 152; and the CFTC, 113; and the FNC, 117; as hostile to Christianity, 114, 151, 164, 168; and the JOC, 149; and the PDP, 111; and Pius XI, 171. *See also* Bolshevism
Marxists, 85, 93, 160
Masons: Combes as member, 41; and *La Croix*, 94; as enemies, 20–22, 35, 36–39, 63, 70, 78, 91, 93, 102, 183; and the FNC, 117; and *France Libre*, 33; and the Separation Law, 45; and socialism, 102; and the Vichy regime, 177
Massis, Henri, 65, 83, 100
Mathon, Eugène, 154
Mauriac, François, 162–63
Maurin, cardinal of Lyon, 124
Maurras, Charles, 4, 11–29, 219*n*7; and the Académie Française, 172; and the Action Française, 24, 104, 178; *L'Action Française et la religion catholique*, 78; *L'Action Française et la Vatican*, 140; agnosticism of, 4, 17, 25, 29, 30, 63, 69, 76, 78–79, 89, 101, 126, 128, 134–35, 140; and Andrieu, 88; *Anthinéa*, 78; Belgian support for, 103, 123; and de Cabrières, 88; and the Carmelite order, 173; and Catholicism, 19, 55, 63, 76, 100; Charost on, 132; as collaborationist, 177; condemnation of, 77, 79–80; and Guiraud, 101, 134; and de Lassus, 67; and du Loû, 89; mother of, 68, 100; *Le Pape, la guerre et la paix*, 84, 86; and Pas-

Maurras, Charles (*cont.*)
  selecq, 124; and Pétain, 176; pilgrimages of, 174; and Pius X, 65, 67, 80, 207*n*20; and Pius XI, 137, 152, 171; polemics of, 70, 143; and Sangnier, 26–27, 72, 74
Maurrasians: and Amette, 67; attacks on, 75–76, 77, 89, 106, 127, 134–35, 140–41, 172; and Catholic Action, 123, 152; and Christian Democrats, 9, 65, 72–77, 87; and church hierarchy, 66, 130; downfall of, 137, 142–43; and *L'Express du Midi*, 101; and the FNC, 102, 138, 139; and the French papal embassy, 86; and Guiraud, 134; and Maritain, 128; and Marty, 129; and Massis, 83; patriotic zeal of, 69, 86, 88, 90, 97; and Pelletier, 72; and Pius X, 69; and Pius XI, 121–22, 125, 127, 140, 173, 175; and the press, 66; and the Second Ralliement, 122; ultra Catholicism of, 68–70, 71, 73, 77, 86, 98–99, 100–01, 103, 132, 183; and the Union Sacrée, 84–85, 88; and the Vichy regime, 178; and World War I, 82, 88
Merklen, Léon, 135–36, 144
Mercier, Désiré-Joseph, 83–84, 88, 100, 103, 130
Merry del Val, Cardinal (papal secretary of state), 43, 52, 58, 61, 122
Millerand, Alexandre, 92, 104
Mignot, archbishop of Albi, 53, 77, 105
Modernism, 50, 71, 77
Monniot, Albert, 56
Montagnini, Msgr., 52, 71
Montagnini affair, 52–53, 61, 67, 71, 74
Montesquiou, Léon de, 17, 19
Mounier, Emmanuel, 153–54, 157, 159, 163, 164, 179–80; *Divini Redemptoris*, 165; *Esprit*, 150–51
Mouthon, François, 33

Mouvement Républicain Populaire, 147, 180
Munich agreement (1938), 161
Murat, Antoine, 190*n*29, 211*n*29

National Front, 160
National Union, 156–57
Naudet, Paul, 8–9, 33, 38–40, 45, 53, 54, 55; *Justice Sociale*, 33, 54
Napoleon, Louis, 5, 182
Napoleonic Concordat, 4, 41–44
Non Possumus, 140–41
Le Nouvelliste de Bretagne, 55, 66, 87, 99, 101, 126, 132

L'Osservatore Romano, 57, 124, 129, 142, 173
L'Ouest-Ecl. ir: and the Action Française, 74, 89, 98, 108, 110, 126, 143; and the ALP, 39–40; and Daudet, 109; and Dubourg, 67, 87; and Maurras, 76; opposition to, 53, 55–57, 74–75, 87; and the PDP, 111; right-wing patriotism of, 38, 85, 90–91, 92, 93, 94; and Sangnier, 114; and the Separation Law, 45; and Trochu, 67, 74, 87, 99, 132, 209*n*17; and the Union Sacrée, 105
Oury, Msgr., 68

Pacelli, Cardinal, 173
"Par tous les moyens," 78
Paris Commune (1871), 23
Parti Démocrate Populaire (PDP), 111, 126, 134, 147, 157, 180
Pascal, Georges de, 65
Passelecq, Fernand, 124
Pays légal, 14, 176
Pays réel, 14–15, 20, 63, 176–77
Péchenard, Msgr., 77
Pelletier, Robert, 72
Penon, Msgr., 88, 100, 130
Pétain, Philippe, 3, 96, 111, 175–76, 179, 182

Petit, Fulbert, archbishop of Besançon, 46, 53, 61, 116
Le Petit Démocrate, 111, 126, 160
Pie de Langogne, Msgr., 52
Piou, Jacques, 13, 37, 39–40, 55, 61, 192*n*16
Pius X: and the Action Française, 66, 81, 121; election of, 41; *Gravissimo Officii*, 47–49, 70; integrist program of, 50–52, 62, 66, 69, 73; *Lamentabili Sane*, 50; and the Maurrasians, 68, 69, 70, 76, 80, 201*n*31; *Pascendi Dominici Gregis*, 50; and Penon, 88; reactionary politics of, 52, 54, 61–62; and Sangnier, 53, 54, 60; and the Separation Law, 49, 91; and the Sillon, 60; *Syllabus of Errors*, 65, 73, 77; and the Third Republic, 42–43, 195*n*6; and Trochu, 56–57
Pius XI: and the Action Française, 103, 123, 125, 131–35, 143, 146, 183; and *L'Action Française*, 122, 152; and Billot, 130; and Briandism, 166–68; and de Castelnau, 154; and Catholic Action, 120, 123, 137–40; and the Christian Democrats, 127–28; and *La Croix*, 133, 136; *Divini Redemptoris*, 164–65, 169; foreign policy of, 106, 114–22, 150, 166–68, 170–71; and the JOC, 137; and Maurras, 174; and the Maurrasians, 123, 142, 173; *Maximam Gravissimamque*, 116, 121; and Sangnier, 114; and the Second Ralliement, 114, 145, 165, 167; and the Separation Law, 92, 116; and *Sept*, 165; *Ubi Arcano Dei*, 114, 120; and *La Vie Catholique*, 112; and the working class, 137, 146, 154–55
Pius XII, 4, 174–75, 181
Poincaré, Raymond, 90, 92, 104, 121
Politique d'abord, 14, 75, 78, 129, 131–32, 140, 211*n*29
Pontifical Biblical Institute, 50

Popular Front, 148, 156, 158–64, 167, 173
Pourquoi Rome a parlé, 127
Press, 8, 9, 13, 16, 56, 109
Protestantism, 20–24, 32, 36, 38–39, 63, 70, 78, 93, 102
Pujo, Maurice, 13, 15, 140–41, 178

Ralliement, 6–10, 13, 34, 35–36, 45, 47, 181–82; and the Action Française, 28–29, 36, 62, 71, 87, 121, 184; and the ALP, 37, 40; and the Christian Democrats, 8–9, 28, 31, 32, 35, 53–54; and *Gravissimo Officii*, 48–49; and Leo XIII, 6, 13, 28, 31; and Pius XI, 92; and the Separation Law, 45. *See also* Second Ralliement
Ralliés, 36, 37, 44, 46, 54, 62, 66, 71, 74, 149, 182
Rampolla, Cardinal (papal secretary of state), 52
Rassemblement Populaire, 158, 160
Réaction d'abord, 15
Réal del Sarte, Maxime, 15, 66, 189*n*24
Reformation, 21–23, 36, 83, 84, 91, 102
Republican Federation, 157
Richard, Ernest, archbishop of Auch, 100
Richard, François, archbishop of Paris, 36, 46, 50
Rivière, Msgr., 100
Rome, 100
Rome: Loubet's visit to, 42, 47–48. *See also* Vatican
Rousseau, Jean-Jacques, 20, 22, 35, 83, 85, 90

Sagot, bishop of Agen, 131
Sangnier, Marc, 9; and the Action Française, 26–28, 72–74, 98, 106, 108, 143, 172; and Alsace, 95; and *L'Aube*, 149; and Benedict XV, 105; and

Sangnier, Marc *(cont.)*
  Dimier, 87; liberal socialism of, 29, 40, 53; and Maurras, 26–27, 74; and *L'Ouest-Eclair,* 39; and the PDP, 111, 147; and Pius X, 60; and Pius XI, 114, 126; and the Resistance, 180; and the Separation Law, 45. *See also* Sillon
Schwerer, Antoine, 132
Second Ralliement, 103, 106, 205*n*3; and the Action Française, 146–47; and *La Croix,* 135; optimism of, 151–52; and Pius XI, 114–15, 144, 171; reaction to, 155–56, 158; as theological renaissance, 149; and *La Vie Catholique,* 112
Second Republic (1848), 23
Semaines Sociales, 7–8, 71, 110–11, 137
Separation Law (1905), 3, 74, 184; and the Action Française, 70, 97, 121; and the Christian Democrats, 53, 62; and the church, 28, 91–92, 96; and "cultic associations," 44–48, 92, 97; and Lemire, 58; and Pius X, 49; and Pius XI, 116
Sept, 150, 164; and de Castelnau, 153; and the Doumergue government, 156; and the Popular Front, 160, 172; and the Resistance, 180; and the Second Ralliement, 150; and the Spanish Civil War, 162; and the Vatican, 165, 174
Service du Travail Obligatoire, 180
Sevin, cardinal at Lyon, 51, 67, 88, 130
Sillon, 9, 33, 53, 73–74; and the Action Française, 26–27, 68, 72–74, 76, 107, 141–42, 144; and the ALP, 40; attacked for liberal socialist views, 29, 35, 53, 67, 87; and the Camelots du Roi, 71–73; and the Congress of Brest, 60; dismantled, 59, 60; and the Jeune République, 107; and Maurras, 76; and Pius X,

Sillon *(cont.)*
  30; and the Separation Law, 45, 46; and Trochu, 55
Socialism, 85, 91, 93, 113
Socialists, 12, 39, 44, 55, 63, 85, 156, 183
Sodalitium Pianum, 52, 105
Solidarité Française, 172
Soviet Union, 161
Spain, 161–63, 164, 166, 167, 173
Suhard, cardinal in Paris, 181
Syllabus (Pius IX), 6, 49, 77
Syllabus of Errors, 65, 67, 69, 73, 136

Temoinage Chrétien, 180
Terre Nouvelle, 159, 163–65, 172
Tessier, Gaston, 149, 157
Third International, 93
Third Republic: and the Action Française, 16, 171, 183–84; anticlericalism of, 23–24, 97, 99–100, 103; and the church, 5, 6, 31, 35–36, 116–17, 183–84; collapse of, 175; and the JOC, 154; and Maurras, 14; and Mounier, 150; and the PDP, 111; and Pius X, 47; and Pius XI, 167; and the Second Ralliement, 155–56; relations of, with the Vatican, 28, 42–43, 86, 108, 182
Thorez, Maurice, 173
Touchet, bishop of Orléans, 66, 84, 124
Tour du Pin Chambly, René La, 7–8, 85
Treaty of Versailles, 90, 97–98, 105
Trochu, Félix, 9, 59, 72, 108–09, 207*n*17; and Dubourg, 67, 87–88; and *L'Ouest-Eclair,* 55–57, 74–75, 87; resignation demanded, 98–99, 100, 132
Turinaz, Charles, bishop of Nancy, 66

Union Catholique, 61, 65, 70, 95, 117. *See also* Keller
Union Sacrée, 81–84, 88, 90–91, 99, 105, 121
L'Univers, 57, 66, 68, 101

Vallée, Jacques, 65
Vallet, Xavier, 101, 127
Vatican: and the Dreyfus affair, 10; French embassy at, 43, 86, 91–97, 116; and the Maurrasians, 132–40; under Benedict XV, 104–08; under Pius X, 52, 54, 61–62, 66, 69, 73; under Pius XI, 114–22; and the Second Ralliement, 114, 146, 154–55; and the Third Republic, 28, 42–43, 86, 108, 182
Vatican I, 52, 182
Vatican II, 3, 181–82
Vaugeois, Henri (founder of the Action Française), 13, 25–26
Vendredi, 159
Verdier, Jean, 158
Vésins, Bernard de, 17, 19
Vialatoux, Joseph, 76
Vichy government, 175–79, 182
La Vie Catholique: and the Action Française, 126, 143; and the Christian Democrats, 110; and the church, 117; and Dabry, 54–55; and Gay, 94, 127, 136; and the PDP, 112; pluralism of, 149–50

La Vie Intellectuelle, 150, 165
La Vie Spirituelle, 150
Vigilance Council, 163
Volunteers of the Pope, 127

Waldeck-Rousseau, Pierre Marie René, 34, 38–41, 43
Working class, 8, 113, 137, 147–48, 154–55, 168–69, 181
World War I, 3, 18, 48, 80–82, 90, 114, 149
World War II, 3, 147, 179–80, 183

Youth movements: and the Action Française, 26, 70, 102–03, 124; and the Camelots du Roi, 15–16; and Catholic Action, 152, 179; and *France Libre*, 33; and Pius XI, 79, 133, 137, 169–71; and the Sillon, 53; student leagues, 15, 64–65, 178; Volunteers of the Pope, 127. *See also* Camelots du Roi; Jeunesse Chrétienne; Jeunesse Ouvrière Chrétienne Féminine

Zamanski, Joseph, 149